You Are Royalty

You Are Royalty

Asserting Our Sovereignty
As We Create Our New Earth

Mary Soliel

12 ✹ 12
Productions

Santa Fe, New Mexico

You Are Royalty

Asserting Our Sovereignty
As We Create Our New Earth

Twelve Twelve Productions, LLC books may be ordered
through booksellers or Amazon.com.

Twelve Twelve Productions, LLC
P.O. Box 22333
Santa Fe, New Mexico 87502
www.marysoliel.com
alighthouse@mac.com

ISBN: 978-0-9890169-4-0 (Paperback)
ISBN: 978-0-9890169-5-7 (E-Book)

This book
is dedicated to you,
the Queens and Kings of our
New Earth coming into being,
placing your divine stamp
onto the world to shift it
forevermore.

Contents

Acknowledgments

To my fabulous royal members of the Michael & Mary group (in alphabetical order): Amy, Carol, Cynthia, Diane, Donna, Jane, Jeannie, Joy, Laura, Margaret, Mia, Rhonda, Robin, Ron, Saramae, and Steinar, who all helped to support me as patrons without pause from when our group began, and remained with me during my journey in Hawaii. We broke away from the formalities and simply became a group on our own. I am grateful to you all and I'm excited to share how you were a part of the magic that I describe in detail, in this book.

To my royal guide Lillian, also known as Lily, who from the other side has deeply touched my life, being an angel on my shoulder since she magically appeared in my life on September 26, 2017. She keeps me lighthearted and joyful with every sweet, synchronistic expression of connection. Lillian took on a role of supporting me in the most gentle and loving manner, helping me to unravel this mission in magical ways.

To the Hawaiian Royalty of the past who helped me to understand Humanity's next steps… only and securely in royal shoes.

To the wild spinner dolphins who became my immediate, royal family in the sea. They taught me so much, constantly piqued my curiosity to learn so much more about them, provided unsurpassed joy and laughter, gained my utter respect and awe, and truly healed me down to a deep soul level.

To my kindred soul friend and queen, Hydee, who serves as a perfect example of working together in tandem for spiritual progression. Hydee was a great cheerleader when I took the leap to the Big Island and she helped trigger the destined message of this very book.

To my beautiful soul family member and queen, Jeannie, who wholeheartedly supports my evolving work with Archangel Michael all these years. Jeannie's extraordinary ways of being and serving of humanity are deeply appreciated by all who know her, most absolutely by me. I refer to her as my human guardian angel.

To my royal friends in Hawaii who each played a role in this story, mahalo nui loa: Angela, Angie, Chad, Chris, Crystal, Eric, Gary, Gina, Hydee, Jean-Luc, Joan, JoanieMac, Lisa, Monique, Natalia, Sheila, Sheoli, Teri, and Therese.

And to my royal friends outside of Hawaii and yet who especially supported me on this journey and with this new message: Anne, Clare, Debbie, Joe, Justin, Justina, Kellee, Lee, and Mia.

To those I love and care about who continue to help me do what I do, as honored and recognized in past books.

And most especially…
~ To our beloved Archangel Michael ~
as well as Jesus, Mother Mary, and Mary Magdalene—my
team from the highest of the High—who support me and
all of us who call on them, endlessly. They help me move
through my challenges, pain, and frustrations, and love
me through all of my imperfections and human trials.

Gratitude to God
for the gift of this lifetime
of all our lifetimes,
where we come to know
who we really are as humans,
and raise the bar together.

Author's Note

To honor their privacy, some names of individuals and identifying details have been changed.

Please also note that this book has not been professionally edited. We are in particularly intense times, and thus, 3D concerns and an urgency to release this book fell by the wayside. Thank you in advance for your understanding.

~ Mary Soliel

Introduction

Life is about to take a U-turn… a U-turn! It is now time. Watch for that sign! The joys will overshadow the sorrows and challenges and extreme difficulties you have endured. You will be making great headway and shifts in these next six months, in particular.
~ Archangel Michael to Mary Soliel, on Mary's birthday of October 27, 2019

Two days after I received this personal message from Archangel Michael, I was on my way back to Hawaii after a short visit with loved ones in Colorado, having moved to the Big Island just two and a half months prior. When Michael said to "Watch for *that* sign!," I knew exactly what he was referring to. He placed that image in my imagination. It was literally a U-turn traffic sign. Little did I know just how magically and utterly unexpectedly it would appear.

On October 29, 2019, I begin to write this very book. While on the plane, about 1,000 words just flew out of me and onto my laptop document. I then closed my computer down to take a needed nap, looked outside over the plane's wing where I was seated, and noticed just a part of a red arrowed line on a white background. It was a decal on the plane's wing, right next to the fuselage. I heard "Look closer." And I realized to my utter amazement and joy that I was basically looking at a U-turn sign, and of all times, immediately after I began writing the first installment of my sixth book. Michael!

There was something about my being seated in seat 18A on both legs of the journey—I felt it. Surely, regarding the numerology, but it was more than that. Had I been in 17A, or really any other seat, I would probably have missed this perfectly timed sign. But I was planted right alongside this U-turn symbolism. Throughout my conscious relationship with Michael, I've noticed how he plants seeds. I may not know what he is really talking about for a couple of days, perhaps months, or even years. But somehow, the answers are revealed in the tapestry of everyday life, and most often in profound and synchronistic ways that you cannot explain away.

What would I do without this angel on my shoulder? I have been in the most impossible fight of my life, and here he is keeping me high vibe, instilling me with drive, pumping me with faith, and somehow making me laugh even seconds after being immersed in moments of despair. He lets me stay there wallowing in negative emotions enough to feel it, understand it, and then shift it. And it may happen countless times until I better learn how to shift the pain on my own. More than anything, Archangel Michael has taught me relentless faith, even when it feels impossible to hold it, and so I do. I clutch onto faith, as if there is no other possibility. As I have said to followers of my work many times before:

"Hope just keeps us hoping. Faith is *knowing*."

And so I *know* my way into each present moment, without pause and as much as humanly possible.

This book is ultimately not about my story. Rather, it is about our story—with mine as merely an example. It is our story as the Heavens help humanity to step it up transmuting the extreme darkness of our world into the unsurpassed power of Light. We do this with our eyes wide open, seeking truths, and seeking deeper levels of love. This naturally leads us to demonstrating unconditional love and forgiveness, inspiration, and relentless faith. Most importantly, we are learning to live from the heart. And that... that is the golden key that will unlock the doors to the royalty that we are.

Chapter One

The Call to Hawaii

Hawaii. Experiencing this mystical land can easily launch one into a myriad of expressions, from utter joy and insatiable curiosity, to emotional acrobatics and profound revelations. I am one who is presently and blissfully immersed in a wide gamut of sights, sensations, sounds, smells, passion, notions, premonitions, and all that comes with living on the Big Island of Hawaii, as I begin writing my sixth book.

While this was clearly my home in distant past lives, I arrived here, in this life, late at night on August 17, 2019. Instantly, I melded with the land and sea, and felt I was simply returning home. It was effortless, as if my cells held memories of this magnificent place. Those of you familiar with my work may have guessed that this was a guided move. I am here just for the time being, maybe six months to a year, or perhaps longer. I have new work to do, I know that—certainly writing this book.

As things unfolded here in these beginning months, I often reflected on my guided trip to Alberta, Canada in September 2017. There, in that gorgeous hamlet of Lake Louise, my life and work changed quite instantaneously—along with those who also felt called to join our mission with Archangel Michael, to carry his sword with him as Michael's Warriors of Light.

Now, after two and a half months here in Hawaii, I know it is time to put forth a new message as we continue our warrior work on the spiritual front lines. I realize that it is about the immense power of the Light and the power within each of us. It's also about the dark, too. Because we still exist in this land of duality. The harsh reality of the extreme darkness now being exposed in these times is nothing short of overwhelming. But this book is mostly about *our becoming who we really are—which is royalty*. May the messages in the following chapters serve as an inspiration to not only persevere, but to carry the torch through these times.

Let's just name the spoiler alert, right off the bat. Light is more powerful than dark. If I had any doubt of this, I would not bother writing this book, to put it bluntly. I would put up my hands and give up, as the extreme dark's effect on all our lives is indeed so enormous, as the skies, the water, the soil, our food, our bodies, and so much more have been poisoned. These forces have permeated every aspect of life, and we are being called to acknowledge the crimes against humanity, to not consent to them, and to transmute these energies.

Several months into the writing of this book came what I near immediately called a "plannedemic," which sent us into overwhelm. I will get into that later, and prefer to proceed in somewhat chronological order. We simply must throw Light over all the insanity and carry our torches with complete and utter faith of the power within each of us, to transmute and overcome the darkness. We can and are doing this, those of us planted firmly on the path of awareness; those of us willing to go down all those rabbit holes to find and recognize the hard and difficult-to-digest truths. But that is not enough. Maintaining our brilliant Light, understanding its true role and power, must go hand in hand with this process.

How many times have you heard the phrase: "The world is an illusion"? I thought I understood the meaning of this famous saying soon after I began my spiritual journey twenty-five years ago. But I didn't really, not nearly to the depth I do now. I had little idea of just how deeply entrenched we are, both in an illusory way as well as in an enslaved way, by extreme darkness. We are so conditioned and indoctrinated over years, over decades, and even over centuries. We all have been at various levels hypnotically programmed by the powers that "be" (soon to be "were"), especially as a result of mass media exploitation in this lifetime, and we are waking from such deep slumber.

If we still believe that all politicians are out to help us, that celebrities are the people to follow, and that every governmental agency is there to protect and serve us—we are in for a rude awakening, in large part. As we awaken to the varying depths of the darkness that are behind all deceptions in many of these areas and more, we realize just how grossly we have been hoodwinked, deceived, tricked, and manipulated.

Many are getting it now, and quickly. And those of us who see through the deceptions are working hard to help others see them, as well. You are probably one of the truthers, the awakened ones. While your heart-felt concerns often fall on deaf ears, however, please never underestimate the quiet but substantial power of planting a seed. When meeting resistance, move onto the next and then the next, while maintaining your energy and Light. My arrival in Hawaii taught me how to maintain my energy and Light, like I never quite learned before.

I was clearly called to the Big Island. While I had visited Maui, Kauai, and Oahu on two past trips to Hawaii, I had never been to the largest of the Hawaiian Islands. And yet, I felt this strong, growing inner pull. About six years ago, I kept hearing the words *Captain Cook* from my unseen friends, especially. Yes, way back then they were planting seeds! When I later learned there was such a place as Captain Cook, Hawaii, named after the famous explorer, I was captivated and intrigued, wanting to know what this was all about. I had this inner knowing that I would live there one day.

When I was speaking at a conference in Colorado in late 2015, I met Hydee, a fellow Lightworker and warrior, and a fire captain of sixty firemen in California! We became immediate friends. Two years later, she told me she was getting married and moving to the Big Island. When I asked where on the island, she said Captain Cook! What?! What is it about Captain Cook?

So, the seeds continued to be planted over years until I just knew that it was time to follow this strong draw to the Big Island—specifically Captain Cook, where I would end up spending the vast majority of my time. Why? I quickly learned that the wild spinner dolphins hung out quite regularly in this area of the island. I immediately knew that meeting them would be the highlight of my stay. I have always been drawn to dolphins, so to swim with them would be a beyond-my-dreams experience. And I would eventually ask myself what is it about this area that attracts the dolphins to spend so much time playing, resting, and working (yes, working) here. I will never stop feeling gratitude for the most blessed opportunity of meeting these wise and fascinating beings. What I did not know was that there would also be very challenging aspects of my stay, as well.

While I was familiar with specific attacks on Hawaii by dark forces, it was only once that I spent time in the physical on this magical land did I witness and feel how much healing these islands still required. This is very sacred land, and it appears to be playing an important role in our destiny. Writing these words causes me to reflect on why I was led to various sacred spots in the world, as well as places also calling for deep healing.

Just five years after my journey started, in 1999, I moved with my family to New Mexico, where the atomic bomb was created and where many spiritual people have felt called to in recent decades. I agree with the theory described in my first book, *I Can See Clearly Now*[1], that Lightworkers were drawn there, unknowingly balancing that regional karma. Fast forward to being in Hawaii twenty years later, where land was taken from the indigenous and not far from where the bomb was dropped on Pearl Harbor, to name two life-altering, historical events.

I was also drawn like glue to the South of France for many years until in late 2016, I finally visited the region

---

[1] Soliel, Mary. *I Can See Clearly Now*. Lincoln: iUniverse, 2008.

and, in particular, the area where the Cathars who revered Mary Magdalene were burned for their beliefs. I shared the miraculous healing and experience there in *Michael's Sword & You*[2]. I even went to the Vatican, when visiting Italy, where extreme amounts of Light is needed, even though Michael knew I really didn't want to go. So, I agreed to take the train from Florence to Rome, but only if I could return in the same day. I didn't see Rome at all, and just went directly to the deemed religious center of the world to transmute the darkness there. Ironically, an earthquake occurred just outside the city on that very day.

Weeks before that trip, I ventured to Abadiania, Brazil, to see who is known as "John of God." The way that trip came to be was so magical and destined, and yet half way through the trip, I began to sense such darkness from him and a couple of others, so much so that I changed my plans and abruptly left five days early. "Enough," Michael said, it was time to leave and I accomplished what I needed to. Although there were many positive experiences, for sure. I met several beautiful souls and enjoyed some profound meditations lasting several hours, something I never experienced before. I was told that the casa sits on a massive crystal bed; the energy there is indeed powerful. However, in December of 2018, the world would learn that the man behind the famous casa is far from the person he is known to be. And that is an understatement!

So many places need our Light and, certainly, you too have been led either out of the country, state, province, city, or down your very street to where transmutation is needing to take place. I do believe in the 100th monkey

---

[2] Soliel, Mary. *Michael's Sword & You.* Boulder: Twelve Twelve Publishing, LLC, 2018.

effect. In my view, this phenomenon is not hypothetical. As Lightworkers the world over focus on clearing and healing these areas begging to be released from the trenches of darkness, we are setting ourselves and the land we stand on free of dark energetic hold to bring in the new. While remote healing is certainly powerful, over recent years I came to believe and experience that these particular types of healing are most beneficial when your physical presence, your literal DNA, is on the land that is calling for healing.

This time, Hawaii called to me. And you will read in the following pages how the Big Island made quite an impression on me. It led me to put together so many missing puzzle pieces regarding the times that we are in right now, and how our very souls are leading us to navigate through the immense challenges that will lead us to our miraculous New Earth.

Chapter Two

The Big Island
Makes a Big Splash

Sometimes I forget that it is not just me in the driver's seat. I work with the Archangel Michael who sees and understands worlds more than I do, of course. And back when my conscious spiritual journey began on October 2, 1994, I was called. Three words came out of my mouth that were not from my own thoughts: "Am I chosen?" Right then a Divine white light came into my right eye—it was the most surreal, otherworldly moment of my life. "Chosen," *not as in more special than anyone else*, but simply that I had a specific spiritual mission before me.

On this monumental day, I had conversations with God for ten hours, and would soon decide that I am here for His will, not my own. After Archangel Michael came into my life on a conscious level, on November 15, 2001, I learned that I had a contract with him. So, while I am a very independent, stubborn, and strong-willed soul, I also work in tandem with high beings watching over our world. I know many of you reading these words do too.

When people would ask me, when are you going to write your next book, I would say something like: "Oh I have no plans to do so now." And then what happens? Michael sends me to Sedona, Canada, or Hawaii in this case. And the book just happens, it effortlessly unfolds, or the seeds of such.

Once I hear the call, I stand up and take it. But the 3D part of me is thinking that it's just too much work and I'm not ready for another book yet. Well, we are all being called so strongly now and in various ways, to the point there is often no doubt what needs to be done. And, certainly, many of us are noticing that our intuitive gifts are growing stronger, so we are hearing the calls much more readily and clearly.

I don't know about you, but I don't have much of a comfort zone anymore. This certainly became clear when I began my warrior mission with our beloved Archangel. And I believe we are all being called to step outside of them, and to definitely stop playing small. Extended periods of consistent comfort can be boring, non-stimulating, while a bit of discomfort and stretching of our limits can lead to tremendous soul growth and a greater appreciation of our daily lives. It can actually create more moments of joy.

From the first day I arrived on the Big Island, I have been faced with many challenges alongside absolute, blissful joy and constant miracles that mirrored the U-turn Michael would soon speak of. Here I am in paradise, and yet it has not all been easy. More on that later.

Archangel Michael has been overseeing my learning every step of the way here. On the very first full day on the island, I was driving in Kailua-Kona, familiarizing myself with the town, and he told me to "Turn here." It was the first time I heard from him since I arrived on the island. About 30 seconds later, I found myself in front of St. Michael the Archangel Church. The statue of him outside of this church would become a place I would frequent. Whenever I would stand by that statue, something magical would happen.

For several years, even though I am naturally quite a social person, I have been reclusive, mostly a hermit outside of my inner circle of friends. However, since living in Hawaii, I took a U-turn and went out there meeting and conversing with many people each day. I truly believe that we are being further pushed out of our shells and comfort zones for more than one reason. We need to get our faces out of our phones, laptops, and social media, and get back to face-to-face communication. Trust me, I have told myself the same, again and again. So much so, that I take long breaks from social media and the computer, and I feel so much happier doing so.

I feel as if we are starving for a return to connection again. We need to hug more, even a stranger you just met (although it's probably best to ask first). We have less touch and connection these days, especially for those of us, like me, who have shied away from the public. However, Michael and the Universe pushed me out there, while in Hawaii.

[This chapter was written several months before the lockdown, quite ironically! And once lockdown occurred, I returned to social media as a way to reach others and spread truths during such chaotic times, while at the same time we were all being physically distanced—forced into reclusiveness, ironically. Clearly, I needed to feel and experience both extremes of connection for a deeper understanding.]

The fact is, I haven't made so many friends in such a short time since college days. When I sought a white used car, in the weirdest, most roundabout way, I found myself with a little (golden) orange one—not a color I would have imagined myself driving in. So, my new friends have come to recognize me on the road.

How many times friends texted me, "You just drove by, Mary!" Well it was pretty funny, I have to say! The Big Island has a very small town feel... everyone knows everyone it seems, and many knew me by my car alone! I didn't want to be conspicuous, and yet it appeared to get me in gear for putting myself out there in a bigger way.

The color orange is known to symbolically represent new beginnings, but I refer to that feeling of being out there, being seen—frankly, no more reclusiveness! Being in Hawaii does remind me of being in Sedona where synchronicity, and, specifically, synchronistic meetings with others are especially present.

I will share some examples of meeting the perfect people at the perfect moments later, but I have had the most magical, spontaneous, educational, and enlightening meetings here, on a near daily basis, and that was quite an unexpected happy surprise. And then there's the not so happy surprises. Let's get some of that out of the way first.

Lightworkers the world over are under attack, especially energetic attack. While no fun, if you are one of them, consider it a compliment because your energy is making a difference in this world. I, personally, have been deeply targeted, so badly so that it has been very hard at times to cope on a daily basis. Impossible things have happened to me as dark energies try to bring me, along with other Lightworkers, down.

However, I learned the hard way through intense experience that the only way to respond is… to stay in your joy and remain in a state of Love. There is no better response. Any other response gives them energy. This is one of the hardest lessons I've ever had to learn, especially being a sensitive soul. I take things very hard on an emotional level. Being a true Scorpio, I feel very deeply, more than most around me.

The dark wants us to fear and hold a slew of negative emotions, for that is their food, literally. It is referred to as *loosh*. If we were all in a state of love, joy, and all other positive emotions, the dark could not exist. (Oh, wow. The lights in the coffee shop where I'm writing this just went out and then back on, confirming that!) And the dark often works through people, knowingly and unknowingly, to upset and bring down relationships, families, spiritual work, and more.

Although this is not fun to talk about or consider, it is empowering to know the truth so that we can stand above the challenges. Because, the fact is, we can be messed with by entities and attachments that whisper things that are destructive, as well. They can make us believe things that are not true. They can make us do and say things that we really don't mean or feel. This is the extreme opposite of what happens when an angel whispers to us, which enriches our lives. Most people don't know that dark entities can whisper to us without our realization, which can end up causing havoc. Hence, with awareness, we can each keep our vibe high and drop these attempts. And with awareness we can more easily forgive others who have hurt us, because they were being manipulated to think or do something not in alignment with who they are or what they truly believe and know!

If something doesn't feel like your own thought, it is probably because it is not your thought! You can then cast the thought aside. When Michael tells us again and again to connect with the heart for the obvious benefits of getting to the truth and our soul's desires, *this is also a grand way to sidetrack any influence!*

So, when we are aware of what is really going on behind the scenes, we learn to temper our reactions. We learn to pause, observe, and make new choices, perhaps. I have learned this the very hard way. But it has been a vital lesson, and we are all being asked to pause more often, slow the thoughts down, and go right to the heart to decipher. To feel our way to truth and appropriate response. This most certainly includes the buffering of our responses to the mainstream narrative.

While on the island, I was confronted with two horrible living situations. The first one, anyone would deem frightening. I was clearly targeted, and yet it did not frighten me off the island. Rather, it only cemented my commitment to my purpose of working with the Light and provide healing for the island, working from this vantage point. I clearly displayed that the perpetrators were not scaring me away and rather I faced it—and this is the big part... I moved on from it. I went back to my joy. This was repeated with a second difficult challenge which left me without a place to call home, again.

Losing a whole lot of money was stressful enough, but much worse was the potential effect on my sense of peace, health, and comfort for a while. And so, I had to start again and again with complete faith and knowing that I was completely protected. We are in warrior mode, clearly. We learn to navigate no matter what obstacles are thrown our way. It's an empowering way to face adversity by going head first into unconditional faith. I guess, that is being an alchemist, right?

Hawaii helped me get used to not having as much of a comfort zone, for the most part. It becomes a learned behavior to maintain inner strength no matter what is occurring outside of you. It truly feels like a muscle many of us are developing and growing now, to step outside of those comfort zones, face challenges head on, and stop playing small.

And so, I reflect on the following. Once you tell God that you are in service to His will, you will surely be in service in unexpected ways. And you will most likely endure some unexpected challenges and lessons to go with that, but as you traverse through them you know they are overseen and for the greater good.

As shared, my spiritual journey began with my stating that "Thy will be done," and this was clearly pronounced once arriving in Hawaii. As I piece together many things, I recall this statement of service, and have no question that I called forth a whole lot of challenges that I had no idea were ahead, on top of traversing through personal lessons very necessary for my spiritual growth.

Some of the lighter third dimensional challenges brought more levity and humility into my life. I tell my friends here that I have lost all grace since arriving in Hawaii. I have done more Lucy Ricardo (the main, comical character of the *I Love Lucy* television show, played by Lucille Ball) stunts getting in and out of the ocean, especially when climbing on rocks—as the Big Island is not laden with only white, sandy beaches. While I have always bruised easily, I haven't bruised this much since I was a little kid, especially in those first few weeks.

While I'm not normally clumsy, this has given me much laughter and the ability to accept all of my shortcomings and many imperfections. Never before had I realized how young my spirit really is until I found myself out there every day defying what my body could normally endure. I feel stripped down to my soul these days, not much to hide and just be who I am. Like never before, I found myself in my late 50s learning to eschew self-judgement and rather embrace self-acceptance. That orange car sure served as a metaphor.

This metamorphosis has allowed me to take a new look at my life—really, my new life within this same life. All of my priorities have shifted and I'm sure yours have too. With so much darkness in the world alone, this affects our choices and decisions, significantly so. It definitely shifts our focus from the synthetic to the richer and more real experiences that life has to offer.

But as we grow ourselves, growing ever closer to our souls, this is the cause of our greatest changes. We are learning to "be" differently. For one, we are moving from relying only on our common sense, to honoring our intuition much more. It's our intuition that is leading us to this new way of being. I cannot say this strongly enough. We need to *feel our way* through life in these times.

Common sense would not have had me living on the very expensive Big Island. And yet, I was guided here by Michael, but also in line with my strong intuition and higher-self guidance. I didn't think too much about it once I made the decision. I didn't even know hardly anything about the Big Island outside of the opportunity to swim with the wild spinner dolphins, which just the thought of made me jump out of my skin with excitement. Hydee and I were on the phone often through our friendship, and once she moved to Hawaii, she was always talking about the spinner dolphins and sea life, but I suddenly realized I really knew nothing else about this paradise.

So, a couple of weeks before leaving, I thought I better start doing some research. I fully trusted there was no place I belonged more than right here, right now—it was simply a deep and unquestionable knowing. Everything I read or watched, I said to myself with excitement, "I'm going to go nuts!" I couldn't believe how beautiful this place is. Everything happened so fast and I recall the excitement I felt with my decision. I just knew that it was time to make it happen. And so I did. I sold my home and car, put everything in storage, and that was that. In recent years, I was learning to *sometimes* throw common sense out of the window—that truly was not my former over-thinking, overly-careful self.

When talking to my angel channeler friend, Jeannie Barnes, on December 2, 2019, we had the following beautiful and powerful three-way conversation with Archangel Michael, who came through Jeannie, as he does every single time we connect.

AA Michael: *Times are requiring different methods when it comes to dealing. What has worked in the past no longer works now. Things have shifted and changed. And so have the way that things work. You are adapting to the new as it should be.*

Jeannie: "The way we used to deal with things isn't the way anymore."

Mary: "So true. What I get, what he is saying is that we are living more intuitively so much more now. It's not going to work using our common sense."

AA Michael: *You are correct. You cannot rely on the mind anymore. It has to adjust to the new world, literally. And you have spoken of this in your books about the new world. Well it's here. It's right in front of you.*

Mary: This is going into the book! Thank you, both!

AA Michael: *You also understand, technology is now a necessity in your world. It is also a way for dark to get in. Be cautious. All beings should be cautious. It is again, new times, a new world. As always, it takes human beings time to adjust. And it's happening so quickly. That adjustment time, that is necessary.*

Jeannie: Everything is so new and we as humans don't have time to adjust.

AA Michael: *Just trust. That's what needs to be now. You are led, you know. In this world, trust is everything. You cannot rely anymore on common sense, but rather intuition.*

[Note: As I was preparing for this book to go to press, I came across something I posted October 15, 2017, in social media: "Following our intuition even when it defies mere logic or common sense… not easy, but most valuable." Surely, AA Michael was starting to plant seeds of understanding.]

On that very day, I experienced something where I consciously realized that I had to put my gut feelings over common sense. It was hard for me, but the feelings won out, even to my personal disappointment. So that gave me chills because I do trust Archangel Michael and I know with my whole heart that the New Earth is here; that we are birthing it into our reality. To trust this and hold the relentless faith is absolutely everything. We are human and we can have our doubts, especially with all of the crimes that continue to be forced onto humanity, but we can choose faith, again and again.

Chapter Three

The Crystal Beings

Being in the water with the wild spinner dolphins has been the unparalleled highlight of living in Hawaii, bar none. I can think of nothing more fulfilling or thrilling than swimming with the wild spinner dolphins, relishing in hearing their sounds, seeing their nods, receiving their healing and telepathing, and so much more. They are magnificent and mysterious creatures! I often refer to them as crystal beings because I feel they emit crystalline energy. Nearly every morning, I'm in the water hoping to see them. My very first experience with them felt very out of body. I could hardly take it all in and I knew that being with these brilliant, loving creatures was positively affecting me in known and unknown ways.

They want to be around us, truly. Time and time again, they would hang around us snorkelers often for three hours at a time—and even longer. I was stunned by this revelation, that they would just swim around and around us, telepathing, communicating with echolocation clicks, whistles, and the sweetest heartwarming "talking" sounds. All while witnessing them sleeping, playing, nursing, and mating—as well as spinning, jumping, and leaping out of the water with outrageous energy and complex maneuvering. It is fully mesmerizing to watch them. The geometric formations they make with movements made in cohesive connection with each other, seem to always exude mysterious messages.

What did this have to do with my work here? They are teaching all of us (human) "dolphin brothers and sisters" so many things. They are healing us as we are hopefully healing them. Dolphins deal with their own darkness in the ocean. When they are captured and sequestered, truly imprisoned for the sake of humanity's enjoyment at a water park or at a hotel pool, or when they are treated nothing close to the magnificence of who they are, they are allowing us endless opportunities to make new choices and to evolve.

Admittedly, we took our kids to Sea World a few times. I adored the opportunity of connecting to the bottlenose dolphins, as well as seeing the killer whales and other sea life. However, once I awakened to their horrific reality, the desire to support these types of enterprises quickly dissolved. And yet, it was these very initial meetings with the dolphins that sparked deep interest and desire to be in the water with them one day. The dolphins are ultimately teaching us the simplest and most vital lesson of all—how to be love.

Are we not being called to see the unfairness and tragedies of how many humans treat ocean life, as well as domesticated, farm, and wild animals, for that matter? And how we in turn are experiencing very much the same thing, as far as losing our own freedom. Is this global karma that we are faced with? [As far as the plannedemic and lockdown that I will address later in the book, I ask, are we experiencing karmic retribution by being penned up like animals, too?] We may think we are free, but we are not. Yet, this will change.

If you read *Michael's Clarion Call* [3], you know that Archangel Michael prophesized a decade ago that the wild will not be so wild—referring to wild animals. We are increasingly seeing the bond between the wild and humans at levels never witnessed before. When I'm immersed in the bliss of being with the spinner dolphins, I easily forget that these are wild animals. They don't act like it! They are the most uniquely engaging and amazing friends one can imagine, in my opinion, who genuinely care about and unconditionally love humans. Our genetics are closely related, I would soon learn. They seek us out, and receive and give information.

It is a most fascinating experience when you immerse yourself in the wonderment and mystery of what is really taking place when with them. Your heart just bursts open and every moment is filled with bliss and often stunning surprises. They are constant art in motion, poetry in motion.

---

[3] Soliel, Mary. *Michael's Clarion Call*. Boulder: Twelve Twelve Publishing, LLC, 2011.

The first time I swam with them, I had rented a kayak in Kealakekua Bay. The man I rented the boat from let me know that the dolphins were definitely around. I was over the moon excited. Sure enough, to my delight I found myself among a fairly large pod of dolphins. A few came right up to my kayak truly checking me out, swimming back and forth around me. I couldn't wait any longer and jumped into the water with my snorkel gear.

Hydee happened to be there, and it was a good thing because she helped me to see them. She would say "Mary, they are right under you," or "They're to your right." Because, I often had no idea as I was almost paralyzed in awe just that they were there swimming around all of us! And something mysterious was definitely occurring within me, finally being in the presence of these beings. You can just wade in the water, and they come right around and beneath you. They were so gentle and beautiful.

That initial experience was so profound that I immediately decided to make it my daily practice to begin nearly every day seeking the dolphins. I wanted to learn a whole lot more about them, and I literally just got my feet wet (pun intended) with this first meeting. What was to come would send me further and deeper into a state of awe and wonderment.

I quickly learned that sometimes they are active and come right up to you, and other times, and most usually so, they are sleeping and stay deeper in the water except to come up for air. If you fear them, they know and will keep their distance. Conversely, if you seek their presence, they will gift you with close connection. They were pretty sleepy on this first swim with them (making only occasional jumps and spins into the air), which was perfect because I was already quite overwhelmed.

You can see this experience I later re-uploaded on the MarySoliel channel on YouTube, titled "Meeting the Spinner Dolphins." According to my new friend Sheoli, when asked how the dolphins recognize us, the dolphins shared: "First we see your light. Next we hear your (vibrational) frequency. Then we see you physically." If you watch this video, you can see them hanging around me while in the kayak, curiously checking me out. They do this upon initial meeting, always taking in information.

A turning point day with them was on November 1, 2019. I must note these numbers of 11.1, [just as 1.11 would also be a magical day on the island.] I had an appointment with an energy healer at 8:30 a.m. and asked her a couple of times if there was an afternoon appointment that week, instead. Mornings are reserved for the dolphins! The appointment needed to remain as it was, and this change in my schedule ended up being perfect; it was divine. We know how that works.

Just minutes before the appointment, Hydee texted me that she saw the dolphins at a beach, which after what happened today would become my favorite place to swim with them. Oh no. Of course, I knew I'd be missing them! Two hours later, I was in my swimsuit and on my way when she texted that they are indeed still there. I got in the water and had a lovely time for about an hour and among several other snorkelers with some very sleepy dolphins, but it was the next two hours that were especially memorable.

Suddenly and somehow, it was just me with the dolphins! Where did everyone go? With that awareness, my underwater camera suddenly ran out of juice. As soon as I realized that, the wild spinners came so close to me. Oh, how funny. Now I cannot capture them, of all times! Yet I also realized the gift in that, so I can just be in the moment with them, not worrying about the distraction of constantly filming. I knew they were well aware of that.

I'd be floating on my stomach in the water and there would be a beautiful line of them coming directly toward me, again and again. They came so close to my body, directly underneath, that I felt sure the dorsal fins on the ones right below me would touch my belly. You never touch them, but they may possibly touch you. It was just me with 30, then 40, and soon up to 50 dolphins or so at this point.

The tsunami alert siren on the hill, just above the beach, then sounded. Luckily, I heard on the radio just when parking the car that there was going to be an alert test, it was the first [and would be only one] I heard since on the island. But no matter, there was no way I was going to leave them now! So I relaxed into the bliss of having dolphins all around me, often coming from all directions. I was spinning myself in the water, poorly mimicking what the spinners do. I literally wondered to myself if it is best to spin clockwise or counterclockwise, as spinning is a wonderful practice known to raise your vibration. Well, the telepathic dolphins heard my question!

Because this one dolphin comes right up to me as if in answer to my question, held still pausing before me, while meeting me eye to eye (with my mask and snorkel on, of course), and very slowly moves me around in a circle, again and again. I telepathed to this crystal being, "Oh my God! Are you kidding me? You are playing with me?!" It was literally making me spin in circles, and, as it just so happened, it moved me in a clockwise direction.

Then a bit later, a different dolphin comes right up to me and again, paused, and looked me right in the eye. It then proceeded to spin me so fast around that I was laughing my head off through my snorkel! I felt like I was five years old. "You are so funny!" I screamed with delight. And it was spinning me in the same direction, so my question was answered in the best possible way.

Yet another one comes out of nowhere and makes a very fast beeline toward me, and changes direction at the last second, just like they play with each other. That took my breath away, too. And they "sonar'ed" me a whole lot. Who knows what is really going on, but I was in awe of every second with them.

It was during these unforgettable moments with the crystal beings that I realized I really have no idea just how smart, amazing, and otherworldly these creatures are. It was among my most surprising life experiences. When I later told Hydee what happened she was so happy for me, and said that they do indeed do this! But she wanted me to be surprised and left some things for me to discover and experience for myself. I was so grateful for her thoughtfulness because I adore happy surprises.

For a long time, I channeled gazing energy through my eyes to the dolphins (my gazing work is described at www.marysoliel.com), as well as channeling energy out of my hands. With any emotional and physical wounds I saw or sensed, I would channel healing energy. That's when I heard the most clicks. Especially when I saw the many cookie cutter shark bites or, most upsettingly, a brand new baby's partly missing tail. And as I channeled the energy, they would often circle around right below me. They are feeling it! If it happened just once or even a few times, I could easily deem it coincidence, but it kept happening and over many future swims.

When I telepathically asked a question of these wise beings, they would telepath an answer. Once I asked a particular dolphin to send remote healing to a friend. It lifted its head with an upward nod as if saying yes, and moved right toward me. They would always surprise me in our growing relationship. Please know I am far from alone in any of these experiences; they love everyone!

I've heard from my dolphin sisters and brothers, especially at this one bay, people find themselves in different dimensions that the dolphins take them to. Is that what happened to me? Because I don't know how so many snorkelers suddenly vanished and then I went into this blissful experience with them, just me with so many crystal beings.

Part of the bliss is being in that state of playfulness with them. They seem to love to make you laugh! It is fun to watch them play the "leaf game," where they bring a leaf to you, and you then swim down and leave it for them. It's like playing "fetch" in the water. An adorable example of this can be seen in my "Meeting the Spinner Dolphins" YouTube video. Towards the end, you will see a dolphin nudge a leaf with its shoulder and then flick its tail to pass it off to me. I couldn't get over that one, and felt grateful that I was able to capture it.

On November 7, Archangel Michael came through with a message:

You are embarking on a time unlike any other in your life or past lives. This time that is coming, and, well, you really are already in it, will bring forth things your soul has never experienced as a human on earth. It is beyond fitting that you are spending much time with the dolphins! They see and know way more than you can imagine. These beautiful creatures are what you should consider as your new friends. Beyond your human friends, Mary, they are going to bring more and more to your life than what you could ever expect. Know this. Know that they are here for you as well as you for them. For they feel your presence, they feel your gazes and healing energies, and they feel my presence through you! This is only the beginning.

One day, I made myself go into a bay that is hard (for me) to enter with rocky shores and waves crashing against them. Much of the Big Island's shores are lined with rock, not sand. The spinners were there and I just had to see them. They hadn't been around for a week, and some believed it was because a pod of teenage male bottlenose dolphins were wreaking havoc with the spinners, raping the females, and one in particular was apparently very hurt. We have been sending it healing Light through our imagination. The spinners are dealing with their own battles just like we are, and on a daily basis.

So, in I went to reconnect with the beings of Love, to send them my love. I got a bit beat up even though going in with such care. By the time I got in, the pod was so much further out there in the large bay, so I began to make the swim toward them. Please come back, I asked. Suddenly, with my masked face in the water, I see five coming directly toward me. I was overjoyed!

One came right up to me, eye to eye, made the sweetest sound saying something, nodded his head upward while still looking at me, and then circled around me. Then more than a dozen followed. It was an amazing greeting! How will I ever leave these beings? I love being out here nearly every day attempting to connect. This unsurpassed joy is a calling I don't want to end.

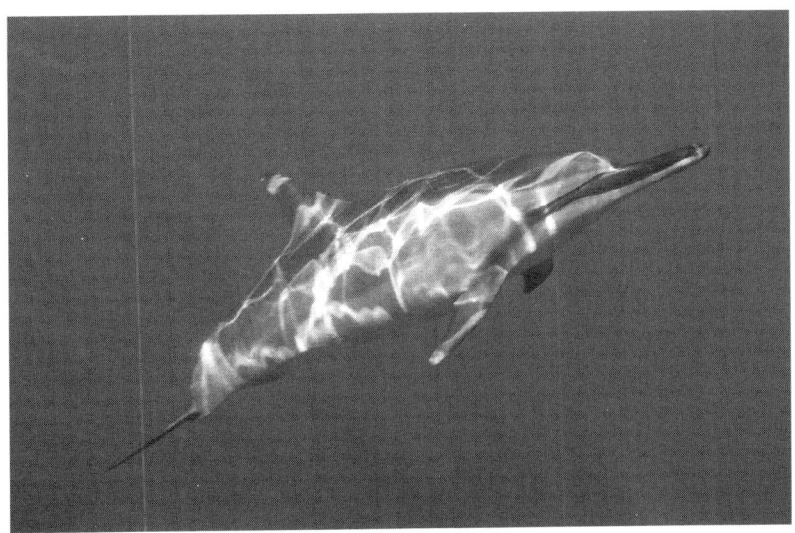

I don't care what anyone says, these beings do want to be with us. They have much to teach us and I am overjoyed to share my observations. When I see my first whale in the wild, it will blow me away, as well, just to be in its immense energy field! The dolphins, whales, and other ocean life are all so vulnerable. A lot of the coral has died, the fish are lessening, and off of these islands many aquatic mammals—dolphins and whales, in particular—have died at the hands of military sonar. I have no question that these beings appreciate all the love and healing we send them. I would send them my gratitude and love constantly, along with so many other dolphin sisters and brothers, always trusting they felt it.

While on the island, I read *Dolphin Dimension*[4] and learned more about what I was not able to articulate or understand yet—just how significant the dolphins and whales are to our world and to our upcoming New Earth.

The author, Therese, whom I had the pleasure of meeting, wrote: "Suddenly everything made sense, I realized dolphins were not only impacting those around them with their high frequency, they were also consciously channeling higher dimensional frequencies onto Earth. An image formed before me and I saw the dolphins setting lay lines of light frequency as they swam. These lay lines extended down through the ocean and into the earth. The dolphins, along with their co-workers the whales, were putting a light grid into place on Earth. The dolphins and whales were laying this light grid exactly in line with the light grid on the dimensional plane above it and every time they swam over the lay lines of the grid, they channeled more light into it. As the light grid on Earth became more and more charged with light vibration, it gravitated up toward the light grid on the dimensional plane above. When enough higher plane light energy was channeled into the grid, Mother Earth, along with all her inhabitants, would achieve the vibration of the next dimension."

How important these incredible beings are to the earth and our destined New Earth, while most of us have no clue. Now what are the chances that on the same day that I read this and inserted this passage into the book's manuscript, I witness a video of a whale performing a spiral movement in the water which created a Fibonacci pattern on the surface of the water? Synchronicity is

---

[4] Therese, *Dolphin Dimension: Adventures with Wild Dolphins*. Kona: Booksurge, 2009.

always supporting the message.

And why is it that so many human dolphin brothers and sisters from around the world visit often and spend day after day seeking to be in the water with these beings? My one friend from Germany made the long trip to the Big Island twice during my seven-month stay! And I knew of more than a handful of new friends and acquaintances who would visit at least once a year.

Perhaps this question can be answered by Therese in her following words. "The dolphins entered my thoughts and told me they needed humankind's help in order to fully activate the light grid. They said that many humans, whether they knew it consciously or not, were already helping to set and activate Earth's light grid. People who were bringing higher frequencies to Earth were helping immensely, the dolphins said, but now it was time for more humans to become involved in the process."

Are we working together with the crystal beings for a higher planetary purpose during these monumental times, many without even knowing it? And, thus, there's this constant desire to seek them out and be in their presence? That sure resonates deep in my heart.

Chapter Four

The Royals Speak

Upon arriving on the Big Island, I was slowly immersing myself as a complete newcomer into Hawaiian culture. I knew little to none about Hawaiian history, and was struck by and deeply touched to see such reverence and honor paid to the former royalty of Hawaii. It felt immediately amazing within my heart to witness this. I knew of King Kamehameha who brought together the Hawaiian Islands, but I was not aware of any of the queens. The main road that runs through Kailua-Kona is Queen Ka'ahumanu Highway.

I quickly learned about Queen Lili'uokalani. This highly revered queen was the first and only Hawaiian queen who ruled the kingdom of Hawaii, and the last Hawaiian sovereign to govern the islands before they were annexed by the U.S. in the late 1800s, and thus Lili'uokalani abdicated her throne.

[It is heavily rumored in present day that Queen Elizabeth abdicated her throne, I later learned while writing this book. Interesting how the tables appeared to have turned. These are both Queens, but let's just say they are like day and night.]

When learning about Queen Lili'uokalani, I came upon this quote of hers which radiates her profound wisdom and depth. "To gain the kingdom of heaven is to bear what is not said, to see what cannot be seen, and to know the unknowable—that is Aloha. All things in this world are two; in heaven there is but One."

If you read *Michael's Sword & You*, then you are aware of the importance of Lily to me, a passed soul who ever warmly communicates regularly with me, and often blesses me with stunning synchronicities. My treasured connection to Lily immediately drew me to Queen Lili'uokalani. The following excerpt describes how my connection to Lily magically began the day I arrived in Alberta, Canada on September 26, 2016, as seen in *Michael's Sword & You*:

When arriving in Okotoks, Alberta for a visit, the magic was set into motion right away. The spirit of a woman named Lillian, whom I never met, came through so clearly saying that she was with me and supporting me. She is the aunt of Leigh, a person I love and am very close to on a soul level. I never met Lillian, also known as Lily, as she passed years ago and lived in Canada. However, I felt a growing connection to her simply because she was so important to Leigh. And here I was, only a couple of hours drive from where she lived on the earth plane.

One of my planned stops in this area was to view the geological landmark Okotoks Erratic. It's the largest known glacial erratic in the world—also known as "Big Rock." I enjoyed exploring this huge and mystical boulder formation sitting unexpectedly so in very flat land, and a fair distance from the Canadian Rockies.

After my visit there, I drove around awhile but was surprisingly and yet clearly guided to return to the rock formation. As always, I listen to higher guidance, and upon arrival I took some more pictures of this fascinating formation. When I *heard* to "Look up" suddenly, I was stunned to see a display of clouds that revealed a being (well, several, when you really look) and with a sword pointing down! The sword is in the upper left quadrant of the photo.

Those familiar with my work may know that I capture images of clouds on a regular basis that reveal Heaven's messages, and published a book celebrating the signs called *Look Up! See Heaven in the Clouds*[5]. So this sighting further validated my new mission with the sword! And it was just a small taste of the magic Michael had in store for me and, ultimately, you.

When leaving Big Rock, I came across a woman walking her dachshund. I clearly *heard* to ask her what the dog's name was. That was a random thing to ask but as always I trusted and blurted out "What a cute dog. What is its name?" "Lily" she said. I instantly

---

[5] Soliel, Mary. *Look Up! See Heaven in the Clouds.* Boulder: Twelve Twelve Publishing, LLC, 2015.

knew that Lillian sent me this validation to prove that she was with me. Had I departed even a minute earlier, I would not have experienced this synchronicity at this most mystical setting.

I left Big Rock and ten minutes later arrived at my next destination, the home I was staying at that night. I wanted to quickly drop off my luggage and get ready to meet my friend for dinner. My timing was perfect. As I parked outside this home, I saw a young woman with her Chihuahua. If you read my book about synchronicity, you know that Chihuahuas have been highly powerful messengers in my life.

As I approached them, I again *heard* to ask what this dog's name was. She replied "Her name is Lily." *Incredible!* Two "Lily"s within ten minutes of each other! And here this Lily lives in the house I was staying in that night. It was a beautiful blessing that both awed and warmed my heart.

Once in my room, I called my kids to let them know I arrived in Canada safe and sound. I excitedly shared with my daughter my meeting of two dogs named Lily, one after the other and very soon after hearing from Lillian. Karen was amazed as she immediately reminded me that two days before I left for Canada, the exact same thing happened. When at this event we attended together, I had asked the owner of this small dog what its name was, and it was "Lily." Oh goodness, that was right, and it made me immediately think of Lillian then, too!

Lillian's magical way of connecting to me while in Canada was so surprising that I hadn't yet put it together that this occurred, as well, just before I left. Asking of a dog's name truly isn't my usual question to dog owners. Lillian must have whispered to me to ask that question even that first time, without my realizing it was her. She clearly wanted to connect with me, somehow orchestrating all of this, and she has been communicating with me regularly ever since. How astronomical are the odds that the three dogs I asked of their name, within three days of each other (and two of those within ten minutes of each other) were all named Lily?

[Note: It gives me goose bumps now as I share this excerpt. Not only because Lily was proving to me that she was going to be my new guide in Heaven, supporting me with Archangel Michael's sword mission, just as she has. But years later, I now realize there is more to it. On the head of the female being in this cloud picture with the sword, taken at Big

Rock, there appears to be a crown! She is most certainly accompanying me on this royal mission that was unveiling itself in Hawaii! I had noticed the crown, but I didn't put it together until rereading this passage I wrote three years ago. So this was a heads-up of what was well ahead, in my view. Two missions were being unveiled here in a single cloud sighting. A second seed was planted, unbeknownst to me.]

Fast forward from this magical trip to Canada that shaped my new warrior work with the Archangel, to his next plans that were incubating on the Big Island. My Hawaii journey began in a synchronistic way, sitting at the airport gate in Colorado waiting to board my plane. This little girl says to her mother that she wants to sit at the window—a seat that happens to be next to me. The mother said that they are leaving now. The little girl comes and sits by me, anyways. Just seconds later, the mother gets up and says, "Come on, Lillian." How many little girls are named Lillian these days? I do believe the spirit of Lillian gave me a wink! Had I sat down two minutes later, I would have missed this. An hour later, I went to the restroom to wash my hands; I turn around, and there is Lillian again, just a few feet from me! Clearly this was a send-off wink from Lily again.

So, my connection to the name of my spirit guide Lily drew me to Queen Lili'uokalani, as if Lily was providing me clues to follow. The Queen's birthday was on September 2nd, 1838, and I noticed when looking up how to spell her name that she passed on November 11, (11.11), 1917, which felt so significant to me. I went to Hilo (on the east side of the island) one early September morning to observe her birthday celebration.

[While editing this very page of the book, I took a break and went to Facebook today, September 2,

2020. I was so engrossed in my work that I had not even made the connection that today was actually the queen's birthday!

I soon see a post from Hawaiian singer and songwriter Amy Hānaiali'i who displayed a beautiful picture of the Queen with this description: "Hau'oli Lā Hānau to our beautiful Queen Lili'uokalani. You inspire me as a Hawaiian woman not only in music and poetry but to push forward every day. To keep aloha in my heart and to always help protect and flourish our Lāhui. I love you my Queen."

I wrote to Amy that this post brought tears to my eyes. I feel so drawn to this Queen, even though I was just a visitor on extended stay in Hawaii. I would eventually realize that I must have been in that lifetime of the Queen. A psychic friend of mine later confirmed what I am sure of in my heart, that I was indeed incarnated during this Queen's reign. This would explain why I feel such love and respect for this queen whom I know barely anything about.]

After the birthday celebration for the Queen, I bought *lilikoi* (also known as passion fruit) at the farmer's market in Hilo. Lilikoi has a wonderful and uniquely sweet, and yet somewhat bitter, taste. You cut the large berry open, that is the average size of perhaps a plum, and only eat the juicy flesh of the fruit. I would even eat the seeds which are high in magnesium, but while avoiding the bitter rind. They make all kinds of delicious desserts as well as juice from this fruit.

The Lily clues were there in the beginning of my Canada journey, and were now leading me to the next steps of my Hawaiian journey, *and it first began with Hawaiian royalty.* The queen synchs then came in like a rushing river with members of my Michael & Mary (M&M) Group!

On October 2, 2019, which just *happened* to be the 25th anniversary of my spiritual journey, Carol from the M&M Group wrote me:

"On my way home Monday, within a short time I saw two license plates that had the word QUEEN in them. One was QUEEN 22, which I've seen before, but I thought it was interesting to see two with that word (I can't remember what the numbers in the other one were)."

Four days later, Carol, who often shares stunning twin synchronicities with me that leave us both in awe, wrote: "Well, this morning on my way to work, a car with a QUEEN license plate passed me. Then, on my way home a little while ago, yet ANOTHER car passed me with a QUEEN license plate (I think it was QUEEN EM)! I'm still not sure if these are signs are at all significant, but I'm going to keep noting them just in case!" Just when I was suddenly experiencing all this royal energy and in tandem with Carol, something happened that revealed the mission and actually led to the very writing of this book!

Hydee texted me one day that she wanted to take me to a sacred site. Well that grew into a plan of visiting four sites in one day, and she said that it was a lot, but that it was guided. I fully trusted what she was getting and was feeling excited about what our friends in the Heavens were up to. So, in the early morning of October 14th, off we went toward the northern tip of the island. While I was excited for this adventure, little did I know just how significant this day would be. Michael and many others were guiding us throughout. We did healings that mirrored the work I did when traveling out of the country for five months in late 2016.

In two of the four places, we simultaneously felt royalty presence, mainly former Hawaiian Queens guiding us where we needed to transmute and anchor healing energy into the ancient grounds. It began at the petroglyphs in Waikoloa—on the "Kings Trail," no less! We could both feel this entourage of Hawaiian royalty of the past who felt perfectly present. They made their presence known telepathically to us both, individually. One of us would say something like "We need to go over there," and the other would respond, "I heard the same." We walked the ground reverently where guided.

Pictured, here we are at the beginning of the King's Trail, which eventually takes you to the petroglyphs.

The last place we visited that day, was the most powerful of all. We felt Hawaiian royalty around us again and also knew that we were part of some orchestrated healing from above. Old energies were being cleared, released, and something new set into motion in this ancient stone circle. I said "We need to walk around these large rocks three times." Hydee said that she heard the exact same request! Once Hydee finished, she laid on a large rock inside the circle. A while later, when I walked in, and with her eyes closed she basically said something like, "Wow, Mary, you just walked in. I can so feel your presence here." Well it wasn't just me but rather a whole entourage of past royalty accompanying me, whom I felt the whole time we circled hundreds of feet around.

I sat on a different rock and meditated for a few moments, and suddenly the most amazing breeze filled the circle. It was not a normal feeling of wind, it was a magical wind. It really revitalized me and I vocally reacted to it. Hydee felt it too. There is only one other time that I felt something like that, such magical energy in the wind, after channeling a message from Mary Magdalene when in Sedona in late 2012. It was as if the air was speaking to me, fulfilling me. (I later told Hydee that it reminded me of the magical wind scenes in *Pocahontas,* because the breeze felt so alive.)

When it was time to leave, both Hydee and I felt extremely nauseous and disoriented. We were actually nauseous throughout the visit but it heightened significantly so, at the end. I had a hard time just getting to the car and Hydee had to drive my car home. It took me a full day to recover from whatever went on there. We both know we were transmuting the energy as guided by past royalty as well as supporting angels, elementals, others—and, of course, Archangel Michael.

And how ironic that the day we went happened to fall on Indigenous People's Day. We didn't plan that and, in fact, we both kept changing the date. This is the same day as Columbus Day, which Hawaii no longer legally recognizes. So the fact that it naturally fell on this day, right there is something to reflect on. I was deeply grateful for the gift of this day, thanks to Hydee's beautiful guidance and trust behind it all.

This book was birthed on this very day without my conscious awareness, but only now in retrospect. This is ultimately why I am here on this island, to glean from these sudden new messages and revelations about royalty, and to then spread them. I truly had no inkling or desire to write another book at this point. I was getting little nudges though, including just a week later from my psychically gifted friend Kellee who agreed that a new book is coming forth.

And a slew of nudges came through members of my M&M Group after sharing with them the powerful sacred sites day with Hydee, and the royal presence before us. Carol described what was happening to her on that very same day:

"My 13-year-old great-niece spent the weekend with us (it was her birthday), and on Saturday, we went shopping. The car with the QUEEN 22 license plate passed me AGAIN, and, while shopping, I saw a T-shirt with 'Queen' embroidered on the front!"

"I still wasn't 100% certain that all of the 'Queen' synchs were anything, but after reading your email, I have no doubt they do indeed mean something! Just wanted to pass that along!"

They sure do mean something. It's important to note that even though I never met Carol in person, and Hydee has never had any communication with her, the three of us were often having the same kinds of synchronicities, even with numbers, and at the same time. Hydee sure had her own share of Queen synchs.

The very next day after the momentous sacred site meetings with Hawaiian royalty in spirit, I went to the first clothing store I visited since on the island. By no means am I a shopper. Yet, lo and behold I happened upon a "QUEEN" shirt. There was just one available and it happened to be in my size. So, of course, I bought it. Clearly, I was led there by my unseen friends. I had never even patronized this popular nationwide retail store chain ever before. I was so excited by this find that I took a picture right then and there, from the hanger.

I continued to be led to royal energy. The first Hawaiian singer I was introduced to via the island radio stations was singer, songwriter Amy Hānaiali'i. It was her beautiful song "Mauna Kea Ku'u Iwi Hilo" from her new *Kalawai'anui* album, that sparked a new love for Hawaiian music. My favorite songs were those that sung for solidarity for Mauna Kea. Being on the island during the Mauna Kea conflict felt significant, as well. I was fully surprised by how deeply this musical language of Aloha touched my heart. By the way, you can see in the YouTube video creation of this song how Amy carries herself, just like a queen.

Without knowing the meaning of more than a handful of Hawaiian words at this point, I found myself feeling into the music and intention of the songs. As I was trying to recall and share another song that especially touched me, I researched on KAPA radio's website and ironically came across this album: *Liliuokalani: Music for and by the Queen*! I am amazed by the continual synchronicities with this particular queen.

The song I was seeking, by the way, is called "Hawai'i '78," originally written by Mickey Ioane while in high school, and later performed by Israel "IZ" Kamakawiwo'ole. In 2019, 40 artists came together for a new rendition (which can be seen on YouTube, as well). *All the giving that the queen has done/She gave all her love to everyone/How would she feel if she saw Hawai'i nei.* These words went right to my soul.

With these building royalty energies, when Amy headlined a concert with other guest artists to benefit Hulihee Palace in Kona—yes, *a royal palace!*—I knew I had to be there. I "happened" to randomly meet her in person, prior to the concert. She walked up to me to ask a question. I was able to tell her how much I appreciate her work, and she gave me a warm hug.

For $35, we were treated to over four hours of fabulous live music and hula dancing. What a treat! This even included "heavy pupus" (appetizers). And what was especially memorable for me was those who were in attendance. And I'm not talking about the human beings, but rather spirits. I am not so much a seer, a clairvoyant, as much as I'm a feeler, a clairsentient. Here we were seated right alongside the ocean at sunset, facing the back of the palace, and so often I would look up at the wide balcony and "saw" in my mind's eye the spirits of past royalty up there; sometimes waving, and enjoying the tribute to Hawaii in song.

I intuitively knew what these queen synchronicities were revealing, that it is time for all of us (men/kings included!) to recognize and step into our royalty. We have been imprisoned and enslaved on this earth, whether we are aware of it or not. And the known royalty of our present time, and that includes much celebrity "royalty," are not all who we think they are. They are far from deserving to be put up on pedestals. Rather, we should be putting ourselves up on pedestals.

Several members of the Hollywood royalty have been compromised. Many are right in our faces displaying satanic symbolism as seen in countless pictures. They are feeding us created and forced propaganda for the elite's goals! We have worshiped false idols who have done the unspeakable, as we will soon learn, if we haven't yet. We need new royalty and it will be comprised of all of us. This makes me recall what Archangel Michael said years ago in *The New Sun*[6]

Everyone will be recognized for who they really are. And in that recognition, it will be understood that no soul is greater than another. The past ways of idolizing and revering the relatively few among you will no longer occur as you see and respect the full magnificence of every being.

While driving on November 24th to a home in the Queen Liliuokalani subdivision, quite ironically, I *heard* the message to really take ownership of my Queendom, to act like a Queen within, the same asserting of our royalty that we are all being asked to master. I was proclaiming myself as a royal and this is what I am suggesting that we each do, within even the most mundane aspects of our lives. Own who you really are.

After that, I went to the coffee shop to write, and Hydee immediately texted me about her dream: "Then, I keep hearing Rex. And Renee. *Rex* means King in Latin and I kept repeating this. I knew it was Latin. And *Renee* means Queen in French! Perhaps the King and Queen unite?! Just looking and I see it also means reborn." The

---

[6] Soliel, Mary. *The New Sun.* Boulder: Twelve Twelve Publishing, LLC, 2013.

messages were being delivered, even via Hydee's dream! So, I called her "Queen Renee" and she called me "Queen Mare."

I shared with Hydee that I was being urged to really own this royalty title. To know who I am and to not settle for less than. And to pass this understanding to all who will hear it! Ever since these early days of this mission, I've been referring to many friends, and even strangers, by their royal titles. Whether they be Queen, King—or Princess, Prince.

Trust me, this is not my style. I am not into looks or elegance or status level in any way, whatsoever. I am fully into casual living, casual dress, casual presentation—being a total hippy at heart—so please understand that I'm not particularly referring to royalty on a physical level. Much more profoundly, this is about owning something so much more mysterious and precious. This is embracing the deepest part of us which is the soul, and to do so in a most benevolent way. To create our New Earth, we have to accept and move into who we really are. *This is ultimately a call to own who we really are, and in tandem with God's endorsement.*

On November 16th, I had an afternoon appointment in Waimea, a Northern town surrounded by stunning green rolling hills, and inland from the coast. I decided to go early so that I could sightsee a bit, and planned to visit well known Waipi'o Valley. It was once home for Hawaiian royalty, referred to as the "Valley of the Kings." It is jaw-dropping gorgeous.

This man I met at Costco, just days before, randomly told me about a restaurant called Gramma's Kitchen, which would normally be a 90-minute drive for me. I thought it was so odd that he would randomly share this, as we weren't even talking about restaurants. Plus, it was so far away. Certainly, there was something to this randomness. So I decided that after I pass by Waimea, I'll also stop at this restaurant in Honokaa for breakfast, because it *just happened* to be on the way to Waipi'o Valley. After ordering breakfast and a coffee, I was astounded to receive this coffee cup with the word QUEEN on it, as well as an image of a crown! Yes, ladies, "It's good to be the Queen."

I asked the waitress if all of their coffee mugs were like this, and she replied that mine was the only one they have. They get their coffee cups from a thrift shop, and so each mug is different, she explained. I then showed her the shirt I was wearing, as I felt to wear my Queen shirt today, and just shook my head to myself. When anything with such astronomical odds as this happens, I often imagine how Michael and my angel team must be laughing, just waiting for my reaction. "Here it comes... now watch her!"

On December 1, 2019, I attended a group meditation wearing my Queen shirt, again. It quickly became a conversation piece with a small group I was speaking with. Everyone really liked it and I explained about the Queen synchronicities, including my finding this very shirt in the very first retail store I visit on the Big Island, and right after several of us began experiencing an influx of Queen serendipities. I then shared that I believe it was all about our stepping into our royalty now.

This one woman, Cheryl, shared to my delight that her roommate made her a birthday cake three days prior, and on the cake it said "Happy Birthday, Queen Cheryl." I asked if her friend ever referred to her as a queen before making this cake, and she said "No!" Surely, it now holds even more meaning for her. And here is yet another example of how the Queen message is suddenly in our consciousness, via what appears to be the 100th Monkey phenomenon and angelic influence! What if that's what the 100th Monkey Effect really is—a result of heeding angelic whispers of guidance?!

A couple of days later, I was at the beach and someone was telling me a story about her family. She said that she told her granddaughter that she was a queen. The granddaughter replied that she was actually a princess and that her grandmother was a queen. I just shook my head to myself. She had no idea about the book I was writing, nor my Queen synchronicities.

I bought a second QUEEN shirt when I realized I was going to be wearing it a lot. When visiting Hilo for a second time, and as I was walking toward the sea, this Hawaiian man holding a Chihuahua mix in his arms approaches me and says, "Queen, meet Princess." "Princess, meet the Queen." He obviously noticed my shirt, and this little Chihuahua/Maltese mix is actually *named* "Princess"! It was all so synchronistic, plus with the dog being a Chihuahua (again, if you read my other books, you will understand why). And the man had hair near identical to mine—a long, salt and pepper, wavy mane. And this happened standing just a block away from Queen Lili'uokalani's Gardens!

Hawaiian royalty continued to be mirrored in various ways while on the island. On December 6th, I was clearly guided to attend the opening night of a movie called *The Islands*. Filmed completely in Hawaii, the film is based on the true story of Chiefess Kapiolani who found Jesus Christ in 1823 through visiting missionaries on the island. She courageously risked her life going to the volcano to demonstrate to her people a true and strong faith in Christ.

What I did not know until I watched the movie was that it was about human sacrifice! Islanders, one at a time, were sacrificed to Pele because their belief was if they did not perform this barbaric task, Pele, the goddess of the volcanoes and fire would take all lives on the island. The royal one showed her people a new belief and way of being. And we are now being shown a new way of being in the 21st century.

Now what are the chances that I'm in Hawaii doing all kinds of energetic clearings on the land and knowing that human sacrifice is one of the horrors that needed transmuting—and this movie happens to premiere when I'm on the island. It was promoted as the biggest movie ever produced in Hawaiian history. I knew I had to attend. I was amazed at how this unfolding happened so naturally and I seemed to be on the island at the perfect time as a revolution and evolution are about to go into overdrive. But the message was ever more profound when I consider where we are as a human species now.

Upon deeper thought into the message of this movie, I realized that even more barbaric sacrifices are happening in present day! While difficult to even write, satanic ritual abuse, adrenochrome creation, and violent pedophilia acts are devastatingly real, and horrifically so with children. The truths are out for those willing to see. And on top of that, all of humanity has been targeted over decades for a slow culling of world population through intended poisons of our food, water, air, vaccines, etc. This is all absolutely barbaric! And most people don't see it. This culling to bring down the world's population (*which they will not get away with!*) is declared and etched into stone at the Georgia Guidestones for all to see.

While on the Big Island, I never went to the volcano area of the island. I had no desire to, perhaps due to a past life experience, and yet part of me still ponders at times if I should have made myself go, just as I went to the Vatican to transmute when I really didn't want to. Yet it may have been too much for me. When I really consider this on a deep level, I realize that the royals, and of course Michael, would have sent me there if I was meant to visit.

Interestingly, the famous young royal couple stepped down from the British royal family in January of 2020. There are numerous reports of darkness in the royal bloodline and many speculate that things will be dismantling within that hierarchy—and it was the first thing I thought of when I heard this news. This feels quite symbolic, a metaphor, actually, that as the old falls, the new Royalty that is evolving humanity will be stepping into being in a whole new way.

When you think of royalty, what words would you use to describe them. Are they entitled, superior, elitist? If you met a royal family member, would you be shaking in your shoes or would you say to yourself, "Oh, there's another human being." Yes, they are people, and this includes Hollywood "royalty" who are souls having a human experience too. In my younger days, I was definitely into celebrity, but not anymore. I can barely even watch a new American movie release for two reasons. I don't like most of them because they are so fake and synthetic and they further us from, rather than elevate our consciousness. And, secondly, I know too much about the dark side of Hollywood. Everything is changing. We are seeing things as they are and as we are.

On December 31, 2016, Archangel Michael came through with this message—planting more seeds! It's a message that is ultimately for everyone.

AA Michael: *I am showing you visions of knocking walls down with sledgehammers, if you will.*

Mary: I see it!

AA Michael: *This is basically what you have, figuratively, done your whole life. Subconsciously at first, and then consciously as you set firm on your path. These walls needed to come down, in the micro and macrocosm of life. And you have completed a huge phase now. It is time to acknowledge this and get ready to build the new. Except it will not be from walls, it will be from pedestals. Pedestals for you all to stand taller, raise higher, connect with us and with each other from a higher standpoint!*

Do you see? This is a way to envision the next steps as you don't have to try so hard to be at a higher level? You are already there. The pedestals are built. And now the desirable will come with more ease. In your personal, professional life... and life outside of you. These are not just words, this is a big announcement and I wish for you to really understand that you are standing at a much higher level. You cannot go backwards, really. It will only get better from here when you see from that higher place.

Mary: Thank you, Michael! I love this! Thank you so much and I am excited for this New Year with you, and our work together. I feel it will grow and be like never before.

As it turned out, 2017 was a year to be excited about regarding my work with Archangel Michael, which would reach brand new heights. The year included extremely rough spots too, learning about and experiencing dark people and interference. While far from fun, it helped me to really understand the mission to battle and transmute extreme darkness. It was later this year that the warrior mission would be given to me, writing and publishing the new book in a rapid three months, and preparing to lead with Michael his Warriors of Light! That took each of us "elevating" ourselves, owning our power. We need to see "royalty" in a whole new paradigm. It is a new kind of royalty, not one that is shrouded in darkness and secrecy. It is honorable and sacred, as we are driven by love, over everything else. Can you imagine such a thing? Well, let me ask you this. Have you noticed yourself to be more forgiving? Are you tempering your anger more easily? Do you find yourself connecting more with strangers and going more out of your way to spread kindness or do more for another? This is what moving further into Love is. It is grand, loving service. It is subtle, and a most natural process in our evolution. We need to buoy ourselves up, as loving, sovereign beings.

Another piece of the royal clues came when synchronistically coming across this:

I, Lili'uokalani, by the Grace of God and under the constitution of the Hawaiian Kingdom, Queen, do hereby solemnly protest against any and all acts done against myself and the constitutional government of the Hawaiian Kingdom by certain persons claiming to have established a Provisional Government of and for this Kingdom.

That I yield to the superior force of the United States of America, whose Minister Plenipotentiary, His Excellency John L. Stevens, has caused United States troops to be landed at Honolulu and declared that he would support the said Provisional Government.

Now, to avoid any collision of armed forces and perhaps loss of life, I do, under this protest, and impelled by said forces, yield my authority until such time as the Government of the United States shall, upon the facts being presented to it, undo action of its representative and reinstate me in the authority which I claim as the constitutional sovereign of the Hawaiian Islands.

Mo'I Lili'uokalani
January 17, 1893

Quite bluntly, the world has been run by bullies. That's putting it mildly. We see this in the macrocosm, but also in the microcosm of our lives. How many children have been targets of bullies in school? It's a huge pet peeve for me, experiencing it as a child, myself, and even at times throughout my adult life.

Bullies work at a level where they have no compassion and are fueled by their self-appointed egotistical power. There is often no getting through to them. If they cannot learn their lesson on how to treat people, their next lesson will come much harder. This is the way that karma works, as you know.

We are in acknowledging and then letting go times. Messages from Archangel Michael have been preparing us over the years to let go of the old, and let go of what no longer serves our evolving selves. And now the former queens of Hawaii are perpetuating the message, seeking healing for the land so that we can start anew. Mahalo nui loa to all the reverent overseeing that touch our lives on the island, whether we are aware of it or not.

Finally, as I marvel over the signs that brought this royalty awareness forward, it took many months for me to realize my friend Jeannie's prophetic nod, just prior to leaving for Hawaii. She was the first human to give me a sneak peek of what was ahead, without my putting it together until months later. Jeannie treated me to a beautiful bon voyage lunch before I left for Hawaii, and gifted me with a warrior bracelet that Michael seemed to help pick out with her.

As we were saying goodbye for now, Jeannie told me that something big was ahead, on the island. She said something to the effect that I am this queen. That I am royalty. This felt way too grandiose to take in. Little did I know that Jeannie was already tapping into my mission. She was actually giving me the most perfect preview of what this mission and book were about, except it is about all of us being royalty!

Chapter Five

Living the Macro Within the Micro

L ife on the Big Island was not all fun and games, and I rolled with some incredibly dark punches amidst experiencing utter paradise. When I arrived on this popular island, I found a place to rent immediately which is most unusual, and was initially very happy about it. The landlord was very unique, but I thought I could handle eccentric and really just wanted to get my Hawaii journey started.

One evening, a couple of days after I moved in, a loud sound and vibration made it feel like a car hit the house, and I quickly wondered if it was an earthquake. Sure enough, it was a tremor. I soon saw the post online, reported at the exact time I felt it. Also, right around that time there was a shooter in Kona that was caught, and thankfully no one was hurt. Things were shaking up, for sure.

Most unfortunately, over time some very weird things were happening inside this studio, that was part of a large house. While avoiding specifics as they creep out people that I share with, I will just say there was hidden video surveillance, my things were moved around while I was out, and all culminating in something very creepy when I finally realized there was a hidden door in this apartment. You can get an idea with just that much information. And trust me, that last straw had me packed up in two hours and then out of the place.

There was something nefarious going on and the people involved knew I was onto something not being right. They wanted to scare me away, but I would not be scared off the island. When I later asked AA Michael what to do about this, he said that that it was in his hands now. He assured me I played my part, I am protected, and I need to let this go and fully move on, which I did.

It took me two months while living in The Manago hotel in Captain Cook to find the next apartment, because I left the prior place when high rent season was about to begin. The new studio I finally found was great for me—it was quiet and in a good location. Even when they erroneously advertised the place over $200 cheaper than it truly was, I went for it because I really needed to get settled and get back to work. After only two weeks there, the next-door neighbor who was a massive hoarder was in denial of a water leak and mold in her bathroom, didn't report it, which then eventually seeped into my place.

The boss at the property management company called me to say that "The job is done." The leak was fixed, she said, and then went on to talk about an unrelated electrical issue in the studio. I said that my office area is literally set in this water soaked carpet and I need to first know if it is clean, gray, or sewer water. She said that she didn't know and that she will see when the bill arrives. I was concerned that mold could develop.

So I insisted that this must be addressed and they have to remove the carpet if there is mold. Sure enough, there was not only water in the flooring but also in the walls. Turns out the renovation company would later tell me that the wall and carpet needed to be replaced. Had I not pushed it, this would have been a much greater mess.

During this most upsetting call, though, the boss was literally yelling at me to run a fan on the carpet. I said that won't do much as there is water under the carpet too, and we are in humid Hawaii, which makes matters worse. We needed experts to assess the situation. Her being a native and in this line of work, she should know much better than myself. Desperate to do something, anything with a very unreasonable and extremely rude person, I ran a fan for 48 hours which led to the releasing of mold spores, my becoming very sick, and I had to vacate the place. To this day, several months later, I am still sick from mold exposure. It can take a year or more to recover.

Both she and another manager were bullying and trying to intimidate me, taking absolutely no responsibility. I was literally sick from mold blown into the air and it cost me mentally, emotionally, and physically, as well as a financial nightmare of over $5,000. I lost all my nearly new furniture, that they wouldn't replace or reimburse me for. I had numerous doctor and supplement bills, and I had to pay for expensive living while waiting to return to the studio. They took several weeks to renovate what was quoted to be less than a one week job. And they never once showed an ounce of concern for my health or how this affected my life.

Shockingly, after weeks of waiting they didn't even replace the carpet, but rather just had the company knock out part of one wall, which made no sense to do that alone. So, I got out of the lease to my great disadvantage, and then got very sick again when returning to pack. This was all about money. Sound familiar? Archangel Michael taught me that the microcosm mirrors the macrocosm, and vice versa.

The message I kept getting was to deal with it, and let go. I would stick up for myself and address what needed to be addressed as things came up, and then move onto new thoughts and positive feelings, whatever it took and to the best of my ability. I quickly realized that this is very conscious work.

What I soon realized was that I was in battle in the microcosm on the island. Just as we, humanity as a whole, are being treated like dirt, as if subhuman, as poisons are forced on us daily from the skies, our water, the food, pesticides, EMFs, etc., I was being treated the same in the micro, treated absolutely inhumanely.

Here I was so excited about it being whale season (January through March), which I was most looking forward to—dolphins *and* whales. Yet for part of it, I was on the other side of the island away from my human and dolphin communities, because it was the busy season and very hard to find anything. After the first six days, I was on my own finding and funding my stays less only prorated rent. The office barely updated me on what was going on and would not answer emails. It was truly unconscionable. And I called them out on it all, which they would still never reply to, nor take any responsibility.

And yet even during all of this, I held onto the bliss, and worked on this book. When my dolphin sister friends would call and check on me, and when discussing the dolphins, tears would come. I couldn't believe how deeply these beings affect me. The dolphins sure helped keep me in my joy and feeling rejuvenated, whenever I was feeling down.

No matter the challenges, I kept a keen eye on the deeper truths here. Making the connections and connecting the dots helped me traverse through the personal challenges, and certainly our global challenges. Truth is king now, and we all must seek it without pause. And along with considering these two nightmarish living situations in retrospect, I refer to one of Michael's teachings that are ever true now:

The greater you see and understand what is really occurring on earth, and has been most especially in recent decades, the harder it may feel to endure. And yet I tell you the way out of this dark grip on precious life is through Truth. Truth—really exposing and understanding the torment subjected on humanity—will free you from the chains of imprisonment you have endured, while most are completely or mostly unaware.

Your courage to seek the truth has never been more needed as you are at a breaking point and turning point. Breaking point as the confusion is so wide and rampant, and often by design. And turning point because you are turning the corner on massive revealing of so much darkness that has plagued your earth. I say this not to frighten you but to ask you to bravely seek and allow the truths to be revealed both in the macrocosm and microcosm. For when you allow the truths of your personal lives to be set free, that in turn affects the greater and more global truths to be set free as well.

When you learn the truth about a dangerous product, say, you are empowered with information that convinces you to avoid that product. When you learn the truths that have been, are being, or about to be revealed on a much more massive scale, you will clearly be making new choices which will have a dynamic and profound effect on and for the betterment for humanity, that which only truth can bring. So seek the truth... in all ways. Bring this actual word 'truth' into your inner and outer vocabulary every day. This is part of the spiritual warrior's way.

~ Archangel Michael on October 18, 2017

Chapter Six

The 2020 Alignments

It is 1.11.20, and I'm in a most unexpected situation right now. I had moved into my studio only two weeks ago, feeling much joy and relief of having gotten settled and back into my routine. As mentioned, that joy and relief came to a sudden halt a few days ago when there was water (and thus mold) leaking into my studio.

Yesterday, I went to seek the dolphins. Sure enough, as I parked, I saw them there in the bay. So I joyfully headed to the water. By the time I got onto the beach, I could no longer see them. This kind man who was sitting a distance away walks up to me and says the dolphins are out there... "See?!" Yes, they were indeed, there in the distance, and I thanked him for going out of his way to point them out to me. I had the strongest feeling to ask him what his name was. I was *sure* that it was Michael. This very morning before leaving for the beach, I read a beautiful post about Archangel Michael appearing through a human. So I flat out said, "Thank you again! What is your name?" He said, "Mike." Oh yes, of course it is. He asked what my name is. I said, "Mary," and quelled the urge to explain the extra big smile on my face.

Later in the day, I had literally just completed writing an email to my M&M group, telling them about "Mike," and was about to send it when I received an email notice of where they were putting me up (for what would turn out to be just part of the time) while they do the renovations. When I clicked on the map for the location, waves of surprise and joy moved through me. On 1.11.20, of all days, and with Michael's energy especially around me during this trying time, I temporarily moved into a condo right across from St. Michael the Archangel Church!

That evening, I was sitting on the balcony talking to a friend on my phone, and at 5 p.m. the church bells rang. Of the many times I've been to this church in Kona, to stand by Michael's statue, which always proved synchronistically magical, I never once heard these bells before. Being located right next to Michael's church for the next six days made my challenge a whole lot more bearable. While I don't attend church, this is a very special place for me to visit—namely, that statue. I know that Michael was orchestrating so much to keep me high vibe through the challenges. And right now, I am just a stone's throw away from his church during one of the most energetically powerful three days this world has experienced in some time. There are no coincidences, as we know.

On 1.11, there was a full moon lunar eclipse. Uranus retrograde ended, and on top of that was an incoming solar storm. As spiritual medium and psychotherapist Kellee White wrote on Facebook, "This is challenging to the opposite alignment of the Sun, Jupiter, Mercury, Pluto, and Saturn all in Capricorn. Capricorn is the Divine Father, responsibility, work, discipline, control. On the

positive side, this brings us all second chances—do-overs! This will bring Light to the planet!"

I don't have the brain for astrology and know next to nothing about it, so I greatly appreciate Kellee's insights as her heads-up always prove meaningful to me. She went on to explain the stellium in Capricorn. "This can cause destabilization in the world. Whatever happens is for the greater good and will bring light and awareness." Then, there's the Saturn/Pluto Conjunction at 22 degrees which Kellee says is huge. "This means a shift in consciousness! 2020 brings a new awareness on a micro level, a social level and a macro level. We will see changes within ourselves and outside of ourselves."

"We are asked to rise above the chaos and in so doing, our marvelous vibration begins to rise! Our intuition grows!" These words beautifully mirrored the same messages that I and so many are receiving. Here I was, being asked again to rise above the chaos in my personal life, rising above much greater intensity than described in this book. So it can be both individual and collective, and how we handle it personally affects the whole, as Archangel Michael teaches.

Additionally, on January 12th, the spiritual community was being asked to send energy to Uluru (formerly known as Ayer's Rock), in Australia which is known to be the umbilical cord of the planet. So clearly, this was a powerful time for the earth and we knew it; we could feel it on deep levels.

Getting back to my story in the microcosm. Some friends told me about the movie *Zeitgeist*, urging me to watch it. I didn't register it in my head though, and completely forgot. However, on January 13, right after the stunning alignments described above, I was reminded by my friends, yet again. I knew I had to listen this time, so I watched it and was quite stunned.

According to the main movie website (www. zeitgeistmovie.com), "The Zeitgeist Film Series is about examining the world we share, the values we hold, the problems we face, along with what we can do to make it better." When it comes right down to it, this movie will help you understand just how deep the corruption of money runs, and how we can shift into a new way of living and being.

Now interestingly, this is what happened to me earlier this day that I finally watched the movie. I went out that morning to take a walk on the sidewalk by the water. Just before I learned about my temporary move to the place right above Archangel Michael's church, which is a 30-minute drive from where I was living, I kept seeing images in my mind of myself walking along the sidewalks in that very area. Was I being guided to truly go there and walk around? Well, once I found about this move, I realized that these were actually premonitions. So, I took my first walk there.

On the one block walk to Ali'i Drive, the main strip in Kona, I strongly intuited I was going to find money on the ground, but even more than I've been seeing lately. The week prior, I saw two quarters right near each other which was quite a find, and I always pick up coins because I render them as symbolic gifts from the Universe, as you may too. Leaving them on the ground is saying no to the gift, in my view. Just after that premonition, I saw a homeless man whom I see so often when driving through Kona. He immediately made an impression on me. I never once saw him ask for money, and I sensed such kindness from him.

I had this strong feeling to go toward the water as if guided exactly where to go, off of the sidewalk and over there on the grass. To my wonderment, there was a dollar bill laying before my feet. I considered it magical, as you could tell it had been sitting in the rain the day before on the powerful 1.12.20. I picked it up and intuited that it was supposed to go to that homeless man, but I didn't see him anywhere.

So I walked along the water, and suddenly there he was! I told him I just found this lucky dollar bill, felt it was for him, and asked if he would accept it. He graciously accepted and responded so warmly, just as I imagined. He spoke something in Hawaiian or Japanese, and shook my hand so gently. There was something about this, and I shared the following with my group:

"Sometimes we feel so intuitively and Divinely guided, and need to trust it. Even though this isn't any big deal giving a dollar to someone who needs it more than me, it was a meant-to-be, orchestrated event for reasons I cannot articulate." I knew this was symbolizing something deeper than I realized.

It was no coincidence that my friends gave me the link to Zeitgeist on that very day, and I later watched it that evening. There was something about looking at the homeless man noticing he had only one backpack of belongings to his name, and yet two American flags sticking out of it! If you watch the movie, you will better understand why this connection was profound to me. Isn't it time for the less fortunate to become abundant, as we create our New Earth, and was this some symbolic gesture stating that to the Universe? Abundance of all kinds is indeed in our future, even though it may not seem like it, right now.

Money symbolism was very prevalent in my life on the island. I was finding coins on a near daily basis, sometimes two or more times a day, in the latter months of my stay. After Christmas, I had a remote healing session on "infinite abundance" in an effort to clear prosperity issues from back into my ancestry, up to this point in my life. *During* the 33-minute session (the practitioner texted me when it began), my dear friends Debbie and Justin who were vacationing in Hawaii for Christmas called me asking if they could take me to the Four Seasons for lunch. What? I don't normally get invited to such fancy restaurants! Turns out that I wasn't able to go, but it brought a Four Seasons synchronicity theme back into my life, not to mention validating that the healing session was immediately working on an energetic level!

Those who are in my M&M Group know about the Four Seasons signs I had while visiting with my mom a year prior. I reminded my mom about the time she took me to the Four Seasons for lunch when I was on a business trip with my parents in Europe. When I was 24, I presented a technical paper I wrote with my father at an international conference in Germany. I reminded her that the celebratory meal was the nicest, fanciest meal I ever had. I'm really not into fancy restaurants and actually prefer casual, but it was a very special and memorable time with my mom, because I knew that she really wanted to treat me while my dad was attending the rest of the conference.

Later that day, after talking about this memory, we drove by a place (not a restaurant) called the Four Seasons! When having dinner that very night, I ordered something at a Chinese restaurant not even realizing the name of the dish *The Four Seasons*, until I was actually ordering it! I was only comparing the vegetables in the different dishes and was stunned when I verbalized the name of the dish to the waiter.

What happened on January 8, 2020 though, was the clincher. To be clear, the following occurred a matter of days after the Four Seasons lunch invitation. I had barely any kitchen counter space in the place I had just moved into, for what turned out to be an unexpectedly short time, and I felt very compelled to stop at a thrift store to see if they had something I can set my toaster oven on. I see this bright yellow filing cabinet and thought it would work. And then I could use the file drawers to store some things. When in expensive Hawaii, and especially when it's not a permanent stay, you make do without worrying about how things look.

As I opened the file drawer, I was utterly shocked! The files were still in there and check out what the *very first file* on the top drawer was labeled: FOUR SEASONS RESORT! Not only on the little plastic tag, but also on the face of the file too. I mean, this was an over-the-top crazy sign. I didn't get the filing cabinet because it was very rusted on the bottom, but I got from it what I needed... the sign! And I took a picture and was able to share this amazing synchronicity with my group, and now you. The fact is, the Universe speaks loud and clear to all of us. And this was an extraordinary sign that needed to be shared as its meaning continues to unfold. But I would come to find that it is clearly about the rich and poor divide coming into balance. More about that to come.

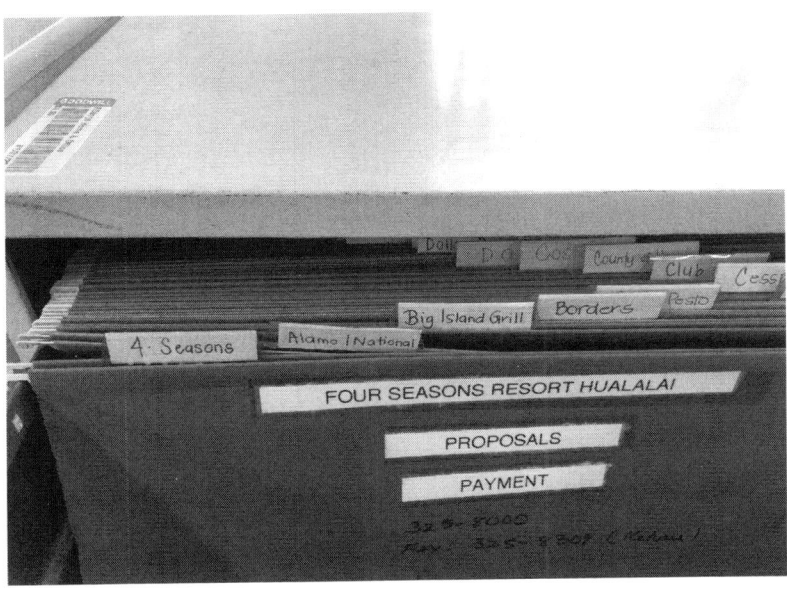

You will find as you continue to read on, that money was a clear and repetitive theme while on the Big Island. Whereas I lost a lot of money, and unfairly so, I gained great riches, symbolically. While I've been sharing amazing signs for over a decade now, I have never experienced anything quite like this. For instance, when this whole prosperity theme was building, I was standing at the cashier paying for my groceries at a store in Kona, and a folded dollar bill landed right onto the top of my left foot. I looked down only to find that it was actually *a $100 bill*, just sitting there balancing on my foot! I wish I took a picture but I wanted to get it back to its owner right away. What are the enormous odds of this happening? And with a $100 bill, no less.

The young man next to me dropped it when going through his wallet, and it somehow floated perfectly onto my foot. I said as I picked it up and gave it back to him, "Oh, you don't want to lose *this* bill!" He said, "Yes, especially because it's my lucky bill, it's from 1988." "Is it valuable?," I asked (surprised that this young of a bill would be). He said "It *will* be."

This made me ponder what was meaningful about 1988? It was the year I got married. Oh, and we went to Hawaii for our honeymoon! But I chose to consider the double digit 8s as being meaningful. As you probably know, 8 represents money and power, as well as infinity when seen on its side. I did later look it up online, and perhaps it was a star note which would almost double the value. But still, I thought it odd he referred to it as lucky and will be valuable. Okay then, well I just let that luck rub off on my left foot! (The left side of the body is known to be the receiving side, to boot, while the right is the giving side.) Here's to abundance for the "common man and woman," who are not so common!

I've been feeling Lily around so often lately, yet I haven't attempted getting a message or anything. I almost always wait for her to connect with me, when she has a message to impart. But, I often know when she is checking in on me. On January 26, right after another powerful reading from Jeannie, I went to Kona to get gas. If you live on the Big Island, you really want to be a Costco member. Gas is at least $4.00 a gallon on the island (at the time of this writing), and you can save about $.70 per gallon at Costco, so it's always worth the trip. Locals and tourists alike seem grateful for the savings that Costco provides here, including myself.

I was the first in line before three cars ahead of me, each pumping gas. The one right in front of me had just parked, and the middle car was leaving. So I moved into the open lane to get to the second pump. The plate that was now in front of me took my breath away. "LILL01." Had I been patient and waited for the person in front of me, I would have missed it, so sometimes impatience pays off—but, perhaps, not usually. Needless to say, once I returned to the hotel on this day, Lillian had a message for me that sure revitalized my heart.

Getting back to the reading I had with Jeannie, as always it was a balm on my soul. As you may know or imagine, it's hard to channel for self, especially regarding personal or emotional situations. What came through Jeannie was so validating, that I was indeed supposed to be in this place that was causing me such challenges, for now anyways. That this was yet more interference from the dark with continual shenanigans, and that basically I am in battle. And what was most touching was when Archangel Michael said through Jeannie that in these times, he is not standing next to me, *but in front of me*, shielding me. These words brought tears to my eyes.

After I left Costco, I went back to St. Michael the Archangel Church, parked in the lot near the statue, and took a picture of his statue from this vantage point. I wanted to have this visual of him having my back, as it is a great vision to behold. To imagine the mighty Archangel right in front of you, shielding you. What better protection can there be? All we each have to do is simply call on him for protection!

I went and ran an errand and then returned, walking on the road toward the statue and about 200 feet from my car. There was nothing on the road, and yet when I got in my car and drove out past his statue, there was a clean, brand new white hat on the ground! It struck me profoundly that it wasn't there in those seconds before that I walked right by there. And then it dawned on me... the "white hats." The white hats are in deepest battle during these times to take down the darkness, overthrowing the deep state, as you probably know. Just incredible! This was a definite message that our beloved Archangel has all our backs. We who are in battle for the Light, in varying ways, are all white hats. AA Michael clearly placed that hat there to provide this message at the most perfect time and ideal place—for us all.

In February, I met Natalia, a doctor who is from a place near Mongolia, and on the island for an extended stay, as well. She is a gifted psychic and healer, while also being an MD—displaying uniquely amazing right and left brain balance. We were both led to Kealakekua Bay a couple of weeks prior, re-meeting for the second time now, and both knew it was by Divine orchestration. In fact, when I visited the bay that second time, I got called away by phone and drove away, yet felt pulled right back only to see her there.

During this meeting, Natalia offered a healing and reading. I returned her generosity with a couple of remote gazings. The focus of her healing was on prosperity because my money is going quickly and I was losing a significant amount of money via the two living situations. I simply want to have the financial sustenance so that I can do my spiritual work without requiring a 3D job.

A few days later, I received a message from Lillian. I am adding this entry two months after the fact, because I went into my channeled messages and found her relevant words. I never put it together until now what happened the very next day that validated this very message! Lillian said that "all I'm going to say right now is to watch from signs from me in the next few days, yet more signs, to prove to you it really is me. And when you go into your heart, you will know." Somehow, I forgot these words!

The very day after Lillian's message, this same friend, Natalia, being such a generous heart yet again, took me out for a wonderful dinner. I told her the whole story about Lillian. Natalia connected to her on a psychic level and immediately recognized her beautiful sense of humor, noting that she likes to have fun with me. Well as it turned out, it wouldn't be just with me. And I was overjoyed that my friend could connect with my adopted aunt, as well.

Once again, the financial prosperity subject came up, and I told her about my friend who has a client who can pull $100 bills out of the air, from another dimension.

Minutes later, we were getting up to leave the restaurant and Natalia looks down at her seat and sees a penny that was surely not there when she sat down! Don't we normally check our seats before we sit? I told her that I was sure it was from Lillian! Yes, as you may know, passed loved ones can leave coins and all kinds of physical things for us. I did not put it together until two months later seeing Lillian's message given just the day before, Lillian told me to look for signs from her!

The following day I was looking at a potential place to live, but it was too far of a drive to the bays where I visit the dolphins. Natalia invited me to come see where she is staying while I was in the area, and we took a walk on the grounds. I told her I felt that penny on her chair was a great sign for her. Just as she replied that it was a sign for me too, a penny appears in front of my left foot! And this was in a low traffic area where hardly anyone is ever around. As I write this, I recall that $100 bill that floated right onto the top of my left foot!

But my abundance of true riches came via experiences in Hawaii, certainly those that occurred when swimming in the sea. Ever since January rolled around, it became common to see the humpback whales spraying water from their blowholes and breaching. I could barely contain my excitement each time I witnessed any sign of them. I had never seen a whale in the wild before, and this was truly a dream manifested. They are such magnificent, gentle giants. And during whale season, you can often hear the humpback singers when in the water, even if they're at a great distance. It is simply Heavenly.

Time and time again, I would film under the water so I could capture the whale sounds. One time, when taking a hearty swim right to the edge where the water gets deep, I was in for a joyous shock. Suddenly, two humpbacks came into view! I had no idea they were nearby. One is directly below me and I can barely contain my emotions. I was in utter awe, and at times crying in my mask, over the massive power and joy felt by being so close to these magnificent beings, perhaps 30-40 feet beneath me.

Now this happened after moving out of the mold ridden place. And even though I was getting tired of trying to find housing and part of me was ready to leave the island so I can better heal from the mold, I told the whales after seeing them that I cannot and will not leave just yet! They inspired me deep in my heart. I could go on and on trying to describe this encounter, but my words won't be enough because it felt utterly surreal and mystical. That whole week following the whale encounter Hydee referred to as my "Whale Week," because my life was filled with extra magic and joy that I felt the whales somehow helped to create. I felt sure they mysteriously helped to raise my vibration, and influence what I then attracted into my life.

Gratefully so, I went on some exciting chartered whale watching boat rides, and something eventful was always occurring, whether in or out of the sea. One piece of the puzzle simply fell into my lap when I was sitting at the bow of the boat talking to a woman who randomly told me that Waikoloa was built by the Rockefellers. Wow, now I get why I feel especially drawn there, to transmute the energies. Apparently, the workers were in the village, and the royalty resided north of there. She just randomly brought this all up, not knowing anything about my work and my new book. And yet it becomes part of this story—more clues being revealed so effortlessly.

I had the pleasure of meeting Gary and Sheila on that boat, although I met Sheila briefly on a prior charter. We bonded immediately and they invited me to their home after we returned to the harbor. They were so kind and generous, and told me I am welcome to any fruit on their land, any time. Fresh tropical fruit right from the trees was like gold to me.

On the way back after the boat ride, I stopped at my storage unit to pick up two copies of *I Can See Clearly Now*. One to give to them, and one for Natalia who told me she appreciated my inspiring her to become more aware of synchronicity. And what happened next will forever make me smile ear to ear.

As I drove up to the hotel for a quick shower before my visit, I was in awe of what was sitting at the curb directly outside the entrance to The Manago. A yellow balloon! (See bottom middle of picture on next page to spot the balloon at the curb.) It was just like the one that adorns the cover of my book! What are the astronomical odds of seeing a yellow balloon mirroring my book's cover—just minutes after I picked up these books for my friends, and right where I'm about to park? As soon as I finished taking pictures, a worker at the hotel picks up the balloon and puts it in the garbage. Had I arrived just a minute later, I would have missed this sighting. I proceeded to take it out of the garbage and put it in my room as a reminder of the power of this synchronicity.

I later realized the metaphor here. I'm bringing my first book and its subject matter out again from the shadows of stagnation, especially ever since Wayne Dyer used the same book title years after mine, which lessened my sales significantly. Anyways, the point is that I'm sharing so much about synchronicity so prevalent here on the island, with the Michael & Mary (M&M) Group, and now you, dear reader, in this very book. The subject of synchronicity, from my viewpoint, is making a huge comeback through me during these highly synchronistic times and while on a most magical island!

After arriving at my new friends' home, I gave Gary and Sheila the book and they got a kick out of the yellow balloon synchronicity. We talked for over three hours on their gorgeous lanai overlooking the Pacific, and realized even more so how like-minded we are. They both immediately felt like family and treated me as such.

Discussing in more detail the work we each do, they asked me about my new book. I told them that only a handful know about it, but I feel to tell them. So I explained that the book is about our becoming the royalty that we really are. In fact, I told them, it is called *You Are Royalty*. When I went on to describe the prevalent Queen synchronicities, and proceeded to call them King and Queen, Sheila said that she has a story for me, too.

She started to explain that she went to a healing dance circle on the Big Island. I knew about this event, but wasn't able to attend. Anyways, when the practitioner got to Sheila, she dropped down to the ground in prostrate position before her feet yelling "Queen!" And she stayed in that head down pose to Sheila's surprise. Sheila is a pilot, and a very strong and powerful soul. While it did not surprise me at all that this is what came through the woman before her, I was still blown away by yet another Queen synchronicity delivered to support this book's message with tremendous ease.

Then Gary, a former policeman, brings up Archangel Michael as the patron saint of policemen. He went on to tell me how profound his connection is to King Arthur and Excalibur! What? If you read *Michael's Sword & You*, then you will realize how synchronistic this was, as well!

No wonder we were all like glue to each other when we met on the boat—this was another Divine orchestration!

Sheila soon ordered my four other books and these people have been an incredible and immediate support to me. You know when people are meant to meet, you are irresistibly drawn and feel it immediately. I felt the same with Natalia, that our paths intentionally crossed, and most certainly with Hydee, of course. I know that you each have your own stories of soul connections and magical meant-to-be meetings. They are so very key, especially during these transformational times.

I was certain that my beloved guide Lillian was behind many orchestrations, and certainly with the coins appearing out of nowhere. And it would not surprise me at all if she was somehow behind that yellow balloon appearing in front of the hotel's entrance at the most astounding time.

When I took this picture in Colorado of an amazing angel cloud on January 19, 2018, it was right after Lillian came through with a message to me, and I was sure that this being was her! It is one of my most cherished cloud photos, among thousands captured thus far.

Look for this beautiful angel's profile of her closed eyes, big hair, and with wings and outstretched hands, as if flying. Even though I wasn't dressed for a hike, I was guided to "Stop now" at one of my favorite close-to-home paths. I saw a huge being in the clouds and joked with my angel team to not make them so big because I couldn't fit it in a single camera shot. Twenty minutes later, and right after conversing with Lillian's spirit, I captured this being in a different part of the sky. I was guided to take pictures as it slowly developed. I obviously knew it was going to be good, but the final "canvas" was over the top; an extraordinary memory. Ask and ye shall receive! And always look up.

After I moved out of the mold ridden studio, I called The Manago hotel in Captain Cook my home, yet again. It was where I first stayed upon arrival to Hawaii. Choosing the shared bath option with two halls of women once more made this a more affordable choice. I eventually converted my little room into a home office. One morning, I said to self that I needed to stay away from the ocean and get to work on this book!

The very moment I had this thought, I get a text about where the dolphins are—no exaggeration here. I had turned off the WIFI on my computer, but because I was expecting some important texts, I left my phone on, but as far from me as possible. Not just because of the distraction, but the cell phone is definitely affecting me more lately. One of my doctors told me that my mold sensitivity has made me sensitive to everything, including EMFs, and to keep the cell phone at a great distance.

My friend notifies me that the dolphins are at my favorite beach. I am usually there at daybreak, and after a month of being away from them due to the living situation, as well as the dolphins appearing to have headed north for some time, I have barely been with them upon my return. And yet look at how I am being tested! I will stay and work on the book. I am overwhelmed with thoughts and information, and simply need to get things down into my manuscript now. I could feel that more clues were coming together, and as synchronicity would surely unveil.

On February 19, I went to the beach before daybreak. I could see about five humpback whales in the distance. So I went into the water. You simply dive down about five to seven feet if there's a male singer way out there, and you should be able to hear. Other times, you can hear them even when swimming at the surface, with your ears in the water. I would never tire of hearing those otherworldly sounds. Hearing them in unison with the dolphins' sounds was the absolute best. While I easily adapt to the new, I couldn't get over all that I was experiencing.

As I was seeking the sounds, thoughts suddenly went to this island friend of mine who told me she worries about me when I go out in the water all alone, and she repeated her concerns to me again, just yesterday. I told her that I'm smart about it, plus Michael is protecting me. Sure enough, a man from Austria joined me just then in trying to hear the whales and I was certain that Michael sent him so my thoughts wouldn't go there. While in the water, he showed me his bag of about five or six Lemurian crystals. at least an inch in size, which he plans to offer to the ocean to attract the dolphins—beautiful.

We weren't able to hear the whales, and yet I was treated to a couple of other surprises, such as my first black-tipped shark sighting. I immediately wondered if that lapse where I focused on my friend's fears for me actually attracted a shark in my proximity. I've seen many sharks from small to medium size in the past six months, and they just go about their business.

The movie *Jaws* ruined it for us all, and a good number of us seem to fear them. I swam with many large docile sharks when in Belize, so that helped me to counter any fear. You definitely do have to be alert and careful. But generally, it seems that just like with snakes, don't bother them and the chances are excellent that they won't bother you. There are many fellow snorkelers I swim with who actually desire to be around sharks, so it makes one see them in a new and honoring way.

My new snorkeling partner named Christian pointed out an adorable baby turtle, so we had fun watching it. He then tapped me on the arm to get my attention, and said that he wanted to gift me with a Lemurian crystal! The usual me would say, "Oh no, you keep them, but thank you!" But since I am consciously learning to receive better, I greatly thanked him for such a lovely gift, and while closing my eyes I excitedly picked out the first one I touched in the plastic bag filled with water and crystals. We then parted ways since I somehow naturally stay in the water for three hours each time, especially when swimming with the dolphins—it's quite uncanny. And it seems to be my limit.

As I was walking out of the water, this beautiful family, all dressed in white, sitting on the beach, struck me. The man was looking through his binoculars seeking the whales, so I approached him to update where I saw them last. They are all from Germany and the woman spoke with me for a long time. She was deeply tuned in and spiritual, and we talked about how tomorrow is going to be a most powerful day, on the 02.20.2020. (It's a powerful 8 day, when you numerologically add up these numbers!)

The woman stated that we are coming full circle, while she drew a circle into the sand with her hand. From Lemuria, to here in Hawaii, back to Lemuria, connecting to it all as we bring forward... and she paused for the words. I said, "The new human?" And she said, "Yes!" There was something so memorable about her marking this in the sand. I shared about the Lemurian crystal gift I just received and she asked if she could activate it. I said that I would be honored by that gesture.

She said that the crystal has been activated to heal my inner child and to not "work." I assumed she meant no conventional work, just spiritual. I nearly laughed out loud because this is the same message I shared with Natalia. So I hold it now, feeling doubly blessed with a gift. And I know that many of us will gather at this beach tomorrow morning.

I have been intentionally transmuting energies on this particular beach for weeks as it is filled with so much Light and extraordinary beauty, and yet dark energies too. Things have shifted, I have felt this increasingly so. This is why I was so drawn to this specific place so often, in addition to the whole area being so gorgeous. I feel it is a hot spot for transformation on the island, in my view, with portals going to other dimensions as I was told on many occasions. The dolphins are definitely doing work in this very area.

So, I was very excited about the next day of 2.20 and the magic that it would bring. Michael recently said to me that there will soon come a great amount of incoming Light that few know about, and I have a feeling it is connected to this. And, of course, this lady tells me that she is connected to Archangel Michael. He keeps bringing us all together!

As it turned out, February 20 was indeed a most significant day, and a full day to boot. Natalia and I felt to go to the very same sacred sites that Hydee and I went to, four months prior. When I was tidying up my car before picking up my friend, I look up and see a crown-shaped cloud! Hydee happened to be driving by *just* when I was taking the picture, which was so funny! There is also a lovely large-winged bird on the right. But it wasn't until sometime later I noticed, to my utter joy, that the word *Love* can be seen above the crown. Stunning! Clearly, the day ahead would prove guided and most significant. The angels were showing us they would support us, again.

After a short period of time at the petroglyphs in Waikoloa, I became so incredibly dizzy that I could barely stand, let alone walk. Why was this a completely different experience here at this particular sight, this time around? It was reminiscent of when Hydee and I provided healing at one of the other sacred spots, as described earlier.

Once we stopped at a particular area within the petroglyphs, without thinking, the following words poured out of my mouth: *We are here to heal the divide, the divide between the rich and poor, the famous and common, the royalty and slave.* Clearly, I was channeling this, and I felt this pronouncement so deeply and would not forget it.

Whatever was going on unseen during the time spent at the petroglyphs felt huge, and as represented by this message that then came through Natalia:

"We came here to remember who we are."

"We are not of this world. We are trusting our hearts, preserving the earth, preserving the nature, preserving the knowledge that has been passed on for generations and generations."

"We are claiming our power. We are claiming our divine heritage."

"We are all God's children. We are here to serve. We are here to serve the Light. We are meant to live in prosperity and abundance, that is our divine heritage. But it has been taken away from us."

"Hawaii… Lemuria will rise again. Lemuria is in our hearts. And by us connecting with each other, and sharing our truths, sharing our love, we are raising the grid. That's why so many of us are being called, having had many lifetimes here. We are helping to raise Lemuria, and raising the vibration."

How beautiful and profound was this message? Natalia summed everything up! And, as mentioned earlier, that woman on the whale watch boat gave me a brief history of the rich versus poor living in this very area. Clues continue to be miraculously placed and unraveling.

Interesting to note that in Waikoloa, just a stone's throw from the petroglyphs are two malls. Closest to it are the Kings' Shops. Further and across the street is the Queens' MarketPlace. It made me smile those times that I drove around the village. As I write this, I recall when I was on the plane to the Big Island, I sat next to a woman who was staying in Waikoloa—I never heard of this resort area. She told me that I had to visit! Seeds are somehow planted without people even knowing, thanks to the angels and universal winks.

Speaking of seeds, I recall photo captures of royalty clouds from years ago. Now I see them as seeds preparing me for these very times and this very book. This angel queen was captured in August of 2014, and I referred to it as "Angel Royalty" when sharing with others. In *Look Up!*

See Heaven in the Clouds, I wrote, "And, in fact, when I saw this stunning accumulation of clouds, it seemed to display angelic royalty. You are looking at the profile of her face (hair, eye, nose, mouth, cheek, and ear), as if standing to her side, and complete with crown. You may see it differently since we all see and perceive in our own individual ways."

And when I saw this crowned and bearded King cloud (seen on the next page) and apparently holding a baby, it struck me deeply. I felt there was something more to this. I love reflecting back after things unfold in my discoveries. It keeps me ever close to the Heavenly beings reaching out, and feeling deep appreciation for their clarity, mystique, and the beautiful clues they provide. At the time, I was just very excited to see royalty expressed in the sky, having no idea they would one day prove ever meaningful.

A week after this powerful healing day, I met with Hydee for lunch. I share the following not from ego, truly, but as a validation of what was going on in my ecstatic and blissful, but also quite turbulent life in Hawaii. She had me in tears, saying how I am this pillar of Light being placed all over the island, and transmuting darkness everywhere. Being so full of Light, I am a target of the dark. And I was seen right away and had this tough living situation and the next. I was being placed all over the island (she named all the places) and willingly followed it, to transmute everywhere I went. She was the first to really name and validate all of what was really going on, which brought me to tears. It softened a lot of the intensity.

On March 5th, I went on my last of the chartered boat rides. The interesting thing was that the angels were residing with us the whole day via the clouds, and this capture was my favorite among many. It looks as if the sweet, winged angel on the left was blowing magic out of her mouth over the ocean—pointing toward meetings, sightings, and yet another white hat sign that would arrive an hour ahead of this cloud appearance!

I shared with you the magical white hat sign when I was at Michael's statue in January. Well, when on this boat, I took mental note of this older man wearing a white baseball cap. I immediately thought of the "white hats" and that unforgettable sign. After we docked and exited the boat, I realized that I forgot my little bottle of drops that keep my snorkel mask from fogging up, so I went back to the boat to ask the crew member for it. He hands it to me and says, "Oh, and someone left their white hat," and gives it to me. Are you kidding me? And he actually used those words. Not their "hat," "baseball cap" or "white cap," but rather their "white hat." So here I am holding this white hat walking all around the parking lot trying to find the gentleman it belonged to. He had already left, as it turned out.

The very next day, a sudden, strong awareness came over me. I know I must leave the island. The mold is getting to me. A doctor told me that it will get into the brain and make me dumb! I didn't like that, and yet it was something I needed to be aware of. And sure enough, it was on this very morning I knew I had to face how much the mold was affecting me. I was suddenly having a hard time knowing not just the day, but what month it was! It scared me, to be honest. This came on so suddenly, and so I decided to leave right away.

At the time the virus "plannedemic" became unveiled, just so happened to be the time I was led to the next place to write the second half of this book. Everything was happening at once. It was becoming increasingly clear that there was another place I need to be. In a weird way, events also made sure that happened, such as the mold exposure. I really did not want to leave this island so soon, but it was clear that it was time.

My first thoughts were about how I could leave the dolphins, more than anything. I would continue my connection with my human friends I've made here, but the dolphins! I told myself to not even think about it, or I would not leave. The emotions were too strong. And yet I knew with every fiber of my being that I had to leave right away. So, I truly could not entertain these feelings, which is against my nature—I always face my feelings.

And yet everything was falling into perfect place. I couldn't believe how magically everything panned out. The preparation to leave was most definitely supported by the unseen. Everything came together and although my heart did not want to leave, I felt I was being protected. If I weren't on the mainland closer to my loved ones during what I knew were very challenging times ahead, it would have been quite hard on me. When in Hawaii, you are far from everywhere.

On March 8, I had my final swim with the spinners. And it was also the most remarkable time with them. One crystal being came right up to me and I was able to capture the whole encounter on video. (See the video named: "Unforgettable Soul Encounter with a Dolphin on 3.8.2020.") Even though I had a few more days here, I just *knew* this was going to be my last swim with them. While I tried to just be in the moment and not think about that fact, my emotions got the best of me and I was overcome.

When this sweet and loving being came up to me with others close by, I lost it emotionally. I cried so hard through my snorkel and at one point, it stood up vertically looking me right in the eyes as if empathizing, but also something more. I was grieving leaving them, but also grieving some deep emotional pain. As always, mixed in with the cries was laughter, too. I ended up laughing and crying deeply at the same time. In these couple of minutes, the dolphin stuck by me and continued to communicate telepathically. Then just like that, they all vanished.

After that extraordinary experience, I continued to swim with them for another hour or two. At the very end, they left doing what is referred to as porpoising, where they repeatedly surface out of the water and swim quickly—a magnificent sighting. It's the quickest way for them to travel, and I have seen them do this only one other time. So it was the most beautiful farewell until we meet again.

Now something otherworldly happened to me after this swim, and I fully relate it to whatever this dolphin did... I lost 8 lbs. overnight! Please realize that I know that you may deeply question how this is possible. It truly was miraculous and supernatural. I ate normally, and even if I were on some wild diet and swam five miles, who loses 8 lbs. in one day? It was during the middle of a 10-day period where it was the only time I had access to a scale when on the island, while staying at an Airbnb for a change of pace. Every morning for five days prior, I noted I was at the same weight. I lost 8 lbs. overnight after the dolphin encounter, and for the next five days I remained 8 lbs. down!

During this final swim, I knew that something magnificent happened. It was a massive emotional release. I could feel something happening that I couldn't describe. When the dolphins scattered in a flash which signified a release, in that moment I felt something had changed within me. And when I got on the scale the next morning I was utterly dumbstruck, as I'm sure you can imagine.

It wasn't until months later, I put this experience together with what Therese wrote in *Dolphin Dimension*:

"After many more swims with the dolphins, I understood that their sonar unlocks emotions that become trapped in the body. The earlier feeling I'd had of getting a 'tune-up' was the dolphins at work using sonar to release unexpressed feelings which had become blocked in my being. My body was simply expressing and letting go of the suppressed emotion. The good part was I was releasing grief without having to re-experience the memories. I felt sad, but I felt better. It was a relief to let it go."

Being a Scorpio, I was more than sad though—my feelings went very deep. Even though it is quite embarrassing for me, I left the sounds on in the video I created. I knew that something very profound happened and I wanted to share it just as I experienced it. But then I did feel a whole lot better.

Later in the book, Therese adds "One of the most powerful ways dolphins heal humans is with their love. It is very healing to experience unconditional love and acceptance. I know from my own experiences that this kind of dolphin healing cures the deepest of soul wounds." And that is exactly what I felt I received on this day, release and profound healing of the deepest of my soul wounds.

And, finally, this I firmly and intuitively believe: "Dolphins heal in ways so advanced that to date we humans have barely scratched the surface of the dolphins' healing potential. As humankind evolves spiritually, I believe we will come to understand more about the ways in which dolphins heal and the extent of their capabilities." Oh how I love this. And this is exactly why I thought that even those who have spent decades with the dolphins have much to learn. Being so new to this, I greatly look forward to understanding more someday.

One of my favorite dolphin healing stories, outside of my own, came from my friend Sheoli. When on her Awakening In Paradise Retreats chartered boat adventures she organizes, this dolphin expert was kind enough to share with me some incredible stories. It didn't take long for her to realize I was a complete newbie to dolphins and whales as I was constantly in awe over every sighting. So listening to Sheoli's stories and learning so much from her was the icing on the cake on these boat charters.

Sheoli told me she had experienced chronic neck pain for many years. Once when swimming with the wild spinners, a dolphin leapt up out of the water and landed on the top of her head. The blow was strong enough to have broken the skin, so Sheoli immediately swam to shore and drove home to tend to her wound. Shortly afterward, she noticed that the pain that used to reside in her neck was completely gone! From that point forward, that pain was never to return—incredible!

It wasn't until later that Sheoli realized the dolphin was actually compressing the vertebrae in her neck rather than what her chiropractors had done. It performed an actual chiropractic adjustment on her neck!

Note: On October 9, 2020, prior to this book going to press, I checked with Sheoli to make sure that this passage was written accurately. On October 11, my dear spirit brother Lee emails me describing his dream that I was in. It seemed to mirror the dolphin healing, in my view! So, the night after writing Sheoli, Lee had the following dream.

He wrote, "You were standing over someone, obviously as a healer, and in front of you was an anatomical drawing of the human physique, both front and back. You were drawing the energy route of where this person felt pain, and the path the energy was taking through their body. The image shifted and the drawing was almost life-size above the person, and you were manipulating the energy, healing, and clearing it. At some point, the person was afraid you might step on them (as in a rough *chiropractic* adjustment) and I was convincing them that you were doing energy healing that would not hurt."

Reading this, I immediately thought of that dolphin. Lee did not know anything about Sheoli or her story about the *chiropractic* adjustment that the dolphin provided! And it did come across as rough, but it took away her pain! Gosh, how connected we all are, which usually goes unseen.

When I do sword and healing work, I often in my imagination extend my physical body's size exponentially, and channel the energy. Say, if I were to send Light to a region in the world. I would enlarge myself in my imagination and use my will to channel Light through my body onto the particular area. I feel that Lee was somehow tapping into this, as well.

I immediately wrote Lee, letting him know that he was really onto something here! I told him that I would put him in the book, wrote the passage above this paragraph, and shared it with him, along with Sheoli's story. He responded, "Wow, that's pretty incredible, Mary! In fact, you WERE much larger in size (doubled, at least) and appearing more in an energetic way, if that makes sense, but I 'knew' it was you! Also, when I was talking to the person, I knew it was going to be hard pressure you would apply, but was assuring her it would not be really painful, and would create the healing she needed."

No matter what people may think about all of this, I know what I felt and experienced with that dolphin's remarkable healing. And it was most especially from this experience that I acknowledged and appreciated on an even deeper level what magnificent creatures these wild spinner dolphins really are. I could truly spend the rest of my life swimming with them day after day, but I know that I have a new mission to follow and it's not on the Big Island for now. I will return to the crystal beings, though, one day.

Chapter Seven

The Big Island Winks

Let me tell you, synchronicity on the Big Island was an absolute constant. I shared daily inspirations, magical synchronicities, and more since February of 2017 with my Patreon group. Just prior to leaving for Hawaii, I closed the Patreon group (especially for privacy reasons) and immediately formed the Michael & Mary Group—also known as the M&M Group. The patrons who were supporting me on Patreon automatically became part of this group. Because I did not know how much I would share while on the Big Island, I didn't want the group to be shortchanged, so I made the group complimentary for six months. However, I ended up posting a whole lot!

In this chapter, you will see a selection of my shared experiences. I find it important to present these as a separate chapter for two reasons. One, to show how magical life becomes when you trust the mission, go with the wind of your soul, and become explicitly aware of the signs along the way. And also, to serve as an example in awe-inspiring succession how the Universe, as well as the angels, repetitively send winks—whether they be seeds, reminders, unveilings, blessings, and more, through each and every day. Also, you'll see how these winks consistently complement each other, and often through additional messengers.

By reading these *informally written* winks in succession, that were being beamed to myself and others so consistently, you will see how the pieces of the puzzle all fit together. They collectively proved to me, and hopefully you too, that the mission of this book is most profound and real. And these signs indicate how this book's purpose is fully supported and actually instigated by the Heavenly realms. These are fun, revealing, and wildly connected. So here we go!

August 29, 2019. *A Chihuahua wink.*

The Humane Society in Kona encourages tourists and residents alike to adopt a dog for a day. Each dog wears an "Adopt Me" jacket. You can take it to the beach or wherever, show it off, and get the dog out there to get exposure and become adopted. Is that a great idea, or what? I told one of my kids planning to visit that we will have to do this!

Today when driving by the Humane Society on the way to the Target store (right nearby), I made a mental note of a must do, and thought that perhaps it will be a

Chihuahua. I then walked into the Target, and within a minute or two I heard on the overhead an announcement asking for the owner of a Chihuahua to please secure the dog in the store that is running around! So, the Chi signs have begun on the island.

September 2. *A Michael wink.*

I went to a beach, north of Kona, to snorkel and relax. Funny thing, I happened to find it just by going with the wind. Without reading or hearing about it, this beach ended up becoming one of my favorites places to visit. It boasts shaded trees to sit under and great reefs to swim in. On the way there, our Ron texted me a picture of a license plate he just spotted. [Note: Ron is a member of this group. He turned into a cloud, number, and license plate watcher years ago, especially after reading *I Can See Clearly Now* and *Look Up!* He is a successful businessman as an owner of over a dozen businesses, and he bought *Michael's Clarion Call* for each of his store's managers! I consider this generous and awakened soul as one of the way showers in the spiritual evolution of business and humanitarianism, as we create our New Earth.]

In this text, he wrote: "Happy Labor Day… GLT 1212… God Loves Twelves." Ron often finds meaning in each letter in a license plate representing a word and that's how he came up with the lovely "God Loves Twelves." I sometimes do that too, and I loved this particular assessment. With letters, I usually sense a single word from the letters that fit the meaning. Such as GLT could stand for *gallant*. (I'll never forget one time several years ago, Ron and I met to play disc golf. Upon returning to the parking lot, next to our cars was a car with the license plate 444 GLD, or 444 GoLD, and we both love the 444s!) Now I didn't see his text until right after I was backing up into my parking spot. And right in front of me was the plate SRD 555. Or SwoRD 555. And Ron is one of Michael's Warriors of Light!

As I was later leaving the beach, I saw two tree trunks hovering over the path, and one of them has the number 12 spray painted on it. Now what are the chances with such remarkable timing with Ron's text? Then when driving away, I see 212 on a white Jeep. 12.12, 2.12, and 12.2, are all symbols of my relationship with Michael, as you may know from my prior writings.

September 3. *A lucky wink.*
I have always loved ladybugs. You too? To me, they are a great sign and symbol to behold. Weeks before I arrived in Hawaii, I texted Hydee a picture of these amazing purple ladybugs, apparently unique to the state. I wrote that I wished to see them there, and she responded that she had never seen one before. I later read that unlike the bright colors on the picture, they are actually a very dark purple.

Hydee and I gathered for lunch today. Afterwards, I got in my car and lo' and behold there is a purple ladybug walking on the inside of the windshield of my car. Just as I'm realizing it appeared to indeed be the purple ladybug I was seeking, it flew right to my seatbelt over my shoulder and hung out for a bit, eventually checking out the car.

September 5. *A Michael wink.*

Once arriving in Hawaii, I heard this song for the first time: "Nobody Gonna Stop Me Now" (Mana'o Company, featuring Caleb of the Green X Micah G; ℗2018 Daniel Spencer-Kennedy). Then again and again. Do you know it? I feel it's a great song for us spiritual believers. Especially the chorus.

If you just believe then you can achieve almost anything/I'm gonna reach for the sky/…

When seeking the link to share with you just now, I noticed that this song was released on 12.12 of last year! A Michael wink for us, right there.

September 5. *A sovereign wink.*

[More than a month before this book became a calling, I sent an article from 2017 to my group.]

"Leading French presidential candidate Marine Le Pen has vowed to 'destroy the New World Order' when she is elected President of France, sending a warning to European elites that she will 'dismantle their corrupt, self-serving institutions with my own two hands if I have to.'" As seen in an article in www.newspunch.com. This Divine Feminine powerhouse in a BBC interview "laid out her vision for reclaiming French sovereignty."

"When I am elected President, I will go to the European Union and say that I want four sovereignties back. Legislative sovereignty: our laws are more important than EU directives. Territorial sovereignty: we decide who comes and stays in our country, we want borders. Thirdly, economic and banking sovereignty: I have the right to promote economic patriotism if I so wish. And of course, monetary sovereignty." As it turned out, Le Pen was not voted in.

The article ends with the message, "Something fundamental is happening: the comeback of nations, of sovereign states, with people, with frontiers. People now want to be in charge of their destinies. For a long time they were prevented from doing so," Le Pen said.

These are powerful words for these very times. How many leaders speak like this? Marine sure sounds like a white hat, a true spiritual warrior. And there's a word that kept coming into my mind since arriving on the island: *sovereign, sovereign, sovereign,* again and again.

September 8. *An MM wink.*

I saw this tattoo on a man's leg at the beach today. It was a large MM and I immediately felt this was a wink from Mother Mary and Mary Magdalene. My friend Mia [who is a member of this group] and I have used the acronym MM to refer to them both, for many years now.

So, when I saw this guy sporting an MM tattoo, I sent a picture to Mia and said "MM wink." She wrote back, feeling it too. A little while later, I went to the parking lot to leave. It was a definite "Leave now" feeling. I got in my car just as a car was backing in, right in front of me, with the plate MMS... or "MMs"—the MMs!

[Notice how this sighting then initiated a string of MM signs to come, as you will see.]

September 9. *A Mother Mary wink.*

Our Laura [also in the M&M Group] responded to yesterday's share about the MM signs: "Wooow Mary! Did you know that on September the 8th, millions of people, Christian Orthodox, are celebrating, with deep respect, joy and gratitude the Virgin Mary Birth Day! No wonder that you saw such significant signs."

Sure enough, I found online that yesterday was the Christian Feast Day of The Nativity of the Blessed Virgin Mary. I am stunned, I had no idea that it was her feast day. Archangel Michael's feast day is 21 days after this one—that I know! Thank you, Mother Mary, for these beautiful signs for our group! And thank you Laura for making this sign many times more joyful and powerful by making the connection—I'm so grateful to know this!

September 9. *A Mother Mary Wink.*

I sent you that picture of a Mother Mary statue which I happened to come across yesterday. Hydee knows of the other MM signs, but not that I stopped at this statue and took a picture. And yet, she texts me from Two Step (a popular snorkeling spot in the Captain Cook area), where she sees the dolphins. Hydee specifically noted that the dolphins were around the Mother Mary statue! I asked, "What Mother Mary statue?" This is a different one, and how I never noticed it before is beyond me. I've been to this bay several times already, but was too focused on what's under water to notice what was on land!

September 17. *A Lily and prophetic wink.*
After my swim today, I was sitting in the shade and this man sitting close by started talking to me. He is from New Mexico. When I told him I lived in New Mexico with my family for five years, he got up to come talk to me. As he did so, he fell backwards straight onto his back and into the sand. He said, "That was graceful, eh?" I responded that I was just telling my friends here that I have lost all grace since arriving on the island—falling on the rocks, into the water, waves bowling me over, etc. We laughed and talked awhile. When I was ready to leave, the man was sitting by his wife at that point, and as I approached them to say goodbye, he asked "Are you psychic?"

Okay, that got my attention. How often does anyone randomly get a question like that, right? So my "antennae" went up as I responded, "Yes, somewhat." He said that he and his wife were trying to recall the name of their friend's dog. Hmmm that was pretty wild that they would summon this total stranger for the answer, right? I threw out three male names and they said it was a girl. Wow, okay, I'm not feeling too psychic today! I said goodbye for now, started to leave, and banged my head hard into a large, low-lying tree branch. I said to the man, "Talk about having grace" and laughed.

When I was half way to the parking lot, I stopped in my tracks and wondered to myself, what if the dog's name is Lily! And that's why this all happened. And that bonk on my head was waking me up. There's something more to this!

I walked all the way back and asked, "Is the dog's name Lily?" The woman said no, but that her friend is writing a fictional book and her main character was Lily! My antennae grew in size, at that point! I told her, that I'm into synchronicity and it seems there's something to this because I felt I had to come back and talk to them some more. And I have lots of signs with the name Lily! Also, I'm an author, as well, I exclaimed.

She went on to describe the character and said it was set into the future, and things were really bad in this country. The lady pointed out that, of course, things are already so bad. So it didn't sound like the future, but rather right now. And the character is working to do good, to help in a big way basically. I asked, "Would you call Lily a warrior?" She answered, "Definitely, yes!"

Now how ironic is this? The chances of hearing about this woman's book that firmly resonated with my own work, and the main character is actually named Lily! One could spend two weeks with these people and probably never hear about this. You know what I'm trying to say. There is definitely something to this. Something more to ponder. Lillian is here with me in my every day, it seems, but today was an especially big wink.

[I look deeper into this stunning synchronicity as I edit this passage many months later. This couple was asking about a dog's name. That is a wink right there! I described to you the Lily signs when Lily first came into my life. I was suddenly driven to ask people what their dog's name was, and three were named Lily in succession, as described in *Michael's Sword & You*. Also, this couple is from New Mexico.

113

Spoiler Alert: At the time, I did not know that New Mexico would be where I'd be returning to six months later to finish writing my book, and here they were from New Mexico! They talked about things being really bad in this country. Things are ever more concerning in this country now than when we met, especially with the virus upheaval. And here their friend is an author, just as I am. She is writing about a warrior named Lily who wants to help humanity. And here I lead a mission of Michael's Warriors of Light, I am constantly seeking to help humanity through these challenging times, and Lily is one of my main guides. This is all quite mind boggling. Are these people for real, or were they beings who appeared to give me a peek into the future, that I'd be writing a book?! Not everyone we see in our reality is human; some visit through human bodies.]

September 18. *A dolphin and Lily wink.*

Here's a fun and synchronous message from Joy [who is a member of this group]:

"We returned from our cruise and I finally had the chance to go through all my emails. I did not connect to the Internet the whole time we were away—just like old times! I also observed so many passengers talking to one another and using iPhones to just take photos! So as we are cruising up the coast towards Maine, I went outside on our balcony to begin my morning meditation and to send prayers, blessings and love to the ocean as I gently tossed 6 tiny pieces of amethyst in her waves. I saw a school of dolphins in the distance but by the time I turned my phone on, they were too far away. I bid them farewell and went back inside. On my pillow was a rainbow! I was so grateful for this sign that the ocean knew I sent blessings and love, and the dolphins were aware of my presence even if I did not get a photo. Later that day I was thinking of you and how much I was missing reading your posts. While off the ship and sightseeing, I see 'Lily's Lakeside' restaurant! So I felt a connection to you even though I had not read your beautiful posts and seen your amazing photos and videos! I truly feel Mary, that you are spreading the light far and wide and the dolphins are protecting you because they know that you are the 'Light Warrior.'" Lightworker and warrior Joy lovingly gave an example of how on some level, soul relationships are always in connection.

September 19. *A cosmic wink.*

When I acted out my latest Lucy Ricardo moment in Hawaii, running straight into that tree branch a couple of days ago, I had this feeling that there was reason for it, as if it shifted something, as odd as that sounds. And then last night I read something very telling.

Here is part of Celia Fenn's Facebook message on September 15:

"As I have mentioned in earlier posts, the (Cosmic) Whales have been working with Humanity to assist in effecting an upgrade to the Heart Center and the Heart Chakra. This is effected through Sound and Sonic frequencies that activate the DNA through powerful Light/Sound Codes aligned with the Diamond frequencies. In my own case, the day after I had spent time with the whales (literally, at a local beach), I fell and cracked a rib. I was in the process of moving house, so it was hugely inconvenient to say the least. Clearly, I needed to slow down and be more grounded."

"But, I was also told that the physical 'cracking' of the rib cage was to make more room to adjustments and changes to the heart frequencies. Like being cracked open to allow more light."

"I have heard of several friends who have had challenges with the physical, and especially the heart, spine and skull. (Yes, first day in my new house I walked into the concrete corner of the stairs and nearly knocked myself out). I am not usually this accident prone, so I am realizing another process at work here that includes physical adjustments and just taking things much slower, no matter what. Remember that in the higher realms, slower is faster and higher....so we need to slow down on the physical plane so that we can adjust to the new higher frequencies that manifest as a slower pace of life."

So according to Celia, adjustments and changes are happening to the heart, spine, and skull, as if possibly adjusting and allowing in more light. (Of course, it can go the other way, too, which I address in Chapter Ten!) Remember the man who fell backwards into the sand flat onto his back, and then soon after I ran my head into the tree branch? Spine and skull, right there. I'm with Celia as far as not being accident prone either, always very careful. [Gratefully, I have not had one concerning injury while on the island, even though I was always pushing myself and had opportunity for it on a daily basis.] I felt with the tree, in particular, that there was indeed something unseen at work here. Fascinating!

It's so interesting about Celia's experience with the whales. I fully believe that the dolphins are providing the very same, assisting in our heart upgrades! My heart feels upgraded every time I'm with them. Also, that's so true about not being grounded. Yesterday, I had a few moments where I felt so ungrounded and even forgot where I am. Oh yeah, I'm here. And that led me to thinking about synchronicity itself. You have to be grounded to experience it, to be in a high state of awareness and very in the moment. And then once it happens, at least for me, I tend to get ungrounded and "in the clouds," as a result. What a dichotomy. Finally, I found Celia's words at the end of her message especially profound: "Remember that in the higher realms, slower is faster and higher....so we need to slow down on the physical plane so that we can adjust to the new higher frequencies that manifest as a slower pace of life."

September 22. *A well-being wink.*
I'm still getting my bearings here, but one thing is for certain. Synchronicity is strong and is powerfully guiding me here. When I went to Two Step to seek the dolphins, I got out of the car and right next to me, getting out at the same time, was a guy in medical scrubs taking them off with his swimsuit underneath. A very nice guy, but I felt the medical symbolism was telling me to move on.

Sure enough, I get close to the water to be certain, and it is indeed quite rough and with the tide unusually high. One thing about the Big Island is that among some of the best places to swim with the dolphins are also very rocky at the shoreline, and with the shifting waves, you have to be careful. There are sandy beaches that do offer more ease, though.

I then got in the car to drive to a "gentler" bay, and randomly see this sweet cow right on the road. Is this another sign to not go to this place either? I wasn't sure. So in my dolphin seeking stupor, I made the drive anyways, and in that downhill road to the beach, in two separate instances, a dog was in the middle of the road. I didn't even get to the bottom and quickly decided to just turn around. On the way back up, there were no dogs in the way, of course.

My spirit wants to do everything, so I'm learning to listen better now. Hawaii made me realize just how young my spirit is, and it sometimes needs to be a bit tamed and more realistic. I am specifically listening to the ocean better, too. On one of my first dips in Kealakekua Bay, I immediately lost my snorkel ripped right from my mask because the waves were that intense. Lesson learned very quickly right there. There was much I needed to grasp right away, especially to always respect the immense power of the ocean. It is way stronger than any one of us.

September 24: *A warrior wink.*

Yesterday was a pretty intense Fall Equinox, complete with my sword raising announcement not being received by warriors. A test email with no warrior announcement went through without issue! I sensed definite interference. And it also happened right after I posted in my newsletter that we have been raising the sword for over a year and a half now (and we did so *without pause.*) Well, as you can imagine, I was not going to miss one if at all humanly possible, and created a different avenue to send from this point forward. I just now went to reread my email I sent this morning, and this is what I see on the time stamp: "3:33 am (33 minutes ago)." I had no idea I sent at that time (my time). This was a most appreciated synchronicity.

September 24: *A Michael wink.*

I just responded to a couple of you who enjoyed my 3:33 am/33 minutes ago synch, look up from my parked car, and immediately see a truck with a plate "MIKE 33"! Thus, it's a wink to us all. I know that a couple of you even refer to Archangel Michael as "Big Mike." Michael knows I need some levity as I continue to be "messed with" energetically, today. Whenever I feel I cannot take another challenge, he swoops in somehow and reverses everything, or at least rejuvenates me, without fail! I share this as a reminder to us all. It is a key understanding, something to hold onto during these times.

September 25: *A shark wink.*

After I posted on Facebook the following message, I synchronistically spotted my first white-tipped shark in the water this morning.

"If it's coming from the mainstream (news or otherwise), like a rushing freight train suddenly everywhere you look, please shun the propaganda and seek the truth. We have all been used and manipulated, hoodwinked and deceived... for centuries, but nothing like during this very time. I used to be gullible, crazy gullible, because I never wanted to see evil, only the good. But we cannot afford gullibility any longer. I had to learn this, we all do. We have to bravely face the dark, acknowledge the truths, and voice it. Question everything. Listen to those blessed gut feelings. Stay positive. Take action and fight for righteousness. Be kind and loving to each other. Don't worry about what people think of you—if they label you crazy, you are probably among the most sane. I care more about you, humanity, and all of life, way more than I care about how you perceive me or how popular I am. For I will always go out on that limb when I need to, in order to protect from harm, and to seek and spread truth in the name of Light and righteousness, as AA Michael has taught me. I care deeply and I know you do too! Follow your OWN drummer. We are learning a whole new way of living and being now, and quickly so. The great news is... in sooo many ways, the dark is dismantling as people wake up, see the deception, and take a stand... you just won't learn about it from the bought out mainstream news. Yet we are in battle and must maintain our strength and power, exuding the highest state of Love to conquer all."

So, this shark sighting was a most validating wink. I put it together, right after taking in the breathtaking sight.

On www.whatismyspiritanimal.com, it says this about the shark: "When Shark circles in as your Spirit Animal, it's time to shut out fear and go for what you want. Shark as a totem animal belongs to those who always survive & keep moving ahead. Call on Shark as your Power Animal when you need to meet life full steam ahead."

September 27: *A New Jersey wink.*
I hadn't been to one of my favorite beaches towards the Northern side of the island in a while. Yet, I felt so strongly to come today. It might not look like it from the picture, but the water was much rougher than ever, and I could barely see the fish when snorkeling. I wondered why I felt so strongly to be here. And also why I felt guided to place myself at a specific spot on the beach. It didn't take long to figure that out.

I met this very nice couple and sister visiting from New Jersey. Right away, I said "I love New Jerseyans!" (Especially the ones in this group, fyi!) The one lady and I talked for a long time. I had no idea she was spiritually minded until I mentioned how synchronous this island is. There was a definite nudge to say that much, and you can imagine where that led. I asked if she was a healer because I could then sense it, and as it turns out, she is. We were very like-minded in our conversation, and she was blown away by the meeting. I told her to check out the tattoo on the lady's back who was going into the ocean... it was of huge angel wings! We both loved the wink.

September 28: *Michael and mirroring winks.*
With this powerful week, our warriors have had some excellent signs and messages.

Carol sent me a picture of a statue of Archangel Michael. She and her sister saw it right around when I shared my Michael statue synchs on 9.22. After taking the picture and driving along, just as she thought that she would send it to me, she sees a plate: CAROL 23. "023" is the number on my car's plate. Carol and I keep having mirroring signs, and even signs for each other. After sending that email, she drove out and there was a Goodyear Blimp in the sky! What?! She pulled over to take a picture of it, and noticed that the time was 12:12! Good grief... amazing!

September 29: *A big Michael's Day wink!*
Oh my God! Oh my Michael!
This morning when in channel and then meditation with Archangel Michael on his Feast Day, he asked me to allow him to lift immense heavy burdens from my shoulders and heart, which of course I did without pause. He asked me to trust him, and that all will be well, no matter how things appear. He then said it was time for some play by getting into the water. I asked him to please send me some dolphins so that we can both swim together with them.

I swam out into the bay a bit further than normal, but it's not very deep in this part of the bay. He directly led me to a particular reef. He whispered to me to turn on my camera. I didn't know what I was to be filming. It was the same kind of fish scene I see daily and I zoomed in trying to find what he wanted me to capture. He then asked me to zoom out. Lo and behold was an immense surprise. I could barely contain myself. A baby whale shark appeared out of nowhere with such utter beauty, grace, and magnificence!

When I got back to the shore, I told some divers putting on their gear where a whale shark was, so that they could see it too. They said it was extremely rare to see one in the bay, and they told me it was a once in a lifetime experience, and I will probably never see one again. (Well I don't believe in those kinds of limitations, but it did give me an idea of how special this sighting was.) A lady overhearing us said that her brother has lived here for two years and never saw one. [I would come to find over time that this was indeed a very rare sighting.]

What a gift as I especially celebrate Archangel Michael on his Feast Day. Thank you, Michael, my deep love and faith are always with you.

If that baby whale shark hasn't been charted on the Whale Shark Initiative Research Program, I will get to name him. If so, I will name him "Michaelmas" (hoping he's a boy), in honor of AA Michael on his Feast Day. I did submit pictures, but Sheoli who told me about this program said that I needed to have captured the left side, not right, to be considered. They compare all whale sharks from the markings on their left sides. I felt to register the documentation, regardless.

[Turned out that while the organization was excited about the footage I sent them, they did indeed need a photo of the left side. Frankly, in my view, that baby whale shark was sent by Archangel Michael—yes, our angels and archangels can do that! I believe it came from another dimension, so it was not meant to be charted. This was one of my best experiences on the island because it was a direct gift from Archangel Michael. You can see the footage of this sighting, just as I experienced it (via the MarySoliel channel on YouTube). I had to re-upload it on May 19, 2020 because three years' worth of videos mysteriously disappeared from my channel while on the Big Island.]

October 1. *A reminder wink from Michael.*

From our Archangel Michael two years ago today, just a few days after hearing his new call offering his sword! I love this so much:

"With this first day of this new month, set your sights on what is coming into fruition for the scores of you choosing love. No matter the intensity as the battles continue to play out, keep your focus on the Light. See the Light in all you encounter as you demand its existence. Breathe in this promise through your choice to be Love. Anything but has not worked for your world. You are really getting this now, more than ever. Every day is a further unveiling of the illusion that needs to be released! All that no longer serves you, nor the collective. The work you are each doing is a success for the collective, do you realize that? We wish for you to honor yourselves for this work, both within and outside of you as you become champions of Love."

("Love is a Battlefield" is playing in the coffee shop in Calgary, Alberta right now after typing this out! I just cannot make this stuff up, and I don't believe I've heard this song in years. Love and Light triumph!)
~ Archangel Michael through Mary Soliel on October 1, 2017

October 2. *An Anniversary Wink.*
Today is the 25th Anniversary of my spiritual journey! Remember when I saw that whale shark on Sunday? Well soon after I returned home from that experience, Joan Ocean emailed me asking if I wish to join her and friends on a chartered boat to seek whales, whale sharks, and dolphins. How's that for timing? I told her I ironically just got home from seeing a baby whale shark at Two Step! I couldn't resist an invitation like this on a hugely momentous day for me. So I said "Yes!" We saw dolphins with their babies, which is the best, but no whales (only seeking to spot pilot and sperm whales, this time of year) and just one juvenile silky shark! It was still a great morning with great people, on this very special day.

October 6. *A Michael Wink for Warriors.*
We had a wonderful gathering for our online "Michael's Sword & You Workshop" yesterday. I talked about how it is very common that signs mirror the call to become a warrior, for others as they did for me. One new warrior

let me know that she firmly heard this call. In fact, she changed her set plans to make sure she could attend.

I woke up to a Facebook message from her. This came across in her Instagram feed just then:

PROGRAMMING

EXPECT SOMETHING WONDERFUL!

Archangel Michael asks that each new day is started by setting the intent of expecting something wonderful and exciting.

October 6. *Dolphin winks.*
This was one of the best mornings here, thus far. Dolphins are incredible. There is so much to learn from these creatures. I'm fascinated by the telepathic means we can communicate with them. This is our future, growing our telepathy, and they are teaching us and encouraging this practice! I telepathed to them as I got in the water early this morning, calling for them, telling them that I have a message from Archangel Michael through me.

Almost an hour later, I still didn't see them and started to head back to shore. However, I was mesmerized by this baby sea turtle and just floated for quite a while watching it. Thanks to that additional wait, the dolphins appeared... and swam around all of us snorkelers for three plus hours! So I just sent out Michael's message that came through me, mostly of Love and gratitude for their presence.

When I just floated and beamed immense gazing love down to them, they would swim in circles under me again and again. The spinners did this repeatedly. They would come up for air right next to me, even a mother and baby so close that I could touch them (but, of course, I did not). The mother and baby telepathed a beautiful message and swam on. When I asked, "Did I hear right?," they took a drastic, unnatural turn back toward me. I am such a novice at this, and yet I am desiring to learn quickly, as much as I can.

The crystal beings started out so serene and subdued (being they were resting/napping), but after a while they were so playful, jumping, spinning, mating, nursing, and sending out lots and lots of those amazing sounds. I would have had a couple hundred wonderful pictures and videos, but my camera was out of battery as soon as I got there. It was actually good thing—so I could just absorb.

October 8. *Dolphin winks.*
A couple of days ago, I shared with you the amazing three-hour long play time with the dolphins. It was extraordinary and opened me up to a better understanding of my purpose with these creatures. I really want and need to practice telepathy with them, for starters. But it's more than that, too.

This morning, I was getting ready to leave for the day and pondering where to go first. I often check one bay, and if I don't see them I go to the next place, and sometimes even a third stop. This time I heard, "Go right to Two Step! We are there!" Did I really hear that? That is where they were the day before. And yet, in the seven weeks I've been here, and at Two Step many times, I never saw them there until yesterday! Could they really be there two days in a row, and they actually telepathed that information to me? I heard it clearly, so I trusted and jumped in the car and was off to Two Step. About two minutes into the drive, Hydee texts me. I stopped the car to read, "Dolphins at Two Step!" and wrote back, "I know! I'm on my way!" She was there when I got there. It never ceases to amaze me how magical they are.

October 9. *Dolphin winks.*

I was telepathically led to go directly to Two Step yet again, to swim with the dolphins, and to leave early. Upon arrival, I parked where I could see the shore, but no dolphins were in sight. Sure enough, within three minutes, six showed up and they hung around for almost three hours. Again, for several weeks I never saw them here, and yet enjoyed their presence three times within the last four days. Trust me, I did not always *hear them*, and yet when I did, it was very exciting.

October 12. *Michael and dolphin winks.*

Today served as a great example of faith… especially in our AA Michael. He is constantly placing people to help me at the perfect times, or giving me the perfect information. And I know that he and/or your angel team do the same for you! It's a matter of us recognizing the gifts, the support, and the love.

I went to Kealakekua Bay this morning to swim with the dolphins after Hydee told me they were there again. It's hard to get to them with rougher waters in this place and, depending on where they are, you may have to swim pretty far. Not that distance ever stopped me, thus far. I found a new way to get in that seemed less challenging with lessened wave activity, but I was a little nervous. On my way walking there, a Chihuahua (I can't make this up!)

comes up to me and I pet it. That serendipity gave me the confidence to forge ahead.

When arriving at this new area, I happened to see a couple of people climbing up these rocks, out of the water. I asked if it was difficult and they said it's not too bad. Well for overweight me it was, as it turned out. Had I not seen a bit of how they were getting out, I probably wouldn't have tried it. Getting in was easy though, you just jump. So I leapt into the water and swam over to the dolphins, and would worry about it later.

After a long swim with more than 20 beauties, I took the long swim back to this place. It was very low tide and extra difficult to maneuver up these rock steps, plus it's ridden with numerous sea urchins in the holes of the rocks, and I refused to get stung. I knew I'd be okay, though. Michael is not only making me emotionally stronger for our warrior work, but moving here to Hawaii, I am building my physical strength, as well. I'm challenging myself each day.

When I am slow at climbing up out of the water at Two Step (literally two lava rocks people use to enter and exit the water) there is almost always someone saying "Need a hand?" I usually say no thanks because I do want get stronger and do it myself. But lately, I have been saying "Thank you!" and accepting the offers when I'm really tired after a long swim, because I also want to pass my test of accepting help.

Because I do have a hard time asking for help, not out of ego but I don't like to intrude on people's lives. This time, I was ready to intrude. However, no one was around and I kept trying to get up onto the ledge. I literally asked Michael for help and imagined someone coming, and just a few minutes later they did. And this is not a busy area—I rarely see people around here. A father and son on their kayak asked if I needed help. I said no rush, but after they get their boat out, yes, if they would please help me. Hilariously so, just a second before the man extended his hand, I got myself up on the ledge, but still greatly appreciated a hand for the rest of the way.

Was I being tested to ask for help, and once I imagined help it did indeed arrive? And they couldn't be nicer about it. I share this with you as example of a test, and especially one of faith. I've had much more concerning things than this happen here, and yet I am always okay.

So while I may totally look like Lucy Ricardo out there each day, I am growing stronger and facing my tests.

October 13. *Stranger generosity winks.*

As I mentioned before, I am working this food delivery job to pay the bills until I find something where I'm not on a cell phone all day. I need this kind of flexibility though for my sword raising mission, spiritual work, and being in the water early every morning (which *is* part of my work). I worked 7 days in a row that first week, 2 - 6 hours per day, and made only $220 (less gas expenses).

When it is busy, it's great, but otherwise this work is usually slow and not really worth my time or gas expenses. But I get these little blessings that keep me going until I step into what is next. For instance, when I made only $6 in two hours, the person who was to get that food order was on the other side of the island and had put in the wrong restaurant, so at least I was fed for free, and luckily it was a vegetarian dish.

On one extraordinary night last week, I had a pretty easy delivery and earned a $10 tip, plus $7 for the delivery—a very nice pay in and of itself. It was pitch dark and I delivered well up into the foothills. When I arrived, the lady was standing at the driveway as it was too dark to navigate the hilly drive. She handed me a bill. I said, "Oh, you already gave me a very generous tip!" She said she knew that but she wanted me to have this. I got back in the car to see she gave me an additional $20! What? I couldn't believe it and basically yelled out into the darkness, "Oh my God, thank you so much, thank you so very much!" I earned $30 tip for her approx. $55 meal? Just over the top incredible generosity.

Then a few days ago, I went to deliver food at this apartment complex. I started to make my way up the three flights of stairs to their apartment. The man and his young son were on their way down with the trash, and took the food. I went back to my car and the man came up to me with an additional $5 tip. I said, "Oh you already tipped me!" (And it was a generous $6 tip for what he purchased, btw.) He said he knows, but I was going to walk up all three stories and most don't do that, and so he wanted to thank me.

I said we all should, it's our job to do so. I look on his shirt, and there is none other than a "444" on the lapel of his t-shirt. [I talk about the magical 444s in *I Can See Clearly Now*.] Really? What are the chances! I told him that he was wearing very lucky numbers, and thanked him greatly.

What I've notice from day one here is that many of the people of Hawaii are generous, super warm, and kind-hearted. I share this as a great reminder that there are always miracles and blessings that buffer and lessen our challenges and frustrations. That's what I always, always hold onto.

October 14. *An MM wink.*

I've been meaning to take a picture and send this to you for weeks. Every time I'm on my way to Hōnaunau and Two Step, where the Mother Mary statue is, and really close to that other Mother Mary statue I was guided to find on Painted Church Road, I drive by this "MM," spray painted onto rock. There is very little if any other graffiti in this area. When you think of all the 2 letter possibilities—and it's MM. I smile every time, and I first noticed it soon after the MM synchs on Mother Mary's Feast Day, as Laura made us aware of. I'm sure MM isn't happy about the graffiti, but glad about the resulting wink.

October 14. *Michael and royalty winks.*
Hydee took me on a journey to four power spots/sacred areas on the Big Island today. [I went on to describe in this message to the M&M group the turning point day that was shared with you in Chapter Four.]

All of this points to stepping into our divine shoes, in my view. We are all much more than we think we are... so much. And we have the ability to heal and transmute wherever we go, certainly as Michael's Warriors of Light!

It was incredible to me that we returned from our mission at 3:17 p.m. to the second... I truly mean to the second, which was when our sword raising was complete today. So as Hydee was driving us back, we raised while on the road and returned exactly when completed. Magical. All with Michael overseeing. I have never been so exhausted and nauseous from a healing mission, by the way, and I've been to many vortexes and power points around the world in recent years.

Now I'm not sure what to think of all that happened today, except that this was by Divine appointment that we go to these places and it felt like much clearing and releasing happened quite effortlessly. If you feel guided or moved to go somewhere, even for just minutes, it is probably because your energy is needed there! We are really ramping up the healing necessary for our earth, as this planet prepares to shift.

October 15. *A Queen wink.*

Carol said that the car with the plate QUEEN 22 passed her again, and then she went to the store and saw a t-shirt with QUEEN on it. I did not know about this yesterday when Hydee and I felt the royalty among us, only Carol's prior QUEEN synchs. I then find my own QUEEN shirt on this very next day after our pilgrimage! This shirt that I bought is something I would not normally wear, but feel to, in honor of the Hawaiian queens, Lili'uokalani and Ka'ahumanu that I know of thus far... and to add focus to the unfolding meanings of the synchronicities themselves!

October 15. *A Prophetic Wink.*

Please read this powerful prophecy. *Just following* a most powerful meditation (AA Michael guided me into) where I saw and experienced the removal of the darkness, minutes later I then synchronistically come across this from Peter Konstantinov Deunov, also known as Beinsa Douno, who prophesized the removal of darkness, a few days before his death in 1944?! How synchronistic is this? Except I saw the removal occurring with water, instead of "divine Fire" as he stated? It was like a forceful "power washing," and it was very liberating!

Here is "The Prophecy." It is very long, but extremely worthwhile! Do not fear; read to the end.

"During the passage of time, the consciousness of man traversed a very long period of obscurity. The phase which the Hindus call 'Kali Yuga,' is on the verge of ending. We find ourselves today at the frontier between two epochs: that of Kali Yuga and that of the New Era that we are entering."

"A gradual improvement is already occurring in the thoughts, sentiments and acts of humans, but everybody will soon be subjugated to divine Fire, that will purify and prepare them in regards to the New Era. Thus man will raise himself to a superior degree of consciousness, indispensable to his entrance to the New Life. That is what one understands by 'Ascension.'"

[I consider what Peter refers to as the "divine Fire," as what is known to be the Solar Flash.]

"Some decades will pass before this Fire will come, that will transform the world by bringing it a new moral. This immense wave comes from cosmic space and will inundate the entire earth. All those that attempt to oppose it will be carried off and transferred elsewhere."

"Although the inhabitants of this planet do not all find themselves at the same degree of evolution, the new wave will be felt by each one of us. And this transformation will not only touch the Earth, but the ensemble of the entire Cosmos."

"The best and only thing that man can do now is to

turn towards God and improve himself consciously, to elevate his vibratory level, so as to find himself in harmony with the powerful wave that will soon submerge him."

"The Fire of which I speak, that accompanies the new conditions offered to our planet, will rejuvenate, purify, reconstruct everything: the matter will be refined, your hearts will be liberated from anguish, troubles, incertitude, and they will become luminous; everything will be improved, elevated; the thoughts, sentiments and negative acts will be consumed and destroyed."

"Your present life is a slavery, a heavy prison. Understand your situation and liberate yourself from it. I tell you this: exit from your prison! It is really sorry to see so much misleading, so much suffering, so much incapacity to understand where one's true happiness lies."

"Everything that is around you will soon collapse and disappear. Nothing will be left of this civilization nor its perversity; the entire earth will be shaken and no trace will be left of this erroneous culture that maintains men under the yoke of ignorance. Earthquakes are not only mechanical phenomena, their goal is also to awaken the intellect and the heart of humans, so that they liberate themselves from their errors and their follies and that they understand that they are not the only ones in the universe."

"Our solar system is now traversing a region of the Cosmos where a constellation that was destroyed left its mark, its dust. This crossing of a contaminated space is a source of poisoning, not only for the inhabitants of the other planets of our galaxy. Only the suns are not affected by the influence of this hostile environment. This region is called 'the thirteenth zone;' one also calls it 'the zone of contradictions.' Our planet was enclosed in this region for thousands of years, but finally we are approaching the exit of this space of darkness, and we are on the point of attaining a more spiritual region, where more evolved beings live."

"The earth is now following an ascending movement and everyone should force themselves to harmonize with the currents of the ascension. Those who refuse to subjugate themselves to this orientation will lose the advantage of good conditions that are offered in the future to elevate themselves. They will remain behind in evolution and must wait tens of millions of years for the coming of a new ascending wave."

"The earth, the solar system, the universe, all are being put in a new direction under the impulsion of Love. Most of you still consider Love as a derisory force, but in reality, it is the greatest of all forces! Money and power continue to be venerated as if the course of your life depended upon it. In the future, all will be subjugated to Love and all will serve it. But it is through suffering and difficulties that the consciousness of man will be awakened."

"The terrible predictions of the prophet Daniel written in the bible relate to the epoch that is opening. There will be floods, hurricanes, gigantic fires and earthquakes that will sweep away everything. Blood will flow in abundance. There will be revolutions; terrible explosions will resound in numerous regions of the earth. There, where there is earth, water will come, and there, where there is water, earth will come. God is Love; yet we are dealing here with a chastisement, a reply by Nature against the crimes perpetrated by man since the night of time against his Mother; the Earth."

"After these sufferings, those that will be saved, the (true) elite, will know the Golden Age, harmony and unlimited beauty. Thus keep your peace and your faith when the time comes for suffering and terror, because it is written that not a hair will fall from the head of the just. Don't be discouraged, simply follow your work of personal perfection."

[The "elite" he refers to is *all of us royal beings,* in my firm view. I always resort to those prophetic words from the bible: "The meek shall inherit the earth."]

"You have no idea of the grandiose future that awaits you. A New Earth will soon see day. In a few decades the work will be less exacting, and each one will have the time to consecrate spiritual, intellectual and artistic activities. The question of rapport between man and woman will be finally resolved in harmony; each one having the possibility of following their aspirations. The relations of couples will be founded on reciprocal respect and esteem. Humans will voyage through the different planes of space and breakthrough intergalactic space. They will study their functioning and will rapidly be able to know the Divine World, to fusion with the Head of the Universe."

"The New Era is that of the sixth race. Your predestination is to prepare yourself for it, to welcome it and to live it. The sixth race will build itself around the idea of Fraternity. There will be no more conflicts of personal interests; the single aspiration of each one will be to conform himself to the Law of Love. The sixth race will be that of Love. A new continent will be formed for it. It will emerge from the Pacific, so that the Most High can finally establish His place on this planet."

"The founders of this new civilization, I call them 'Brothers of Humanity' or also 'Children of Love.' They will be unshakeable for the good and they will represent a new type of men. Men will form a family, as a large body, and each person will represent an organ in this body. In the new race, Love will manifest in such a perfect manner, that today's man can only have a very vague idea."

"The earth will remain a terrain favorable to struggle, but the forces of darkness will retreat and the earth will be liberated from them. Humans seeing that there is no other path will engage themselves to the path of the New Life, that of salvation. In their senseless pride, some will, to the end hope to continue on earth a life that the Divine Order condemns, but each one will finish by understanding that the direction of the world doesn't belong to them."

"A new culture will see the light of day, it will rest on three principal foundations: the elevation of woman, the elevation of the meek and humble, and the protection of the rights of man."

"The light, the good, and justice will triumph; it is just a question of time. The religions should be purified. Each contains a particle of the Teaching of the Masters of Light, but obscured by the incessant supply of human deviation. All the believers will have to unite and to put themselves in agreement with one principle, that of placing Love as the base of all belief, whatever it may be. Love and Fraternity, that is the common base!"

"The earth will soon be swept by extraordinary rapid waves of Cosmic Electricity. A few decades from now, beings who are bad and lead others astray will not be able to support their intensity. They will thus be absorbed by the Cosmic Fire that will consume the bad that they possess. Then they will repent because it is written that 'each flesh shall glorify God.'"

"Our mother, the earth, will get rid of men that don't accept the New Life. She will reject them like damaged fruit. They will soon not be able to reincarnate on this planet; criminals included. Only those that possess Love in them will remain."

"There is not any place on earth that is not dirtied with human or animal blood; she must therefore submit to a purification. And it is for this that certain continents will be immersed while others will surface. Men do not suspect to what dangers they are menaced by. They continue to pursue futile objectives and to seek pleasure. On the contrary those of the sixth race will be conscious of the dignity of their role and respectful of each one's liberty. They will nourish themselves exclusively from products of the vegetal realm. Their ideas will have the power to circulate freely as the air and light of our days."

"The words 'If you are not born again' apply to the sixth race. Read Chapter 60 of Isaiah, it relates to the coming of the sixth race, the Race of Love."

"After the Tribulations, men will cease to sin and will find again the path of virtue. The climate of our planet will be moderated everywhere and brutal variations will no longer exist. The air will once again become pure, the same for water. The parasites will disappear. Men will remember their previous incarnations and they will feel the pleasure of noticing that they are finally liberated from their previous condition."

"In the same manner that one gets rid of the parasites and dead leaves on the vine, so act the evolved Beings to prepare men to serve the God of Love. They give to them good conditions to grow and to develop themselves, and to those that want to listen to them, they say: 'Do not be afraid! Still a little more time and everything will be all right; you are on a good path. May he that wants to enter in the New Culture study, consciously work and prepare.'"

"Thanks to the idea of Fraternity, the earth will become a blessed place, and that will not wait. But before, great sufferings will be sent to awaken the consciousness. Sins accumulated for thousands of years must be redeemed. The ardent wave emanating from On High will contribute in liquidating the karma of peoples. The liberation can no longer be postponed. Humanity must prepare itself for great trials that are inescapable and are coming to bring an end to egoism."

"Under the earth, something extraordinary is preparing itself. A revolution that is grandiose and completely inconceivable will manifest itself soon in nature. God has decided to redress the earth, and He will do it! It is the end of an epoch; a new order will substitute the old, an order in which Love will reign on earth." [Source: https://dailyoccupation.com/70-year-prophecy-earth-swept-extraordinary-rapid-waves-cosmic-electricity/]

The new continent Peter refers to that will be emerging in the Pacific must be Lemuria rising. Please do not go into fear reading this prophecy, on the contrary! This is what we are here for. Let me repeat his words which I also feel, down to my very soul, that "it is written that not a hair will fall from the head of the just." Back when I channeled Archangel Michael and published *Michael's Clarion Call* in 2011, all about our New Earth, I did not know about this prophecy. Not until today, right after my meditation on the same subject! There was much new information in our book together that was hard for me to put out into the world, and yet the validations have been repetitive ever since. My faith in our wondrous spiritual destiny is untouchable, and I hope it is for you too.

October 29 *A Lily and Michael wink.*
First of all, I don't think I communicated clearly in my last email. I've been in Colorado only visiting for a few full days, and will be returning to Hawaii today to find a

new place to live. A couple of you thought that horrible living situation caused me to change my plans, but I belong in Hawaii for now and that situation only confirmed and heightened my need to transmute such darkness into Light. While far from fun, just like the unfortunate situation before our mission with Michael's Sword was unveiled, had they not happened, I would not have had the understanding and resolve to take on the mission. I have lots more to say about that once I begin writing the book (and once I get established again).

On the way to Colorado, I was seated on the plane next to a young woman from Jamaica. When she saw me coming down the aisle, she said she just knew I was going to be seated next to her. We ended up talking the whole way from Phoenix to Denver. She asked what I do, so our conversation got spiritual right away, and we both knew our meeting was by Divine appointment.

She is clearly on a very awakened path, and it was interesting that her plane was cancelled the night before, and yet she felt that it was all perfect. At one point, she was telling me how her 5th grade teacher was a huge inspiration in her life. I kept *hearing*, "Ask what the teacher's name is!" That sounded funny but I trusted the whispers and asked for the name. "Her name is Lillian _____" Lillian… unreal! Then she said that her hotel and conference were in Westminster! I told her that is the city I am staying in, too! So, this synchronous meeting was a fun way to start this trip home.

Yesterday, my alarm for our sword raising went off as usual at 3 p.m. (Hawaii Time). I was distracted and forgot to reset it for 7 p.m. (Colorado Time). I was later watching something with my son and completely lost track of time. Suddenly, I heard Michael say "Sword raising." I look at the time and it was exactly 7:00 p.m.!

October 30. *A Michael and book wink.*

A personal message from Archangel Michael:

It's my first full day back in Hawaii. I went to Two Step, didn't end up getting in, but just to see if the dolphins were there. As I was beginning to leave, a Chihuahua mix walks in front of my car. (Most of you know about the extraordinary number of times this has happened to me, from *I Can See Clearly Now.*) I get back to The Manago, and that same man I keep running into and whom I offered my advice to in order to help sell his car, tells me about this book I need to read about manifesting money. I did not bring up this subject. And he was very insistent. I got outside and he comes looking for me to give me more info about the book. There is definitely something to this.

[This was an early clue of many, on this theme of clearing the prosperity divide in the world.]

AA Michael said this to me: *You are becoming a strong magnet to your desires now. So if you wish to put meaning to this synchronicity, let that be the meaning. Infuse your life with this knowing and feeling. As you ponder your new book, know that just as with our sword mission and book, I will be firmly placing before you, magically, the very path and understanding of this new project.*

We are a beautiful team, you and me, and this new book will be a further testament to this fact. I love you, Mary. Please find happiness, find joy in your moments now. And then weave them together into a beautiful tapestry that is your life now.

November 3. *A dolphin nudge wink.*

I shared with you my unforgettable day with the dolphins on November 1st. Having mentioned on Facebook that I gazed at them, prompted four gazing requests right away. It seemed this was a nudge from the dolphins, as crazy as that may sound! They are magical!

Here are the testimonials from two already:

"I had nausea for several days which is why I decided to see if you could gaze for me, because I haven't been able to eat. I wanted to tell you that my nausea is so much better and was able to eat last night." ~ M.D.

"Thank you so much. I felt a palpable and powerful shift in my being this morning. I feel I am in the process of quite a shift and your gaze, the energy of dolphins, and your kinds words feel so supportive. I am still feeling the effect of the session. As the day has gone on, my nervous system feels more calm too, which I appreciate. The stress of the home buying intensity was resulting in such a charge in my nervous system and inability to sleep. This afternoon I fell into such a deep and blissful rest." ~ S.B.

P.S. Ron just texted me a picture of a car with a plate 4444JGD. So perfect, and today my total at the coffee shop was $4.44. I bet others of you had a 444 sign today?

November 5. *A healing wink.*

This morning, I was with a sweet pod of 24 wild spinners for three blissful hours. It's uncanny how often it turns out to be three hours, most every time. Sometimes it's hard to get an accurate count of the precious beings, but not today since they were quite sleepy. Every time feels like some kind of healing, understanding, energetic download, geometric/numerical displays and messages, etc. And I always give as much as I can back, too—much love, messages from Michael, gazing and healing energy.

November 8. *A group wink.*

I went to the water hoping to see the dolphins this morning, but wasn't feeling they were around. However, I was feeling strongly to go for a swim regardless. When I got in, I *heard* to go *this* way, not my usual way. As I swam out toward the magical place where AA Michael brought me that baby whale shark, I came across this group of five women. They were very quiet at first—turns out they were meditating in the water!—and then laughing heartily. I just had to pipe in, "You are the happiest group of snorkelers I've ever seen." Well, as it turned out this meeting was by Divine appointment. I was guided right to them and I knew it.

These five ladies are part of a Sound Healing workshop and flew in from the Mainland and Canada. *And* they are all planning on joining our sword mission! Unbelievable. There we are standing up in the water in our clunky snorkel gear talking to each other, and their questions led to my work and what I'm doing on the island. When one woman said that she was from Alberta, Canada, I had a huge smile on my face. That is where AA Michael presented this new mission to me, I stated!

We all felt so bonded and these ladies were so kind, that by the end of our gathering, we are saying "I love you" and things like that. Two lived very close to where I lived in Colorado! There was such like-mindedness and of the same tribe type feeling! They asked me to say a prayer out loud for them before we parted ways. I was so honored. Of course, it included a request for the dolphins to appear for my new friends.

November 13. *A Michael wink.*
Hydee and I met for lunch yesterday. We were talking about the importance of visualizing our New Earth, and as you know we are raising the sword to our New Earth now, every single raising. As you also know, AA Michael is always stressing the utilization of our creative imaginations, including during our sword work. Hydee was telling me about this art gallery in Kona that exhibits some ethereal paintings, so we spontaneously decided to drive into town and see them. Once there, she realized that the best place to park was at Archangel Michael's church. When we got back to the car, we caught sight of

what looked like an inverted eagle outlined by a cloud, right above his statue! You know that many consider the majestic eagle as a sign of his presence.

November 13. *A social media wink.*
I went to a coffee shop to work on my new book this morning. After a few hours, I heard "Leave now," even though I could have worked longer. I always trust that though, because as we know amazing or meant-to-be things always happen. As I'm starting to leave, a Facebook friend from Europe recognizes me, calls out to me, and we sit and talk for a long time. She had just read my post earlier while at the coffee shop, and she had no idea that I was on the Big Island! She recognizes me in those quick seconds walking by. What are the chances?!

November 18. *Queen winks.*
Just wow. On the same day (November 16th) I experienced the Queen sign with that coffee cup on the

way to Waipi'o Valley, and just like the same kinds of signs Carol has been noticing, now Laura sees QUEEN on a license plate! I knew this was going to be one very contagious sign... and now with Laura. These signs are just as much for the guys/Kings, as this is about all of us becoming royalty now.

Laura wrote me this morning: "And I saw a car that pulled in front of me, with a QUEEN plate on it! When I saw this, it impacted me so much and I wondered why. I burst into laughter, feeling that something is behind it... Now I know why, xoxo. And I am also under the number of 11, every day. I am seeing it almost continuously..."

When I asked about more detail about the QUEEN plate, Laura responded: "Yes Mary. it was just QUEEN, gold letters on black background. I saw it on Saturday afternoon, while driving to work. I guess the same day you saw it, right?" "Yes," I responded! "And the picture of it is not the fact itself but the state of consciousness I suddenly experienced in the second I saw it. The car came across from the right lane, went a little bit in front of me, then it went to the left lane, for the freeway. I don't know who was in that car because the energy, when I saw it, was like wiping the energy around in such a way that it shocked me, lifted my energies to the sky and I suddenly felt like a queen! It was like a sudden, awakening moment that I can never forget, that's for sure."

Laura continued, "Interesting is the fact that, in the next days, I suddenly re-experienced that QUEEN moment while driving through that very place! It felt like I went into that Queen bubble for a few seconds, as it happened when I first saw it, but less intense, yet queen-like. Hey, and I am just noticing now that the 're-experiencing' stopped after I wrote to you about it, hmmm..." Let's keep it going!

November 18. *Royal winks.*

Goodness. Laura experienced much more! "Ha... and this afternoon I was driving to work. After I passed the point on the street where the QUEEN car appeared last week, a truck changed lines and I tried to pass it but just couldn't. The way things happened, made me pay more attention to that truck, and guess what? I was able to see, on its wheel protection sheets and then on the side, an imprint saying 'ROYAL TRUCK.' It was black letters on gray rubber... I exploded in laughter, sending thanks to the universe. Then I remembered seeing, before leaving the house for work, a little decorative black pillow hung on the bathroom door of my rented house, having a gold crown on it. Then, I came to work to assist a lady that is from UK (she just became a 101 year-old on Nov 8th). She likes to watch videos about the royal family sometimes and today was one of those days, see?"

November 23. *A Michael wink.*

Earlier this week, Michael whispered to check out the headline at the newspaper stand. I haven't read newspapers for so many years, but listened and was overjoyed by headline. If you didn't see it mentioned in this morning's raising announcement, here it is from *West Hawaii Today*: "Hawaii County Bans Herbicide Use."

This is huge news for the Big Island and hopefully it spreads far and wide. So often while driving, I wonder what they are spraying with so much of this gorgeous, tropical vegetation, and I wonder how it is affecting all of life here. You every so often encounter workers spraying alongside the roads, especially in the lusher areas, as they are trimming and spraying to keep up with the constantly growing vegetation. I'm always avoiding the newspapers, thus was glad I listened; I would have missed this news.

On a side note, Laura had another Queen synch! She wrote that she had a reading from someone in India, "and the reader said that my name, Laura, is a name of a Queen!" So amazing! Also, how ironic is it that a man from India read my palm last weekend?! On the same day, I was served that Queen coffee cup.

December 4. *A number wink.*

I was on a three-month waiting list to get a post office box in Captain Cook. I checked in yesterday, and they said that several boxes recently opened up and that most on the waiting list will be offered one, surely me. The last few post office boxes I set up, the number was computer generated and you couldn't ask what numbers were available and were just assigned a box. Although I did luck out when the computer at the post office in Sedona assigned me "P.O. Box 2244."

With this smaller post office, I asked if by any chance I can pick from the boxes available because numbers are important to me, that I believe they carry meaning. All three workers there were helping me get the right one, either triple digit or in ascending order. They were so kind and respectful of my wish. And I was very happy with the numbers: P.O. Box 1234. This box opened just the day before.

December 6. *Royal and prosperity winks.*

This is a long post, but I think you will get quite a kick out of it. Yesterday, two studio rentals came up as I actively seek them on a daily basis. One was on *Queen* Kalama Ave, a block from *Princess* Ke'elikolani Dr., and less than a mile from (*King*) Kamehameha III Rd! Wow. I think this is just a royal wink and this place isn't for me, however I'm still going to check it out. I just had to share because this is one royal filled area!

This morning I went to the coffee shop just prior to joining Birkan Tore's online Prosperity Class. I walk in and got a big hello. I was so surprised to see three women from the meditation the night before, when we talked about my Queen shirt. And here I just happened to throw the same shirt on to go get coffee. They thanked me for the reminder!

Just before the prosperity class began, one of you wrote and asked for my PayPal address to send me some love. Oh, how that touched me, and the timing of it! I have been working hard to clear my past and distant past money issues so I can stay on this expensive island.

Back at the hotel, I was overjoyed to see Birkan on Zoom holding his Chihuahua mix, and with a statue of our beloved AA Michael in the background. As soon it was completed, our Ron sends me a painting of Archangel Michael that his loved one took while in Italy! Just wow. I love when synchs all blend into each other, and with each other as messengers.

P.S. I was just finishing this email and about to send it. A lady dropped several coins at this coffee shop I'm now working at (drinking tea, though). From where I was sitting, I could better see where the coins were, and I guided her to them. I told her I felt it was a wonderful sign and went on and on about it, because her money was "exploding" all over the place. She was just staring at me in shock by my words, and yet really getting it. I told her that I'm literally writing about prosperity and the fact that happened was not only a great sign for her, but that I feel I was a messenger for her, as well. As it turned out, this was indeed a message she needed.

We introduced ourselves to each other, and Marta kept saying "Who are you? Who are you?" I said I am just a person who is here to acknowledge her with a message.

She said her wallet keeps busting out. I responded that maybe it is time for a new and bigger wallet, to tell the Universe that you are ready to receive and accept more! She was blown away by that and asked if she could sit and talk to me. I said yes, of course. She was so courteous and thoughtful, and kept asking again and again if I was sure. I said absolutely, that this is by Divine appointment! So, she got her coffee and sat down.

Marta stated several times she feels she knows me. I said that this is soul recognition, and that I felt like I knew her too. I asked if she sees even just a penny on the sidewalk, does she pick it up? She said yes, always, and her husband does the same. I explained that I do too, that I want to have enough money to live on from my spiritual work so I took this prosperity class today. After a long talk, we parted ways.

I stopped at Costco which was less than a mile away, and when parking I see a personalized license plate SO FR33 (SO FREE?). I had just explained to Marta about the master numbers 11, 22, and 33. I also shared the Queen synchs. And then I took it deeper, sharing that society has been enslaved for eons of time and we need to free ourselves. And this is the license plate I see right after that, so I emailed a picture of it to her.

Getting out of the car, I find a penny and a dime on the ground outside of Costco. Next, I go see that house on Queen Kalama St. (I was right, it is not the place for me.) And I'm talking to the owner and see a penny on the ground right by us. I said, "Oh you should pick it up!" She responded that it has been there for four weeks and no one has picked it up. She said it was mine, so I took it.

December 10: *Queen winks.*
Hold onto your hats with these royal synchs from Laura! "I felt to buy a white blouse, with some imprints on it. I

liked the shape of it and didn't pay attention to the details, but later, while in the line to pay, guess what? It was all printed with an artistic 'Queen' word."

Just incredible! And yet there were other Queen synchs too, but with this one… wow!

In another email today, Laura wrote:

"While driving, I felt to chant Lakshmi mantra, the goddess who brings the golden age and the Royalty…"

"As a result, minutes after, while I was still thinking about those syncs, a truck changed lanes, going in front of me for a while. I felt a kind of sudden joy and I moved my whole attention from my thoughts to that truck. First I saw a crown on it, then a blue bumper sticker but I didn't pay attention to it because of the traffic, yet, something was pushing me to look closer and BINGO, I got the whole picture). Then I saw the numbers on the plate ending in 55. But when I was able to read the blue bumper sticker, it cracked me up with such incredible joy, laughter, and much more…"

"It was all aligned to You, Queen Mary, because the bumper sticker said: 'I brake for interesting cloud formations.'"

"For me, it was The Crown, the Numbers and the Clouds Day, a Mary Marry day). What are the chances to get the three of them together?," asked Laura.

I responded to Laura that I was just so blown away, and that I feel these royal signs are for her, and now all of us in the group to also glean from. But it is funny, I haven't had a Ford car since the very first car I bought, a Mustang, and then bought a used Ford decades later, here on the Big Island! And the Crown? I have never noticed that emblem around the Ford logo, have you?! With the 55 (a recent influx) and oh my gosh, that bumper sticker!

These are such wonderful, royal synchs! Thank you, Queen Laura!

December 13. *A Michael wink.*

While we didn't see whales from the boat charter and swam just briefly with spotted dolphins, we did arrive back in the harbor at exactly 12.12! That had to be a wink from Michael.

Actually, this happened twice, where we docked right at 12:12, and this second time was yesterday, on the actual date of 12.12!

December 13. *Green-tinged penny winks.*

I told you about the green-tinged penny by my driver's side front tire when I went to see the apartment last week, and then another green-tinged penny right after that, when I arrived at the property management company to hand in my application.

Well, when I went back to sign the lease yesterday, right by my door getting out of the car was a penny with white tinge. Unreal. But today, I was astounded. I went to the apartment complex to leave a note for the present renters about something we discussed. I got out of my car and was stunned to see yet another green-tinged penny right in front of me! That is four penny sightings, all associated with the apartment.

[These were incredible clues of what was ahead, unbeknownst to me—mold in the apartment!]

December 14. *A dolphin wink.*

Many of us are feeling the magic of this powerful time, certainly these last couple of days.

Yesterday, the dolphins were acting most unusually. You know that sound you hear when a condensed number of seagulls are chiming in chorus? That is very similar to what the dolphins sounded like underwater. While I've heard these loud sounds from them before, this was unusually intense and loud. Their behavior was different, as well. They were consistently congregated in large groups touching bodies as they swim. A few were, of course, mating—dolphins mate so very often—yet they were mostly just in this continual, close huddle while making very loud sounds of excitement for a long period of time.

When they come up for air, it is normally at a gradual angle, but this time they would often shoot straight up while sounding out, appearing to be in jubilation. At one point, there were 10 or 11 of them closely huddled, coming straight up from the depths right toward me. As they took their collective breath alongside me, it took my breath away. The ocean has been really churned up the last two days and I probably shouldn't have even been in the water at this time, but I felt so called. Things feel very intense, in general, and yet ultimately in a good way.

After I got out of the water, I texted a friend that they are still there and to come, that something is up and it's unusual. She was on her way and later told me that it was one of her most epic swims with them, and she is a veteran swimmer with the spinners—just like me seeking them every day, as well.

Do the dolphins know something that we don't know?

December 14. *A shooting star wink.*

Just wow! Talk about magical. I was driving in the dark this morning and saw what looked like a shooting star, but only no more than 30 feet from me. All I could think is that it was Heaven sent. It had a sparkler quality to it. I was several miles North of the Kona airport where it is simply untouched, lava laden land. And I realized that this is the third time this has happened in my life.

Michael whispered to check my Facebook memories a little later... I was utterly gobsmacked. Six years ago, in 2013 *on this same date of December 14*, I posted on Facebook:

"Oh my, what a SYNCH!"

"I just walked toward my kids' rooms starting to tell them what happened this morning, that on my way home from the gym while still dark, I saw a VERY low shooting star. It was clearly a shooting star but made no sense how low it appeared to be... I was beyond intrigued! And just as I'm starting to share this (without yet mentioning the star), my son comes out of his room holding this! It's a balloon I gave him for this college graduation months ago! Even this synch crazed woman who has experienced a ton of synchronicity in her years was utterly star struck."

What are the chances of this occurrence on the very same day, years apart? I will always marvel over this divine, repeat sign.

December 27. *A dolphin pod wink.*

Prayers really do work. Today was the day my visiting soul family, Debbie and Justin, and I set aside to attempt to swim with the dolphins. With dolphins being wild animals, of course there is never a guarantee you will see them. Sometimes you see the spinners days in a row; other times, days and even weeks can go by without those beautiful, shiny gray fins in sight. As word got out, there ended up being 11 of us gathering, getting up early, driving as far as 90 minutes, renting snorkeling equipment... oh gosh, please be there dolphins.

I was shocked to learn that Justin actually shaved off his beard in order to wear the snorkel gear! Debbie had never seen his chin in the over 20 years they have been married. Oh God, please... the pressure! From the night before, I was praying to God, Michael, everyone I could think of, including the dolphins, of course.

We arrived at the beach with no dolphins in sight. I suggested we all go in the water and just keep calling for them. About ten minutes later, a pod of about 30 dolphins suddenly appeared. They were very sleepy and oh so serene, and we all just floated above them, respecting their space, and yet in their beautiful energy. They hung around for hours and later got more active.

Believe me, I pray every day for the big stuff in this world and while raising Michael's sword with him. But this was a great reminder to keep the faith and ask for help to manifest what we want to see in the world, as well as in our personal lives.

December 31, 2019 *A 12:12 a.m. wink from Michael.*
For Everyone: *Can you just let go? Can you let go of the pain and frustrations that many of you endured through this past year? Holding onto it will not serve you now for you need your energy and emotional well-being for what is ahead. While chaos in the world continues, in the microcosm things are going to open up big time in your lives, collectively. The Universal energies are supportive of monumentally profound shifts and many of you are already feeling this. You are feeling this unexplainable inner excitement. Truths are coming forth at greater speeds now, and on personal levels you are feeling lifted and supported. There is a magical underpinning present in your daily actions, understandings, interactions, all of it. Ride this wave of renewal knowing that the Universe has your back through this profound new year, no matter what challenges arise. Hold steady with faith and let your intuition reveal what is next for you.*

January 6, 2020. *An ICSCN wink.*
I had one of the best swims with the dolphins today... about 50 of them and just me for at least an hour. Then a

lady swam over to me asking if I would take pictures of her with the dolphins. She explained that she had been coming here for 15 years and never got a picture with them. The juice on my camera was running quite low, and this was an epic day with the dolphins, but how could I pass up this heartfelt request, so I took several pictures for her.

Later on, she asked how to contact me so I could send her the picture files. Being in the water, we had no phones or paper and pen, of course, so I told her my name. I said if she forgets, just internet search "Mary" plus "+" that popular song title "I Can See Clearly Now," and she will find me—I told her it's the title of my first book. I just *knew* that this was an orchestration. And the next words she uttered proved it. She said, "Really? That song 'I Can See Clearly Now' was running through my head this morning!"

January 6. *An upside-down dolphin wink.*
I had such an incredible swim with the dolphins yesterday, and I posted my favorite clip on YouTube for you to see. This dolphin was not only spinning me in circles, but while on its back! It also appears to be mimicking my laughter. Simply amazing.

There is so much to talk about regarding the dolphins. Things go much deeper than the fun at the surface. But the fun is an important part, too! And I honestly feel that watching these videos of them does something for the viewer. It's mystical.

January 6. *A Michael wink*
From a conversation with Archangel Michael…

Mary: I want to know what the dolphins are saying. The sounds they make are so fascinating. I could listen for hours and sometimes do, as you know.

AA Michael: *This will not surprise you, for their communication is very positive, clearly joyful. Outside of necessary information for their well-being, they often communicate their feelings and you are hearing a compilation of individual feelings in chorus, creating their own symphony of emotion.*

Mary: Oh, that is so beautiful, no wonder I want to immerse myself in this. And I know that I am far from alone in that feeling.

January 7. *A download wink.*

This morning, being the first in the water, I had a glorious swim with a pod of 8 wild spinners. I know this may sound funny, but sometimes I feel I'm receiving downloads from them and have to take a break. For instance, I was out of it for some days just before New Year's and couldn't go in at all. My dolphin brothers and sisters here say they have experienced the same, at times.

January 8. *A favorite author wink.*

Here's a synchronicity for you, or perhaps it was a Michael wink, putting a thought in my mind to *make* the synch happen!

I was just thinking about Dr. Brian Weiss, one of my favorite authors who I feel is simply the real deal. Immediately after, I felt to go to my Facebook memories and saw this there, one of my favorite quotes about deep soul connection. The title of the book this quote is from is a phrase that also went through my mind just yesterday. May we hold onto love as fear takes a back seat during these shifting times. And may we especially embrace the leaves on our twig.

"I like to think of soul relationships as similar to a large tree with a thousand leaves on it. Those leaves that are on your twig are intimately close to you. You may even share experiences, soul experiences, among yourselves. There may be three or four or five leaves on

157

your twig. You are also highly and closely related to the leaves on the branch next to yours. They share a common limb. They are close to you, but not as close as the leaves on your own twig. Similarly, as you extend farther out along the tree, you are still related to these other leaves or souls, but not as closely as those in your immediate proximity. You are all part of one tree and one trunk. You can share experiences. You know each other. But those on your twig are the closest."

"There are many other trees in this beautiful forest. Each tree is connected to the others through the root systems in the ground. So even though there may be a leaf on a distant tree that seems quite different from you and very far away, you are still connected to that leaf. You are connected to all leaves. But you are most closely connected to those on your tree. And even more intimately connected to those on your branch. And almost as one with those on your own twig."

~ Brian L. Weiss, M.D., from *Only Love is Real*[7]

January 14. *A spirit wink.*

My next-door neighbor when growing up was so strong in my consciousness today. I finally questioned to myself if Ruth is still here on this plane. She is around 90 by now and we lost touch at least a decade ago.

I looked her up and immediately learned that she died *on this very day* of January 14, three years ago. Unbelievable. Clearly, she was connecting to me. It was nice to know and feel that. As mentioned in a previous post, our intuition and psychic abilities are growing so strong now, *and we are being led to trust them* like never before.

---

[7] Weiss, Brian L. *Only Love is Real.* New York: Warner Books, 1996.

This makes me ponder the fact that in the last couple of years, my pediatrician growing up comes into my awareness every so often, including just a couple of days ago. While he was well respected and thought of fondly by my family, he was not a family friend or in my life other than as a little girl for doctor check-ups, and yet he checks up on me in spirit every so often. Given my sensing Ruth's presence right on the anniversary date of her passing, I am confident of what I'm "getting" about my former doctor, because I don't recall even thinking of him in even the last couple of decades, and I was surprised I even remember his name.

Funny thing, I remember the nurse even more than I do the doctor. I don't recall a whole lot of my childhood, but I can still see her very distinctly, giving vaccinations to kids in this long, narrow hallway. And I did not want one. I understand my feelings better now as these immunizations would one day grow dangerous, as they have caused untold damage, and we learn what is actually in them. Anyways, when things such as this happen, with the sensing of visits from the other side that prove meaningful or serendipitous, it gives us more confidence to trust our intuition and psychic gifts.

[While editing this entry, I was inspired to look the doctor up online and was surprised that Bryce died at the age of 88, the same age as both of my parents when they passed, and just three days from the anniversary day of both my parents' passing— they both passed on the exact same date five years apart! I can only imagine that my parents' spirits reunited with the doctor's. And perhaps that is why he checks up on me. Who knows?]

January 21. *Penny winks.*

So much has been going on in my life and too much to get into, but I will say this much. As you know, I felt I needed to be in this studio and was loving it for two weeks, and yet I am going through something quite unexpected. I have been on the other side of the island since the 16th, since it's hard to find any place to stay on the tourist side during high season, and as I wait for the place to be renovated.

They had to move me out of the condo by Michael's church after only six days there. And because I wouldn't accept this next place they were moving me to where I had to meet a man in a vacant apartment to get the key to a different place (all felt very odd, and the management company completely lost my trust), I was left to find and pay for my own stay, and during high tourist season!

Remember all the crazy signs with the green-tinged pennies? That was cluing me in to the mold issue. I knew there was something to the green, moldy appearance, and that is why I felt to share in detail with you. I am in battle in the microcosm for what occurs in the macrocosm so widespread—lack of responsibility, gross inadequate treatment, lack of concern for one's health and well-being, bullying, manipulation, unconscionable unfairness, being ripped off financially, and on and on. If I told you how I'm being treated, you would not believe it.

I know that with Michael by my side, everything will all work out. When I was placed right next to Archangel Michael's church, that was the balm on my soul to endure this. His telling me through Jeannie that he is standing in front of me gave me further comfort! And the lessons I'm learning are huge and necessary: holding faith, watching my reactions while staying in my joy, putting my health first, and taking just one step at a time… and certainly more to come.

January 24. *A blissful wink.*

Last night, out of the blue, I suddenly felt very unwell. I had horrible back pain and could not get comfortable, whether lying down or sitting up. It was hard to breathe and I was heating up quickly, I had to have the fan blowing right on me or I couldn't stand it. My breath got weird and labored and I had these uncontrollable vocalizations, while hoping people couldn't hear me through thin walls at the hotel. I must have sounded like I was dying. Not to sound dramatic, but I even questioned if I was having a heart attack. I wasn't panicked, just extremely uncomfortable, and thinking I had to go to the hospital, but couldn't drive and didn't want to be taken by ambulance.

It was then that I called out for a million angels. Within what seemed like thirty seconds, all symptoms subsided and I felt this most incredible relief. Not only did I suddenly feel myself, I felt better than normal. I felt blissed out?! I did. I had a smile on my face for a long time after. I had energy again. What on earth was going on, just what was that? I kept *hearing* over and over… "Kundalini Awakening." I would never have come to that conclusion; it was given to me. So I looked up several online sites, and that is clearly what I experienced. When I read about uncontrollable vocalizations, I knew for sure.

Have any of you experienced this before? I'm sure some of you have. I feel elevated, cleared, and released from some 3D issues. I'm still figuring this out… but I feel to share with you.

January 24. *A royalty wink.*

While I'm not ready to divulge the title of my new book yet, you must know that it has to do with our shared

Queen synchronicities, as this message regarding royalty has come up in so many ways after arriving in Hawaii. And we are seeing and feeling it from others, too. We are all tapping into the same Universal messages, and this is a message so many are apparently getting, including Celia Fenn, as you can see below. I was just blown away to read this... and it may explain things you are feeling and experiencing, and certainly my kundalini experience yesterday. I think we have all felt our calibrating to new energy, especially since 1.11 and 1.12. And here's more royalty validation!

From Celia Fenn on Facebook today:
"Ladies...and gents.... don't forget to pick up your crowns as you strut through the Aquarius Gate with confidence and power! The Queen and King are entering the Kingdom of the New Earth! As we move towards the 2/2 gate under the powerful frequencies of Formalhaut and Regulus, we are certainly feeling the increasing energies and the shifts between 'normal' brain wave patterns and the higher Alpha and Theta patterns that are activating. As we evolve to become Fully Multi-dimensional, we are also evolving to be able to modulate our brain wave frequencies depending on the frequency grid in which we find ourselves."

"This is how we enter into the Golden Age of Peace at the Aquarius Gate. When we are in Alpha state we are in that peaceful state of meditation, and when we are in Theta state we are almost in a trance like dream state. Recently, you may have found yourself tired and sleepy, just wanting to rest, or sit and stare into space, or forgetting things or words you would normally know. This is when you have shifted into another brain wave pattern at a higher frequency and your brain is not working in linear narrative mode any more. You may feel disconnected and lost, grasping for meaning... Don't worry, you are not losing it, your brain and body are simply being realigned to be able to carry multiple brain wave patterns in your multi-dimensional state. Just make sure your Crown is on straight before you pass through the Aquarius Gate!"

January 23. *A matrix wink.*
I was meditating yesterday and witnessed, in my third eye, quite a show. It was a grid, either blue or green lines. I can't remember because it wasn't the only vision I saw. I sensed it was the matrix. It was a knowing. Within an hour after that, my friend over the phone used the word *matrix*, having nothing to do with my experience, but she used the word in another context. This is a word that I don't recall her using before.

A couple of hours after the meditation, Hydee sent me this esoteric article:

https://eraoflight.com/2020/01/27/andromedean-directive-202-phase-5-team-aurora/

I was stunned to read: "Third eye activated - seeing the matrix, the dark web, astral planes and heavenly realms." I wrote her back describing what I saw in meditation, what I felt was the matrix, and she responded: "That's wild! I kept feeling to watch *The Matrix* for the last month or so and finally did yesterday! I haven't seen it in 20 years." So around the same time that I was seeing the matrix in my meditation, unbeknownst to me Hydee is literally watching *The Matrix* and also sending me this article. This was all pretty surreal. Perhaps you can relate to this too?

January 30. *Triple dragonfly winks.*
I decided to go right to the studio, finish packing up everything, find a storage unit, and move everything into it this morning. When I walked out of the hotel and went

to my car, there was a golden orange dragonfly flying all over the top of my same colored car. When I arrived at the studio, and brought the first load to the car, the *same* colored dragonfly was all over my car. If that weren't enough, believe it or not, my friends, when I came out after putting a load into my storage unit, the *SAME* colored dragonfly was all over car for the third time.

Instead of green-tinged pennies moving into this place, it was golden orange dragonflies moving out! Dragonflies represent transformation, and orange represents new beginnings. I was happy as a lark, even when in the midst of a most unpleasant move. I saw so many 888s and 555s in a row, it was crazy. I know many of you are having wild synchronicities too, these days!

Then I got in the car and went to Kealakekua Bay, and met who would be my new friend Natalia. She, like me, has not been able to settle into a place. We both felt that things are shifting now. A Chihuahua then walks right up to me! I told her how I always seem to have Chi signs, but today, the dragonflies were really talking. *Just then*, a lady walks by in a dress with the print of many dragonflies! Okay, things are shifting! Phew. Anyways, it was such a synchronous day that softened things and to get ready for the new.

My dear friend Crystal and her boyfriend were also being moved around from place to place. Being without a kitchen for months (except during those two weeks that I had an apartment), I would see this young woman nearly every morning at a favorite coffee shop where she works as a barista. We soon became like family. I would stop and get a coffee, we'd talk about spiritual things including the dolphins, and then I'd go for my swim—it became a tradition over months. She is wise beyond her years and spiritually gifted. Crystal isn't her real name. She gave me the nickname Gloria because she said she wanted to sing "Glorious" every time I walked in, and so I named her "Crystal" because she is definitely a crystal being with beautiful crystal blue eyes. These names stuck!

When I found the apartment that I stayed in for only two weeks, Crystal and her boyfriend found a place at the same time, just hundreds of feet from me, same town, same side of the street, and were also forced out after only two weeks, too! They were not treated well or with respect, either. We never figured out what on earth was going on, but we believed that easier times were ahead.

January 30. *An Understanding Wink.*
Wow, everyone, this warrior is really in battle again. I should have held onto that first white hat by Michael's statue, by the way. And having this visual of Michael in front of me shielding me [described in Chapter Six] to help me persevere is big for me right now. If and when

you call him in, you too may like to use this as a visual, as well, for it feels divine. I am totally okay, I am very strong, and I know that this is a necessary mission and Michael is helping me.

There is no doubt that this is battle in the microcosm that mirrors the macrocosm. The themes are treating humans inhumanely, cheating people financially, not taking any responsibility, bullying, lying, dishonoring— you get the idea. We are not being treated like the sovereign beings we are evolving into. This is my book! So, I get why this is happening, and I am on it.

Look at the crimes against humanity, in general. We are not being treated humanely. When Michael said that I was meant to be in this place for the time being, it was not at all what I thought and I believe it was to relieve my mind because this had to play out. I keep recalling those green-tinged pennies! And thus I needed to battle through this experience.

January 31. *A penny filled wink.*
So interesting... The property manager during the walk through (I stayed outside) to close out my stay at the studio was horrible this morning. He didn't want to hear about how my almost new furniture was now unusable and had to be pitched. He didn't want to hear that the mold is still in the carpet they won't replace, as the restoration company told them they need to. Or that the small job took weeks longer than it should have, and all at my expense. When I told him I got sick again when I returned a few days ago to pack, he had absolutely no response and didn't care. I was starting to tell him that I went to the eye doctor for new glasses yesterday, and the doctor brought it up himself, asking if I knew why my eye tissues were so inflamed. The doctor asked if I was exposed to something lately. I said I had severe mold

exposure. He said that would do it! And yet, the manager drove away in his jeep leaving me standing there, right in mid-sentence trying to get through to him. He then stopped his car a hundred feet ahead to light up a cigarette—great that he could find relief for himself while I wouldn't get physical or emotional relief for months.

I went to the bank to deposit the security deposit and pro-rated rent (that's all I got for my expensive three weeks of stay), and on the way walking in I see four pennies! Every time there is a valley to traverse down, I am lifted to the top of the mountain. Yes, these four pennies did just that, with mere symbolism!

January 31. *A warrior wink.*
When having lunch with Hydee today, I was talking about Michael's warrior mission, basically saying that warriors are needed now of all times. Hydee said, "Oh my God, look at this guy's t-shirt" and she saw it right when I said "Warriors"! I turned around and saw:

"WAAARRIORRRRSSS"

And on the back "STRENGTH IN NUMBERS"!

The year depicted on the t-shirt is 2017, which is the year our mission was revealed at Moraine Lake in Alberta, Canada! And in my newsletter today, I reminded everyone that "Archangel Michael has said, one working with him is like thousands working without him." Strength in numbers, indeed!

Once recovering from the shock of the most perfect t-shirt at the most perfect time, I asked the guy if I could take pictures of his fabulous bright yellow and blue shirt.

I then went on to basically say to Hydee that I'm seeing some Lightworkers being influenced without knowing it, feeling that the dark is already defeated at the top. This makes them give up the fight, thinking job done (Oh! I just now realized this mirrors the "job done" with the leak in my studio, when it was far from done.) Or they are simply being influenced to give up, in my opinion. And I said that now, of all times, is the time to step it up, as I do believe we are progressing toward that tipping point of awareness!

I just adore when someone else is with me to witness synchronicities with such astronomical odds of it happening... it is so much more fun. Just as I'm sure you all do, as well.

February 1. *A personal power wink.*

Lately, I have been pondering the actual power that lies within each of us. With a powerful leader who once spread peace in the world, his actions positively affect people in those times which ripples out to the present and into the future. Doesn't his work make an imprint that shifts the world eternally? And don't we all have this same kind of power?

When my father, an engineering professor, was honored at his retirement dinner, I had the privilege of speaking at it, on behalf of my family. In it, I quoted Henry Brooks Adams: "A teacher affects eternity; he can never tell where his influence stops." I then went on to proudly describe my dad's influence as a most celebrated professor.

And we all have this same power! We are all impacting the world each and every day, which does affect eternity. We are affecting each other with our thoughts, feelings, words, and actions—and certainly with our vibrations. You can just sit in the middle of the city not saying a word to anyone, and your positive vibration is quietly but absolutely making a difference that you will never know about. There is power in just being. When we are conscious of this, it helps us to make even greater attempts to put more good out into the world and to serve others as much as we can.

Of course, because we exist in duality, there is the flip side to all of this. We all can put out less than positive influences out there, as well, for it is part of being human.

There is also the extreme negative. All it takes is one dark man to create a toxin or perform an action for evil purposes targeting the masses, and the repercussions are utterly massive, also affecting eternity.

With Love being more powerful, we will win this game. But the more conscious we are, the quicker we attain what we are here to achieve in this world. I feel like I'm preaching to the choir here, as you all know this. But frankly, I needed this reminder myself.

More to come on this subject, but I feel Michael wanted this much shared today as I woke with these thoughts. Perhaps because we are in the 2nd month of 2020... and 2 represents duality. We have 2.2.2020 tomorrow and then 2.20 and 2.22.2020 coming up too! Exciting times, for sure.

February 2. *An orange dragonfly wink.*
Yesterday, I went to visit Angela who works at a store in Kona. I told her about the housing challenge and yet all the positive signs, especially about the three orange dragonflies that were hovering over my orange car at the hotel, over my car at the apartment building, and over my car at the storage place, all in the same day. After leaving the store, I went to my car only to see an orange-colored jeep next to it with a plate 144!

I decided to get a bite to eat, and texted the picture to Angela. This golden orange is a rare color of cars, but my new German friend visiting here said it's a hot color in Europe. I still don't like sticking out, but this made me feel better. After lunch, I felt so strongly to go back to the store. My friend was typing on her computer.

Angela said she was *just* writing me back and looked up, and there I am. She then described what happened five minutes prior to my return. A woman with her two kids came into the store, which made Angela look up and then see an orange dragonfly flying in front of the shop! These ripple synchs offer goose bump moments. I rarely see these dragonflies here, up until now. So I'm passing the orange energy forth to you to see what happens next!

[It's mid-September 2020, and I was editing this part of the chapter and took a two-hour break. My friend Mia from Slovenia messaged me that this person she knows just moved to the Big Island. I wondered why she was compelled to send me a picture of his reddish-orange Jeep. She wrote: "Not sure if it is orange or red. It reminded me of your car!" This man whom I happen to know of is clearly on a spiritual mission, as well.

Now here is the really crazy thing. The friend who just rented this jeep is best friends with Angela. By the way, I did not meet Angela through my friend in Slovenia. They don't know each other and yet have a connection to this same friend. We let the enormity of this synch sink in, and were simply astounded. Seven months later, Angela's best friend would be driving an orange jeep, that I made notation of months before. My picture of the orange jeep with "144" next to my car was like a clue of what was ahead. Mia and I talked about this for about an hour, and laughed and rejoiced. Metatron's energy seemed to be behind it all.

Mia is one of my dearest friends and she channels Metatron. Certainly, Metatron was behind all of this, back in February through today. He was probably behind the orange-colored vehicles that Mia's friend and I were each driving. Mia just told me that orange is actually the color that is associated with Metatron! It seems that each time that Mia and I connect, everything is so magical. After taking in these synchronicities, she messaged me: "It is like we are in a bubble of magic." I responded, "Totally! We are in 5D" at the *same* time she wrote "New Earth Vibe." Exactly. I will talk more about navigating between 3D and 5D energies in Part Two.]

February 3. *Palindrome and Lily winks.*
How was your 02.02.20? I was pretty excited about it. I went to get a coffee to go and told the owner of the coffee shop all about the very special palindrome day. As I walked out, I told her to expect miracles, and there right

before me on the walk were 2 shiny quarters, again. They were not there when I walked in!

I went out for my third boat ride since on the island and saw about 6 whales (one a baby and mama), it was so thrilling and heart opening. For the third time, we docked right at 12:12! I went to pick up carry out, but first called ahead and ordered by phone. The cashier asked for my name. I said, "Mary." She said, "Lily"? I laughed to myself, in awe! I said, "No, Mary." She repeated the order and said "... and it's for Lily." Okay, I will be Lily! Hahahaha That's pretty unbelievable, considering how important that name is to me!

When I got there, the woman asked for my name and I said it's "Mary," but told her I think the person who took my order thought it was "Lily." Sure enough, "Lilly" was still on the order. She crossed it out and wrote, "Merry." So much fun, although I didn't want her to cross out the name. Later in the day, Lillian came through with a message!

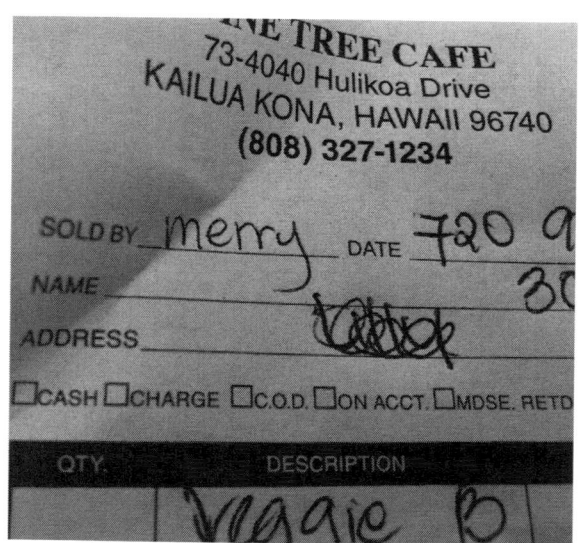

The name "Lily" doesn't sound too much like "Mary." There was definitely some ethereal whispering going on here! I love my adopted Aunt Lillian so incredibly much.

That evening, I picked up a salad at the grocery store. Checking out at the cash register, we talked about the magic of the Palindrome day and the bagger knew all about it, to my delight. And the total came to $8.88 on this powerful 8 day! Let's expect the magic of 02.02.2020 continue into this day, as well.

KTA EXPRESS - KEALAKEKUA
81-6602 MAMALAHOA HWY., KEALAKEKUA, HI
STORE 323-1916

02/02/2020   16:49:15
Total: USD$ 8.88

February 4. *A non-complacency wink.*
Yesterday, a friend emailed me: "Have you watched Mark Passio on Natural Law? He used to be a Satanist/Occultist and he has evolved, and now is exposing them and their powers. He is showing people the way to manifest through the heart, mind and gut aka emotions, thoughts and actions in alignment and then wrapped in caring."

I found his lecture on Natural Law on YouTube, decided to watch with discernment as always and given his past—and was wowed. I won't try to sum it up and let this speak for itself. It is a time commitment of over 8 hours. I'm 2/3 of the way in. I agree with most everything (except on a couple of points), but this is mystery school kind of information. This is in direct alignment with our sword work, seeking truths, and taking action! And I agree with much he says about the dark side of the new age movement, as I addressed in *Michael's Sword & You*.

Very ironically, just before receiving this email, I met with an acquaintance from Germany. She insists that evil does not exist in her world, at the level she vibrates. I was bringing up new age beliefs that were erroneous in my view, and that while we all have different roles in this massive shift we are going though, I feel that we all do have to recognize the dark, in order to transmute it. We simply are all being called.

Complacency is so widespread, and I like that Mark calls humanity out on this. He is gruff though, and very direct. However, as I have said myself, it is "Rip the band-aid off time." I am seeing too many Lightworkers giving up or saying we already reached the tipping point. Although I never heard of this guy before, the timing could not be more perfect.

When he was touching on the very themes of my new book, I realized how destined I was to watch this now—not that I needed the validation as it is constantly validated by so many sources, but it is always appreciated and supporting!

February 5. *A prayers answered and 1212 wink.*
Our fellow warrior from Sydney, Australia shared this most excellent news!

"I just wanted to let you know that the rains are coming at last!"

"We are expecting steady showers and some heavy rain all along the east coast for the next 5 to 7 days which will be so helpful in extinguishing most of the fires."

"So this is a big thank you to you, AA Michael and all your Warriors – as it seems our prayers will be answered!"

Let's keep it up!

Tonight, I submitted testimony to oppose two 5G bills they are rushing through the Hawaii State legislature tomorrow morning with little notice. I also attached 11 pages of links to educate those voting! When completed and ready to submit, please check out the number of characters I typed to make my point known, and to my awe... 1212.

ᴐnths. With this much concern the

ᴈ, it is ALL of our moral obligation

se and we must have the courage

Characters (with HTML): 1212/20000

Update: Even though the testimony we provided was unanimously opposed, both 5G bills passed.

February 6. *A boogie board wink.*

I have been told that I must really take it easy as I heal from this mold exposure on top of so much intense stress over the last two plus years. Therefore, I've been spending extra time by the water, the last two days, and finding every way I can to find joy, feel young, and just be in a most loving state.

This morning, I was watching this courageous boogie boarder do amazing feats by surfing on it, even hydroplaning on the wet sand as the waves come in. If I could just hold onto the board without getting toppled with waves, I'd be quite happy. I thought it would be nice to have a board to just hold on to as I wade in the waves, and maybe try to ride them a bit to feel younger.

As soon as I arrived at the *Queen's* Marketplace in Waikoloa later this day, Hydee texted me. I laughed at the timing because she, too, is experiencing the royalty signs. I went into the grocery store, and in the tourist section was a boogie board for a whopping $60. I thought I'll take one for free? That truly was my thought because I didn't want to spend money on it. I am not a shopper and yet felt driven to look at the tourist merchandise. I then walked down the next aisle and saw nice baseball caps, for only $5.99? That didn't make sense. I saw one sporting an image of a turtle which made me think of my son who loves turtles. I pointed the "deal" out to the couple next to me and they thanked me, as they didn't see it, and proceeded to both buy hats. I said, "Can you believe this deal? The boogie board on the next aisle was $60!" They said they saw that!

I went to two beaches after that to watch whales in the distance. As the sun was beginning to set, I felt magnetized to the trash cans, as absolutely weird as that sounds. I did have a tiny bit of trash, but I truly thought that something was up. Lo' and behold, sitting on top of the trash can is an adorable boogie board, and in fine condition! It immediately became mine. And remember the turtle hat and boogie board connection, there was a large turtle design on this board! Yes, what a deal.

This is a reminder to ask and ye shall receive. This happened all in the same day. Let's manifest the big stuff for our world of course, but had to share this little miracle with you all.

February 12. *A Sun wink.*

Our talks with Michael can always bring peace in a myriad of ways. People continue to ask me to ask Michael things on their behalf, to which I always respond that he hears you just as well as he hears me. I trust that everyone in this group firmly knows this.

Last night, I was awake due to loud noise and the mold situation continuing to be symptomatic. I asked Michael for help. He said "You are going through a whole lot, Mary, and yet the sun continues to shine on you." That is exactly true. He went on to describe an immense Light ahead for us. After this, I picked a card online, at www.powerfloweressences.com, from Isha Lerner's Inner Child Deck. And it could not be more apropos: "The Yellow Brick Road" card. The description begins with: "When this card appears in your reading, a burst of spiritual sunshine can enlighten your mind and warm your heart." This card is for all of us.

February 12. *A slew of winks on a special anniversary day.*
Today was fueled with incredible synchronicities, with
Michael and more! This cloud sighting took my breath
away on the 2-year anniversary of our warrior mission
with Archangel Michael!

And I saw this at 1:11! I then received an important
warrior call at 1:23. Thank you, Archangel Michael! This
is for all of us proving again these words I quoted from
Michael this morning, from *The New Sun*:

*Many feel they just cannot take another day and then
something suddenly occurs that gives them strength. They feel
replenished by some occurrence that makes them feel not so alone
and, rather, supported.*

Oh how true this is! I always count on this. After
being in a "Help me, help me, help me, God!" state of
mind last night, today was pure magic! God and our
angels hear us all. When I sometimes wonder what to

share with you (although it's usually very clear thanks to synchronistic winks), past messages from Archangel Michael fill my head. These feelings make me want to also quote his words from *Michael's Clarion Call*:

You will gain much joy, and benefit in endless ways, by pushing the envelope in how you connect and work with your angels.

This horse head-shaped cloud was seen on the way down to the beach, and wowed me first thing.

On this particularly magical day, I saw my name everywhere (even on a guy's shirt at the bank). Some of you may recall what I said about seeing and hearing your name suddenly, in *I Can See Clearly Now*. I needed a shift away from so much dark attack trying to bring me down, as many Lightworkers and Lightwarriors are experiencing, and the shift is indeed happening today.

A friend often visualized me in a baby blue convertible years ago. That always stuck with me, my being a free, independent spirit. I needed to stop and make a phone call today, so I got off the road onto the shoulder, and this baby blue convertible is in front of me, and also with the same 023 in the plate as mine!

I then went to meet with a lady on her organic farm about a possible rental, but it ended up being about something totally different. As three wild turkeys (great totems) walked next to my parked car, we realized our meeting was about other things.

This lovely lady told me that male warriors would bring pregnant women to have their babies on her very land in the distant past, where the warriors would keep them safe and protected. What are the chances of learning this, and on this special day?

She, too, is connected with Archangel Michael. And I found it simply stunning when she began talking about warriors, and here, on this special two-year warrior anniversary day! I was dizzy with the synchronicities and Divine orchestration, and told her that I would share this in my new book. The afternoon then ended with a beautiful double rainbow sighting.

February 13. *A reminder wink.*
I just now came across this conversation with Michael from a few years ago.

Let me say first... I have never really been a seer or a hearer (physically seeing and hearing) of the "other side," as much as I have always greatly desired this. Only on rare occasions. I channel Archangel Michael telepathically, as you know. I don't "hear" him with my physical ears, as some channels do.

Well, something interesting happened this morning as soon as I sat down to channel Michael. And this kind of thing has, is, or will be happening to all of us, at different times, different ways. Because as the veils thin and our energetic vibrations rise, more and more of this will become commonplace. And this is why I'm sharing.

Mary: Why do I hear a man snoring right now? What is that sound? It comes and goes. Is it from the spirit world?

AA Michael: *That is indeed from the spirit world. You are able to hear better now and we are sending you a gentle example of how you are now able to hear inter-dimensionally.*

Mary: Wow, that is amazing! I welcome all gentle inter-dimensional sounds, sightings, etc., from the highest of the high.

AA Michael: *Ask and you shall receive. There will come a time when this won't seem so odd to you. You will know just what is coming from another dimension and will welcome it.*

Mary: I really most want to see inter-dimensionally, as you well know.

AA Michael: *Yes, indeed, and it shall be so. For you and all of you, as you know.*

Note: Once we stopped conversing, the snoring completely stopped!

February 14. *A new friend wink.*

Yesterday, my friend Chris introduced me to Monique, his friend visiting from Holland. We spoke briefly and the dolphins showed up for only a few minutes and then left, so I went in for a swim to hopefully call them back. When I came out of the water, Monique was just going in. Had the timing been off by a minute, we probably would not have spoken before she goes back to her country today.

This meeting was clearly by Divine appointment and I would soon tell Monique that she would be in my book, with her permission. When we first met, I was distracted by the quick dolphin visit, but was soon sure of the angels' setup when we crossed paths at this next point of meeting, because of the synchronistic timing. Besides, we both felt it.

We talked about so many things, the light and dark sides of Hawaii. This often comes up in conversation with Lightworkers called here. We all feel and assess it pretty much the same. While the paradise aspect of these islands is obvious, there is also a potentially challenging aspect. I have written about this in my book already, as well as to you, group members.

I felt such kinship with this new friend, and thus felt comfortable sharing such private, deep matters with this "stranger" when she brought up a relevant subject. I *knew* she had a message for me, that the angels were working through her. Just when I'm telling her my personal story, a yellow butterfly flew above her head—clearly, an affirming sign.

We stood there for probably 45 minutes in such deep conversation, both really appreciating the Divine orchestration. It wasn't until the latter part of our discussion that I realized the brand name on her wet suit was... "Mares."

I told her that some of my closest friends call me "Mare," and my last name begins with an S! MareS. It felt like another cosmic wink. Monique said that she wants to look up my books and stay in contact.

[More about our Divine appointment in Chapter Ten.]

February 15. *The equine wink grew meaning.*
When arriving at the beach yesterday, I was sitting in the car for a bit when someone knocks on my car window. It was Monique, the woman from Holland! She was leaving the island that day and so I didn't expect to see her. We gave each other a big hug as if long-time friends. Then she, Chris, and I sat on the rocks and spent some quality time watching the whales in the distance.

Remember, I sent you the horse cloud capture I saw on the way down to the beach, the day before Monique and I met? It turns out that she is an equine therapist! Clearly, this was a sign of our necessary meeting. It turns out that Monique caught sight of that very cloud!

February 16. *A Mares wink.*
When telling Chris about connecting with Monique, including the "Mares" sign with his friend, he said he wasn't familiar with the scuba brand name. Just as he said that, someone wearing a Mares scuba wetsuit walked by. We laughed. Heightened synchs for us all, these days!

February 18: *Money winks.*
I found two pennies by my car when stopping at a store prior to meeting Natalia to go on a chartered boat ride. The first thing she tells me when we meet at the harbor is that she just found a dollar bill on the ground! She said she never finds money like this. Coincidence? Or is it the Heavens, namely Lillian, showering us with gifts?!

February 21. *A dizzy wink.*

Did you feel the unique energies of the 2.20.2020? I was so dizzy when I woke, and at varying intensity throughout the day. And also this morning, somewhat. I spoke with several others who were either dizzy and/or nauseous, knowing or feeling that something was up.

Just over a week ago, on 2.12, Michael said to me, in a personal channel: "Wait and watch for the incoming Light. This is not known by most, but you will be experiencing a download of immense Light that will create a most significant turn of events."

When that German woman from the beach talked about the significance of the 2.20 the day before and Lemuria returning (drawing it in the sand), my thoughts went right to Michael's words to me. This was the day, and sure enough, I haven't been this dizzy in a while! I met a friend at the beach before daybreak. As soon as I got there, the dolphins swam by real close, so we got on our snorkel gear and had a good swim with them.

I kept having signs to take it slow because I was dizzy and had to just stand up where my feet could touch in the bottom to ground. But I simply needed to be in the water and in the dolphins' energy. Even where shallow, the sound can travel such distance and we could hear a whale singing. It came fairly close to shore again—right where it drops off into deep waters. So, I felt the cetaceans were assisting, and showing us they were.

February 22. *A royal wink.*

What a wonderful numerological day—02.22.2020! And check out Celia Fenn's Facebook post on this day! This whole Queen, King, Royal theme was new to me until October, and as you lived through it with me—synchronicity revealed it all. And yet many are all getting this same message! Look at how many of you too were and still are experiencing queen synchronicities! It's so exciting.

This mirrors Natalia's powerful channeled message around this same time, as well as my own feelings about how we are here to serve the Divine. Here is Celia Fenn's message, who lives in Cape Town:

"Today is the 22/2/2020."

"Another powerful number sequence that closes out the series of '2' energy transits in February 2020.

It is the only one that falls outside of Aquarius, in the sign of Pisces.

It is also the only one that adds up to a 10/1 rather than an 8.

It is a new beginning of a New Path.

It gives us the opportunity to fully integrate the power shifts of 2019 and early 2020 by stepping into our Queen or King Energy.

In the New Earth, we return to the original path of the Avatars Yeshua and Mary Magdalene, and express our Queen and King energies through 'Royal' service to the Divine Light. We live and express the highest energies of Love and Self-Empowerment.

To be 'Royal' means to be in service to the Divine and to the Community.

As Way Showers, Light Warriors and Light Workers, this is our Mission as the Journey of 2020 unfolds.

May you wear your Golden Crown of Christ Light with Dignity and Grace!"

February 22. *A crown cloud wink.*
While on the boat today, I saw what felt like another crown cloud with a beautiful royal angel centered above it! I don't know about you, but I find these clouds extraordinary and I cannot doubt that this work is so

heavily supported. I'm learning so much, so fast, and the book is coming together.

So, it looks like the crown is going to be the main symbol of my new book since it is now coming up more often, especially since meeting that man with the crowned king on his t-shirt right after I created my first video talking about my new royal book!

February 25. *A huge mother and baby whale wink.*
Gratitude abounding! I kayaked around a gorgeous momma and baby humpback whale in Kealakekua Bay for at least an hour and a half this morning! They came so close to me. I stayed in the same place the whole time and just observed. It was extremely thrilling—I couldn't have been more overjoyed! (Video can be seen on my YouTube channel.) And check out the surreal rainbow sun and magical water sparkle orbs toward the end!

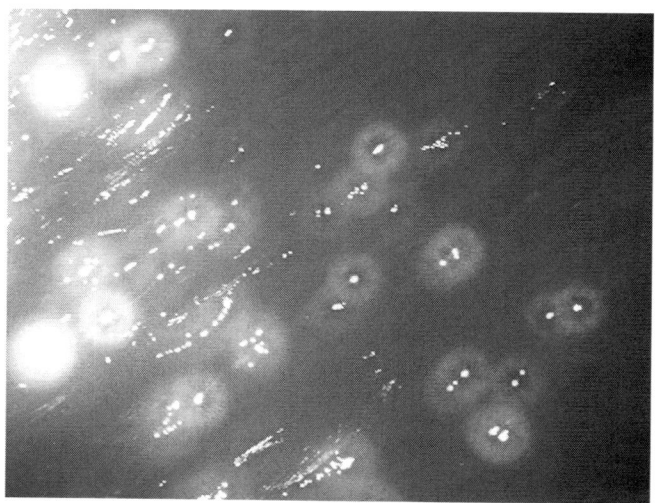

February 26. *Transmuting of energies wink.*
This morning I had a long spiritual discussion with a friend at the beach. It's a beach where I have transmuted

energies repeatedly, over weeks. A place so beautiful, and yet holds some negative, surprisingly intense energies. It's such a dichotomy, alongside the Light.

My friend is a warrior too, and we were blown away by everything feeling so synchronized, that we seemed to be transmuting just sitting and talking about things that needed to be talk about. For instance, there are a few bullies that ruin people's experiences at this beach (as well as at other locations). They scream at, threaten, and have even had physical altercations with snorkelers. This includes tourists who may be here for that once in a lifetime vacation trying to enjoy their time with the wild spinner dolphins.

Once, many weeks ago, I was having such a great time with the dolphins, but Michael said to "Leave now," and when I arrived at the parking lot, I knew why. I was to calm and validate someone's horrible experience with this one bully. The young woman I was comforting was a very sweet soul—I met her while out swimming with the spinners. And, sadly, she was so shook up by the bully's awful behavior toward her. Sure enough, she needed some hugs and to be told that the behavior had nothing to do with her personally, that this woman has ruined many a vacation, and to please try to let it go.

The woman left feeling much better. Had I not listened to Michael, and got there even a minute later, she would have left extremely upset. These upsets have been occurring well before I arrived on the Big Island, and while I haven't been harassed, I've witnessed and heard a lot about it myself. Whether it was the spewing of anger or even physical punches at innocent people, by at least this one, that I know of. She feels she owns the dolphins, truly. It has been hard to watch.

There are snorkelers who definitely do need to curb

their behavior and let the dolphins sleep, for example, but so many are being unfairly judged and harassed. To be in bliss with the dolphins, contrasted with being jarred by the yelling and worse, was frustrating. We should all be allowed to be in quiet bliss during our sacred time with these incredible beings.

Well most interestingly, the bullies at the beach seem to have disappeared or least calmed down. No more harassment at the beautiful beach for now, I'm sure to everyone's relief. [Note: Several months later I was updated that this beach remains very peaceful.] Spreading light and transmuting energies really does work! We have noticed the energy is much different at this beach in recent weeks. No wonder I meet so many Lightworkers there, often visiting from other parts of the world. We are all doing our part, perhaps some doing so consciously, while others not aware.

I feel such happiness that this harassment has seemed to end, for the sake of everyone, including the dolphins! Remember that incredible swim I had with the crystal beings on November 1st, when everyone just vanished and I had the company of up to 50 dolphins by myself? Well just before everyone somehow disappeared, the three bullies were all in the water with me. Clearly, there was something to this.

The one woman swam right to me complaining that the other woman was harassing her, pointing at her while telling me, making a scene. Then that woman swam to me complaining about the other. I told them both we are so blessed to be with the dolphins, let's just be happy like they are and have peace, please. I swam away, and soon after is when everyone suddenly disappeared and I felt as if I was in another dimension!

February 27. *Heads-up wink.*

Several friends on the island are reporting heightened drama, responses, road rage, etc., in the last few days. I've noticed it as well. I was just driving normal this morning and someone drives up next to me at a light, yelling at me, and I had no idea what I did or what it was about. Then someone got upset with me about something that made no sense. I honestly said that I have no idea what she was talking about; she backed off and was real sweet again. Kind of funny! Learning to go with the punches.

February 28. *An Excalibur wink.*

Hydee and I were out having coffee today when this guy comes up to us randomly talking about Merlin and King Arthur! Our mission continues to validate itself and strengthen!

February 29. *Coin winks.*

I've been working on healing and transmuting the rich/poor divide in many ways, certainly when returning to the four sacred sites with Natalia. And I'm making the association, again, with this micro/macro connection, that a great majority of us are struggling to make ends meet and we are so very done with this. Life is not meant to be lived in this way. Too many are in the same boat, and most certainly there are many Lightworkers like me struggling to focus on just their spiritual work.

This is why I think I keep finding coins on the ground nearly every day. Just the day before yesterday, it cracked me up because there was a quarter next to my car door, right when I'm coming out of a bank! I find this to be incredible. Truly, I barely found a penny in the first months I was here! And now it's basically on a daily basis, and sometimes several coins!

And I'm going to assume that this, like the royalty signs, has been or will be contagious with you! When I see a coin, I pick it up with great gratitude, as if the value is exponentially more than it is. And that is actually quite accurate, because it is often a gift dropped from the Heavens!

March 1. *Coins hiding in the sand winks.*
Just wow. This morning, I went to the beach and sat in the car for a while looking for the spinners. When I opened the door and put one foot out, I see this right in front of my toes. I uncovered the other hidden coins in the sand, and there was 47 cents. By the way, the jpg. of this photo is IMG.39.39, or 12.12 (when you add up the single digits).

The 4+7 adds up to an 11, which stands for illumination, as you know. It had rained last night, and the coins were mostly covered in the sand, so it felt like I was revealing a treasure. The little girl in me was excited. As a messenger, I feel this further validates symbolically that we will succeed in breaking this divide of abundance, and, most importantly, we will become sovereign and free. Even though it doesn't seem possible right now with the top 1% still causing mayhem (but not for long!).

My whole day was made in these coin finding moments, and I couldn't wait to share with you! This email takes up 7.07 lucky megabites. Oh my gosh, I'm in my hotel room packing up to move to an Airbnb for the next 10 days while I still look, and just now "Somewhere Over the Rainbow" is being performed live by a band at the farmer's market across the street. Magical. This is a sign especially meant to be shared, because deep in my heart I feel that this metaphor is for all of us!

March 2. *More coin winks on same day.*

WOW... after the coin treasure yesterday, on March 1st, later in the day I went to the laundromat. I picked up 13 more cents from the ground when walking in! Or so I thought.

Actually, the one "penny" is a darkened dime, so that's 22 cents total. And one penny is a 1940 wheat which is valued at least 35 cents! So magical. Thank you, Michael and angels! Look for the coins... expect them!

March 6. *An I Can See Clearly Now wink.*

Carol wrote me just yesterday that her husband recently said, "I have a song going through my head – 'I Can See Clearly Now!'" She asked him if he had heard it recently, and he said no!

Today, the very next day after hearing this from our Carol, I was at the bank finally cashing a check for money owed to me, received only partial payment, but it is something. Right as I walked to the teller, "I Can See Clearly Now" played on the overhead!

March 7. *A Lightworker wink.*

When I was working with my second doctor regarding this mold illness, he emphatically stated that mold *IS* darkness. It works to permeate the body and brain, and that I must work to rid of this, which I have. I would come to learn that Lightworkers are targets for mold. That may sound "out there," so just bear with me.

Yesterday, I had lunch with Eric, a wonderfully bright and jovial young man I met on a boat in recent weeks. We felt immediate connection... that soul thing where you are sure you have met, but as you share details of your lives, it turns out there was no prior meeting *in this life*. Eric was telling me more about something he initially shared on the boat, without having known about my own mold exposure and experience.

Eric was renting a house on a different island with friends, and the home held dark energy. He literally saw this energy with his eyes. When he and his roommates one day found mold on the walls and proceeded to completely clean it up, the very next day it fully reappeared! I made an immediate connection with what my doctor said, that mold *is* darkness. This doctor, too, had severe mold exposure when he lived in Colorado! We're all Lightworkers.

Getting back to Eric... he went to this Hawaiian Priestess who said that very dark things had happened on that land a long time ago. He moved out of the house. Yet his Light was needed there for that time, just as many of us are needed in certain places, clearing and transmuting, and perhaps not knowing that we are in most cases! What are the chances this guy would tell me this story, before he had any idea of what my experience was?

March 8. *Bittersweet winks.*

The night before last, I knew it was time to leave. I've been noticing a difference in my cognitive abilities and focus. I can write just fine (or do I? I hope so! haha), but I'm forgetting the day and even the month, believe it or not, and can't keep my focus for long—I never experienced anything quite like this. Common sense may have said to stay during volatile times with the crazy virus panic and not even travel now, but my heart, my gut, my soul, and certainly Michael all said: "Leave now!" So, I'm flying out on the red eye on Wednesday night and I'm so excited to reunite with my family.

I love the Hawaiian people with their beautiful, loving hearts, and cannot begin to absorb yet what leaving here is going to feel like. But leaving these magical crystal beings whom I can't skype or pick up a phone with, I just lost it emotionally while swimming with them today. They are so magnificent that I could easily spend the rest of my life being with them, learning more and more trying to understand them and what they are *really* doing for this planet. I'm crying now as I write this; they just touch people so deeply. I'm one of countless who feel this deep connection to them. I'm so glad I have the videos to share with you and everyone, because you can feel and glean a lot from them.

Chris, knowing it would be hard on me when I leave the dolphins, said that I never really will be apart from them. They are a part of me as they are with everyone they make connection with—it continues on. He said when he got back to the mainland they were immediately in his meditations and dreams. I have already experienced this, so I know he's absolutely right. I will hold onto that message. And it has been a wonderful experience to bond with many dolphin brothers and sisters, over the great mutual love of these beings.

I'm excited to reunite with loved ones for several days and then will be on a new adventure as I heal and really take care of myself. Much more to come. Where I will go next always offers much to write about and is very special too. Granted, it is much different than Hawaii!

Well, I hope this finds you all well and coping with the worldwide pandemonium. We don't feel it much on the island yet. All I heard is that they are out of hand sanitizer everywhere, but I'm sure it is more than that. We're kind of sheltered here, though, at least at this point. But I'm sure I will experience it more when I get back to the mainland so I can delve into what is really going on. I will find a place to live quickly, and stock up, since I'm starting over again. Wishing you all a most beautiful Sunday.

March 11. *Car wink.*

I sold my car to a used dealership two days ago. I decided that cars bought on the island should stay on the island with the moisture and the issues that can come with humidity. Of the three main salesmen there, they were all named Ryan. What are the chances? They were born around my time, when Ryan was a fairly uncommon name. Yesterday, while organizing things in storage, I noticed the instruction booklet for the car. I had taken it out to read it and forgot to put it back in the glove compartment. So, I took it back to the dealership and here it was less than 24 hours later, and the car is all nice, clean, and ready to sell. There was a young couple looking at it in just those few minutes I was there, and I felt strongly they would buy it. Sure enough, not even a few hours later I see them on the road in the unique colored car. What are the chances? Plates stay on the car, even when you sell. Plus it's one of the most easily recognized cars on the island, pretty much.

Surely, I told you just how small town the big Island is? I have synchronistically run into so many people I know, last minute, as I get ready to leave. I will miss the magic of this island, but, of course, the magic is everywhere.

March 12. *A so long Hawaii rainbow wink.*
I left Kona on the red-eye last night. Everything fell into place so magically. I never watch the news but happen to learn at the airport that there's a US travel ban from Europe to the US. All the sudden shifts in our world certainly added to feeling all the rush to leave. I could feel the urgency to get home during such uncertain times. I'm very grateful to be on the mainland now. I spontaneously decided to leave the island on the evening of the 6th, and left on the 11th. Natalia left the island just hours later, also feeling the same!

Just before I got onto the Queen Ka'ahumanu highway to head to the airport, I opened up Carol's emails that shared her Queen synchs, including her seeing a KONA license plate! I was stunned not only because I was just getting on the Queen's highway wearing my Queen shirt right by the place I bought it, but I see this amazing double rainbow so striking that I must share. Thank you, Carol!

[My deepest appreciation to Carol who hugely and joyfully supported the royalty message with her validating, extraordinary signs, from the time the mission was just unveiling, right to my island journey's end. I will never forget.]

Well I'm about to board Flight 888 for home! How is that for perfection?! I hope you are all keeping a high perspective and holding relentless faith through these wild times.

March 13. *Queen and quarter winks.*
I didn't have time to write everything out about Carol's queen synchs when about to board the plane, but wish to expound on it, because it was pretty incredible!

Carol was playing the word QUEEN in the "Words with Friends" game yesterday, and then sees the KONA plate when leaving the FedEx store on the same day I'm leaving Kona. Not only that, but she was at FedEx on Monday which is the *same day* I was at Kona FedEx to ship my desktop computer back to Colorado. And I haven't been inside a FedEx store in many, many months! They were experiencing what sounded like mercury retrograde ramifications, which made her return to FedEx on Wednesday. And that is when she saw the KONA plate on this same day of my departure! We certainly are connected.

It is great to be home! I am deeply grateful that I was able to travel back as you have to wonder if they will be banning additional flights, since they are from Europe to US! Anyways, so far so good with everything. I need to find a home and a car pronto, and I'm sure that all will fall into place. When my son picked me up at the airport at lunchtime today, he was putting my luggage in the trunk and right behind his car was a quarter! Here we go again… just astounding.

March 13. *A Michael wink.*
Michael had a message for me after I returned to Colorado.

Mary, my beautiful warrior and friend. You have done well! So well, that I am so proud of you for your strength and determination to follow the clear flow of what is next for you. And it will be grand, as you deserve this. You have felt in your heart both the pain and relief of leaving the Big Island. You are already feeling relief at a level you didn't realize until you came back. And here, back on the mainland, you will thrive. The dolphins have made sure of this! That healing by the one and supported by the pod, was monumental and instrumental. Yes, a release of untold proportions.

~~~~~

While I don't like to have regrets, I do wish I absorbed more of Hawaiian culture, learned to Hula dance as I planned to, swim just a few hundred more times with the spinner dolphins, and partake in the beauty and understanding of the depth of the Hawaiian language. Reading a profound book that Hydee gave me while on the island, *Change We Must* [8], by Nana Veary, I reflect on a specific passage:

"'Alo' means the bosom, the center of the universe. 'Ha' is the breath of God. The word is imbued with a great deal of power. I do not use these words casually. Aloha is a feeling, a recognition of the divine. It is not just a word or greeting. When you say 'aloha' to someone, you are conveying or bestowing this feeling."

Alo Ha, Hawaii, with my deep love and honor. I see you and will miss you, for now.

---

[8] Veary, Nana. *Change We Must: My Spiritual Journey.* Honolulu: Institute of Zen Studies, 1989.

PART TWO

Chapter Eight

The Awakening of the Royals

The awakening of the royals occurred, in large part, most dramatically and unexpectedly in 2020. Unbeknownst to most of us, we began on some level preparing, in earnest, for our new lives on a New Earth as free and sovereign beings. What sparked this? A virus. And what I personally and immediately believed to be a "plannedemic," designed to bring humanity down and create a dark new world order, where our enslavement would worsen to unfathomable degrees. But we will one day see realize that those nefarious plans backfired.

Go down this rabbit hole and you may find that the created virus was designed as a culling of humanity, that largely failed. And its other purpose was to bring down the U.S. and the person that many us believe is most bravely after the deep state—President Donald J. Trump. Yet the virus plan ended up forcing much of the global population into sudden lockdown which would spawn the beginning of true human evolution, and yet at a great cost to all our lives—especially, of course, to those lives lost.

Eons of time have led up to this very moment in our history where we are living the period that the book of Revelations spoke of in the Bible, and yet is being greatly rewritten as we set forth on a new path for all of life. We are here to experience the lifetime of all our lifetimes. This will be the lifetime that we free ourselves from enslavement and tyranny, and co-create a New Earth that will never again be run by extreme darkness.

Please bear with me as we discuss the necessary reality before us. *We cannot move forward into our royal lives until the evil is acknowledged and removed to prepare for the arrival of a completely different existence for us.* I don't enjoy talking about these things whatsoever, but frankly, we have no choice at this point. Part of our Lightwork *is* facing evil. As much as we may not believe it exists, it simply does, *but not for much longer, as long as enough of us awaken.*

When writing *The New Sun*, published back in 2013, I asked Archangel Michael that burning question:

Mary: I can hear your answer before I ask this one, but when exactly will we be firmly rooted in the fifth dimension? Some believed it would occur on December 21, 2012.

Archangel Michael: *There is no answer to this question yet. Aside from what you may hear from channels and prophets, this date is not set in stone. It will be revealed to you when things truly are set in stone, so to speak. But within eight years of your time, life on this planet will indeed be very different.*

Eight years from when Archangel Michael gave this message would be early 2021. That is next year (from this writing) that "life on this planet will indeed be very different." We are nearly there, dear readers! And look at how much our lives and the whole world have changed, just since March 2020. I have recalled these words so often, certainly since the appearance of the virus when life was suddenly changing so drastically for all of us.

I would often question just how would this all come to pass where we, with our earth, would evolve into the New Earth. Archangel Michael made it clear to me that some things would change in the blink of an eye, while other changes would occur over time. Even now, most of humanity still has their collective heads in the sand, so how will we reach that tipping point of awareness? How will we establish the desire to create a whole new way of being and seeing? Outside of the controllers and those directly involved in the creation of such mayhem, I don't think any of us knew just what we were in for in the infamous year of 2020. I would venture to guess that the majority of us were completely shocked.

The whole world shut down under the guise of the coronavirus. *Virus* means poison or venom in Latin. *Corona* is the Latin term for crown. It is also the aura that surrounds the sun, as seen during a total solar eclipse, as we know. How interesting. Our evolution is being made possible through what Archangel Michael calls the New Sun—which is the Galactic Central Sun—that is working through the sun that we know. AA Michael refers to this Sun as "New" because it is new to most of us.

Is this the dark's deliberate attempt to poison the crown, to falsify it, to fully snuff the royalty that we really are? They are well aware of the Divine plan for us to continue to raise our Light quotient, move into a New Earth, and enjoy an age of love, peace, and freedom. And so, they continue to do everything they can to put a halt to our evolution. They have attempted over decades now to block the sun from us via weather manipulation. Our sun is life. All of life is alive because of the sun. And then we have the New Sun, the Sun beyond the sun which cannot be blocked. We see the sun as brighter and whiter in recent years. The sun is where it's at, the key to our evolution. Our bodies continue to receive Light upgrades, whether we are aware of it or not.

What is most exciting is the coming Solar Flash that will bring us to our New Earth, despite the dark's attempts to stop it. Surely, Archangel Michael is referring to the Solar Flash regarding those instantaneous changes that are ahead. Check in with your intuition and consider how you feel about this. The sun is changing as well as our thoughts about the sun—we are more drawn to it. We have received growing amounts of Liquid Light from the New Sun, preparing us for our evolution. The lower vibrations will not be able to handle the Light, and thus they continue to try and stop our evolution. They need our fear and negative emotions to survive. Once we elevate ourselves with more Light, they won't exist here.

Archangel Michael gave us this beautiful metaphoric preview in *Michael's Clarion Call*:

Think of yourself as flowing in a river of love. There are rocks that represent hate and anger and other qualities that oppose love all the way down the river. You can continue your flow past the rocks and stay in the flow of love, or you can get stopped by the rocks and stop the flow. The further you continue down this river, you meet less and less rocks. They don't even matter at this point because you are so cleansed and full of love that they couldn't affect your flow even if they tried. This is the way it shall be.

I asked, "Do we continue on this river in the new age?" *The river grows wider until it becomes an ocean, as each of your individual rivers feed into this ocean, and there you will be surrounded by love. The river is but a distant memory, and you are no longer touched by the negative influences. The ocean represents the oneness of all brought together in love and Light, and there you will have attained the peace your hearts desired for all your lifetimes.*

Until then, we are truly in a fierce battle of Light versus dark—good versus evil. The dark have attacked humanity on every level. They have even attacked the seat of the soul, poisoning the pineal glands of many through fluoride added to the water and many toothpastes. And now they are going for our crowns? I must point out that *ovid* means "sheep" in Latin. They consider us all as sheep. Not only that, but the virus name assigned also stands for Certificate Of Vaccine ID. Yes. All planned so that the evil software billionaire can unleash his deadly patented vaccine on humanity? So, I personally never use their name for it, and rather only call it "the virus."

The dark are masters at symbolism. They take all that is sacred and hijack it. There's all kinds of symbolism embedded in this latest virus set up which many, including myself, believe was several years in the planning. After all, weren't we warned that President Trump would be dealing with a pandemic years before he did? That U.S. doctor in the spotlight who was a prominent player in causing the whole world such harm was either psychic or doing what the dark always does. They announce their plans ahead of time, out in the open, and for all to see.

On March 15, I sent to my two groups my thoughts and feelings about what was occurring back then, just before things started closing down and the craziness was getting all too real:

This worldwide, unprecedented challenge can affect humanity very positively, as well as negatively. This may grow our spiritual connection, and God knows so many are so out of touch with the nonphysical for far too long. Our priorities are going to be reset immediately, certainly from material needs and wants to being grateful for "enough." Simplicity will become king. Many have slowly worked toward this, but now we have an incredible catalyst forcing us into change. We will be getting back to simpler ways of thinking and being, not clouded with the unnecessary and synthetic. Perhaps with more home time on our hands, more people will seek truth, as this is forcing all of us to ask a lot more of the difficult questions that most are too afraid to seek. It can actually force us into confronting the truth and taking action, as many more of us are needed on the front lines. We may actually care more about the poisons forced on us and say "Stop! No More!" Ultimately, this disaster will evolve us quicker than anything else could. Don't you think? We simply have to get our new priorities straight and rethink a slew of things. We are having to get very real with who we have been, who we are, and who we are becoming. As challenging as these times are, it is also a most exciting time for us, being that as much of the collective as possible is finally waking out of its deep sleep, as we make the internal and external changes that drive us forward on the path to our New Earth.

Reading this, I somehow feel led to recall the anti-gmo marches that I attended year after year in Boulder. I was beyond dismayed that even in consciously aware Boulder, so few appeared to care. There were maybe a couple dozen protestors and that was it. How can people, most especially parents, not be aware of the dangers of gmos? And how can they not be vitally concerned? It was probably because parents are too busy just trying to survive, often with both parents working at least one job each. Yes, this lockdown will give people a breather they maybe never had, to take a good look at their lives and the broader picture—only to find that *things are not what they seem.*

Eventually, nothing will stop the necessary truths from emerging. Most everyone is going to eventually have a good idea of the level of extreme darkness that has brought such harm to all of life and the earth. Finally. It is difficult for any of us to wrap our minds around the depth of this darkness, *most especially* the rampant, horrific sex crimes done unto children, in many cases by elites, political and religious leaders, celebrity, etc.—people you may not ever have imagined. But the only way through this evil is truth, and full exposure of it, no matter how uncomfortable and dreadful to hear about. We owe it to the child victims to understand the absolute horrors of their experiences. And even those of us fighting for the truth for years will never understand and know it all, for it is so complex, far reaching, and unspeakably evil.

I do worry about the many people who are fully clueless about the level of such darkness in our world. Most are going to be in for a massive shock, especially when it comes to the crimes against children—the rampant pedophilia, child sex trafficking, adrenochrome creation and use, and satanic ritual abuse. Many of us have spent years learning about this. But it is time for more to start understanding, in my view, no matter how uncomfortable. *The truths will truly set us free.*

Yes, the truths are coming out and better to hear it from people who come from a place of love before the big announcements come. You certainly aren't going to hear it on mainstream news unless it becomes fully overhauled. The words of Archangel Michael in *Michael's Clarion Call* ring in my ears, from a decade ago. I had no idea the level of darkness that he was referring to at that time:

There will be shocking and upsetting news of the darkness that has resided among all of you. And many of you will be glad you never knew about it as it would have been too hard to bear knowing about. It would have ripped at your sense of well-being. But know that this battle is almost over. Always think, feel, speak, and act with love and Light. This is your protector. Love and Light will never fail you.

Had we known what many of us now know, back nearly a decade ago when Archangel Michael gave this message, it would have been so hard on our hearts to hold this for so long. On April 7th, I posted Michael's message above on Facebook and added in my words:

"And since I shared that, I see on an even deeper level just how beneficial this is for our evolution. The dark was using us for their continuing plan to bring down humanity, but I do believe it is totally backfiring. Yet we all must do our part to be aware of TRUTHS and stop feeding on the lethal mainstream narrative (until it's taken on its ear)... please, please, please. In the microcosm, I see that people indeed are seeking the truths more, as they do finally have time on their hands to do so now, and realizing that things really have run amok. When I used to post about 5G in the past with a heart full of concern that we must be aware, just a handful would read and pay attention to it. Now, I'm seeing plenty more. That makes my heart soar. We simply must wake out of the slumber we've all been led into, like with the poppy fields in *The Wizard of Oz*. Ding Dong the Wicked Witches Will Be Going Away. We must demand our freedom and stop being led by the extreme dark. We must wake up so that we can be the Sovereign Beings we are designed to be, and truly are deep within. Let us set ourselves free and create our destined New Earth with joy, excitement, and the Heavens cheering us on, and helping us incredibly so. These are such challenging times, for sure, but it's also ever so exciting to be alive right now. What an honor for us all to be a part of what the Universe has never experienced before, at least from the perspective of this planet. We are moving into an Age of Love."

Note: In the Summer of 2020, I learned from various corroborated sources that Trump banished the Chinese version of 5G which is known to be deadly. And in its place is a Nikola Tesla-based 5G that is not only safe, but actually beneficial and supportive to life. This may sound far-fetched, yet look into John Trump (President Trump's uncle) and his connection to Nicola Tesla! Please God, may this be true—and true for the whole world!

We have endured decades of being sprayed from the skies, and so many can look at those foreign lines day after day, year after year, in our once beautiful skies and still not see it. Cognitive dissonance is alive and well, certainly with geoengineering, as well as with so many other crimes against humanity. When a healer told me about chemtrails and geoengineering soon after the turn of the millennium, I was in absolute disbelief myself that the government would do that to us. She insisted on our taking baking soda and sea salt baths way back then, to help dissipate the effects.

Over time, I saw that she was exactly right. It would be a while before I learned of what we were being sprayed with—including barium, strontium, and aluminum—but I never forgot her words and continued to keep looking up. We are breathing in nanoparticles day in and day out. And here we are 20 years later after I first heard of this, and the world and all of life are still dealing with it. In some areas, we are witnessing a dramatic drop in this practice dangerous to all of life. But in other parts of the US and world, the criminal spraying continues.

It may be the truths about Hollywood that will bother people the most—sad to say, when we all should be most upset about crimes against scores of children. Yet we have spent decades collectively praising the celebrity royalty—false idols in many cases. Many (not all) of the most beloved stars are not who we think. Many are not to be put on pedestals, whatsoever. Hollywood is filled with grave darkness. Mel Gibson tried to tell people the truth, and got vilified for it. We are talking pedophilia, sex crimes, adrenochrome usage, satanic indoctrination, etc. Once you know, you cannot un-know.

Clearly, it will be hard to watch the same movies and television anymore. Some time ago, I got rid of most of my favorite DVDs (except for old ones or foreign films), and let me tell you—I have loved movies since I was a kid. They had to go, though. Not just because of the programming, dark symbolism, and indoctrination behind them. But because I could no longer watch the actual actors in them. We can't just hate on them because we don't know how these stars came to behave in dark ways—whether they were mind controlled, sold their souls, cloned, and yet some may truly be dark people. We are talking extreme evil, in many cases.

If you don't know what adrenochrome is, you perhaps need to understand for children's sake. You will then understand the disgusting symbolism in *Monster's Inc.*—it's very sick. You will also realize why Google's *Chrome* is called just that, with a 666 designed into that logo. The dark puts all kinds of darkness right in our faces; in songs, movies, television shows, gaming, and the worst—in children's programming, movies, books, educational tools, and toys. Many of the worst tragedies in our world caused by dark forces were first displayed, by the way, especially via popular television shows and movies, and unbeknownst to most people. It is their way to always give a heads-up of their nefarious plans.

The dark permeates pop culture trying to indoctrinate us. They target most especially the youth, and certainly through music. Over decades of effort, they have touched all aspects of life, and once you are aware, you can eliminate it as best as you can from your daily awareness and presence. Great new businesses in the future will focus on wholesome, moral, and beneficial products and viewing for children! But nothing is like getting outside and "programmed" to nature!

We simply have to face the fact that the extreme darkness of satanism and luciferianism has been running our world, and permeating all aspects of life. I personally went from not wanting to see it and denying it to myself, to actively researching to gain awareness. Then once I was given Michael's sword mission, I eventually realized that most nefarious actions on the planet stem from beings (and, clearly, they are not just human) connected to these dark religious belief systems.

As we fight in this dimension, we know that a massive battle is being fought in the heavens with dark entities. The only way through this reality we have been held victim to is by acknowledging truths to then set ourselves free from this matrix. It is all coming down now. But we can no longer hide our heads in the sand in the midst of the great reveal.

Therefore, the diamond in the rough of this virus forced on humanity is an awakening that humanity has never experienced before. The benefits of this virus mess will end up far outweighing the tragedies. And, believe me, I am not belittling the loss of life, loss of businesses and livelihood, and the temporary loss of our human ways of being. Absolutely not! *But life continuing the way it has would have revealed much more grave consequences.* The old ways were not working. The rampant, hidden darkness running the world is now being exposed, and this absolutely had to come to a stop. We simply had no choice but to wake up. And, frankly, there are still many fast asleep. This is why there are so many truthers spreading awareness.

Once enough of us have awakened to the evil running this world, and we stop consenting to their influences, we free ourselves for a new experience on a New Earth where evil no longer controls us! And Love takes its place. Love wins. God wins. We win. And with all that we were subjected to—enslavement, lack, deception, dishonor, poisoning, cheating, etc.—we will then experience its extreme opposite!

We are heading toward a destiny well beyond our imaginings. Freedom. Truth. Abundance. Excellent health. Free energy, like Tesla discovered long ago. Cleaned up water, skies, soil, and food. And so much more.

The glories of the Golden Age will be more wondrous than any one book, or speech, or course can describe.

~ Archangel Michael, from *Michael's Clarion Call*

Chapter Nine

Enchantment in the Desert

On March 11th, I was excited to get home to Colorado, but without a place to call home. It was becoming increasingly clear in the final days on the Big Island where I would finish writing this book—in New Mexico, *the Land of Enchantment*. I didn't think too deep into it. I felt my way through this decision. And I found angelic and universal support magically setting the stage for this move with much ease and joy. I gained a certain feeling of peacefulness I was craving, and that this land always provides.

After a fairly quick visit upon arrival in Colorado, I felt such urgency to get down to New Mexico to find a place to live because I could *feel* the lockdown just ahead. So I left on March 16th at 1 a.m. and made the six-hour drive down. What I would soon find is that this journey and new beginning was to be fully blessed and overseen, in ways I truly did not expect.

Returning to the Land of Enchantment after having lived there from '99 – '04 with my family, felt like an inner yearning was being satisfied. I am a wondering soul, and yet I was not done here. If you read *I Can See Clearly Now*, you know that my connection to this land never left my heart. And you would also know that there is a reason why throngs of Lightworkers have been drawn here over decades, as described in this book:

"We can also be pulled toward places for unexpected reasons. I learned from *The Light Shall Set You Free* [9], that New Mexico holds the karma for the creation of the atomic bomb. Yes, not only people but also places, cities, states, and countries acquire karma, which manifest though the Law of Cause and Effect. Karma says that for every action, there is a reaction. People, without knowing why, have been driven to settle in this region to balance the karma and provide accelerated healing energy to this area. I read this just after feeling the pull myself, a perfectly timed sign, one of the countless New Mexico signs that proved to be validating."

I knew I must reconnect to this land, and the reasons are still unfolding. For one, there is plenty of darkness that still needs transmuting here. Not just because of the past atomic bomb creation, but before arriving I learned that there are major underground bases known to be in this state (as there are under so many states and

---

[9] Milanovich, Norma, and Shirley McCune. *The Light Shall Set You Free*. Albuquerque: Athena Publishing, 1996.

countries). Just like, prior to my arrival to Hawaii, I was shocked and upset to learn about the prevalence of child trafficking on the island. Once arriving in New Mexico, and the mandates began spreading, I became aware of dark leadership in this desert state. Clearly, darkness is begging to be transmuted across the globe and why millions of us are being called to specific places.

Upon arrival to New Mexico, I was open to various areas to live. However, I kept feeling I need to be in the high desert of Santa Fe. I was not interested in being right in the heart of town, though. So I asked God for a place in the rural part of Santa Fe, ideally, and a home that had the rustic New Mexico architecture I love and feel comfortable with, *and more*. That is just what I got. I found the place the day I arrived, saw it and quickly signed a lease, getting everything I desired and more.

There were so many renters interested in this newly built studio that the owners scheduled viewings every hour, then every half hour that first day. My appointment was at 12 p.m., and these most lovely new landlords immediately decided to rent it to me. I moved in just three days later. I had only a car's worth of belongings, and would not move everything from my storage unit in Colorado for a few months, as it turned out. At the time, I wondered if they were going to shut down state borders, since I had read reports that it was a possibility. So, I just made a quick trip to get one more car load and happily lived with less. Tremendous ease with a living situation! It all fell into place, and magically so.

Now I share the following even though on the surface it may appear mundane. But I use it as an example of what happens when you go with the wind of your soul, and in a state of trust in and connection with the Universe. Everything falls into place. On March 21st, I bought a used car from a dealership on the last day dealerships were open, only to be closed for what would be two months. Had this not happened with such incredible timing, I would have had to keep my rental car all that time—which would have proved expensive.

Mine was the final sale of the day, and with very nice people. Everything was falling into place in the nick of time. It was only because I was so full of faith and going with the wind of soul, everything was occurring with ease. This wasn't me before. *I was always way too much in my head with concerns, overthinking, and worries!* Anyways, all this ease and joy made up for the horrible living situations experienced on the Big Island. Archangel Michael kept telling me that ease was ahead in my personal life, and it was indeed.

The funny thing is that I love Subaru cars and was excited to look for my third one. But when I rented a car from Colorado to come down to New Mexico, the rental car rep said they were out of the standard cars and that he would have to upgrade me. He asked if the Volkswagen Passat would be okay with me. Absolutely, I said. I'm not real big into cars. I just want something comfortable and a nice ride. Well I soon realized that this car offered the best ride ever. I fell in love with this car and suddenly wanted a Volkswagen. Destiny seemed to lead me to purchasing a 2013 VW Jetta wagon, not expected and yet it fell perfectly into place, and just in the nick of time! Amazing. And it isn't orange.

By the way, I actually found this car the same day that I signed my rental lease—it was a very full first two days—but I was too busy getting things to set up my new place. I hardly had any food and as I said, I could feel the lockdown intensity. I had to start from scratch with most everything since I gave away all my stored food before leaving for Hawaii and most of my things, in general, were in storage. So I bought what I absolutely had to have and spent time figuring that out and shopping while the stores were still all open.

I was ready to buy the car later that week, but there was a recall on it. They would fix it and have it ready the next morning. I was told that due to the recall, the car's engine was covered for 150,000 miles! What a nice bonus. And so, I am loving and appreciating every facet of this experience.

There was a stunning juxtaposition to be gleaned from, between experiencing the new surroundings and feeling joyfulness and relief in my personal life, and observing the lockdown that began just a few days after arriving, and to my shock. How was this happening? How was this so sudden, like wildfire, seeping into every business, with safety measures very quickly going into place and refining, reviewing, and replacing these measures for those deemed more appropriate?

How people were falling in line so fast is what I found most stunning. Truly, it felt robotic and people were often emotionless, just going with the flow of the sudden shift as if under a collective spell. I guess most people were in shock? How were people complying so quickly, not questioning anything? My gut was screaming, "This is not right!" But I went with the 'rules.'

Before I even left Hawaii, I stated in a YouTube video I created on February 29th, "Please don't get caught up with mainstream news and all the fear and hype about the latest virus. If you really go down that rabbit hole, you know that this is not something... that is not fabricated, we'll put it that way. It's all by design. It has been done before. Please don't get into the fear of it. Just do what you can. I mean, I don't worry about the actual virus. What I worry about is everyone's reactions to it. And, you know, we all have to take care of ourselves and do what we feel we need to do. But don't go into the fear, because that just heightens everything. It takes us where they want us to be—to be in fear, be in the conquer and divide energy, getting us all upset with each other. Just so done with that. Let's just love each other. We don't have to go to tea or have lunch with everyone, but let's just have peace. Keep moving toward peace. Being neutral as much as possible. Being open to new beliefs. And being in a state of love in our hearts." I could see and intuitively feel all of this *before the crisis really hit*.

So much was coming together in my personal life in those first couple of weeks in the Land of Enchantment, truly so effortlessly that I felt I was living in 5D. What? In the midst of this chaos and while many are so full of fear over this virus? Yes. I was actually excited during this time because I could feel on so many levels that this is what it is going to take for humanity to shift, even though a most difficult and uncertain journey was ahead for us all. This world could not afford to continue down this same path anymore! We are being woken up like never before... finally.

I was so high on life and realized this is what living in 5D feels like. Everything comes with ease and high vibration. And then something would happen to bring me right back to 3D, but I would choose again. I felt as if I, in this same body, was experiencing two different dimensions. Maybe it's 4D and 5D. How do we know for sure? I just know that life was feeling very different, and it was privately felt, an extremely wonderful kind of different. I hope you know just what I'm talking about!

As many of you know, a global meditation occurred on April 4th, perhaps the largest organized meditation ever. The positive energy that was created during this event from reportedly tens of thousands of participants (but who knows the actual numbers), was nothing short of miraculous. What a massive benefit of world lockdown—Lightworkers and Starseeds had little excuse to not participate.

The world is changing so fast now, and certainly the results of this meditation will catalyze the changes. We really are beginning to recognize our power, as individuals and as a collective. We are delving into our abilities to co-create, as we imagine our New Earth into being. We are also imagining what our new lives within these lives will look like.

For several years, I felt that in my new life within this life, I would create spiritually-based movies. Whether they be documentaries or uplifting fictional stories to help anchor in the New Earth remains to be seen. I have no background in this work, and yet I feel driven to follow this passion.

We are conditioned to learn and glean from videos and motion pictures, and when you have movies teeming with violence and darkness, it is so bad for humanity's collective consciousness. So, I would like to break into this and provide powerful, positive messages, even if just on a small scale, and then see where it goes.

A few weeks into my stay in New Mexico, I suddenly pondered another reason why I am here. This state has been a burgeoning mecca for American movies. New Mexico's landscape has been a prime movie location for motion pictures, starting decades ago with the old westerns. So being here has gotten me more and more excited about working on my first movie project— perhaps some time next year. Again, I am starting from scratch, and yet I desire to reach people in this creative way. Things happen for so many reasons, and this is what I am suddenly feeling about my move to this enchanting land.

Around when the anticipated global shift of December 21, 2012 came around, I recall speaking about this most violent apocalyptic movie starring a huge celebrity name, that was about to premiere. I was praying this would just stop. How have we become so conditioned to violence and chaos? We have perpetuated it by paying money and supporting these films. Well, as we grow our vibrations, these movies will simply cease to exist. As related earlier, Hollywood is falling now in many ways as the truths of the level of dark, satanic practices that flooded much of this industry get revealed. New movies with new subject matter are going to flood the market, I have no question.

This leads me to a memory. Back when I found out that the famous Wayne Dyer was authoring his new book with the same title as mine, *I Can See Clearly Now*, and seven years after I published it, I was quite shocked. One of my readers sent me a radio interview where he discussed that he was writing a book (also) on synchronistic life experiences and set to be published more than a year after this broadcast. I immediately wrote the publisher as well as Wayne Dyer, and sent them each a copy of my book. My concern was that our books have the same title on the same subject, and with him being so famous it could affect my book's exposure.

I was pleasantly surprised to receive a call from the publisher. He was very kind and told me that our books are very different (I still haven't read Wayne's book, but I took the CEO's word for it). He said that Wayne Dyer will know who I am and he will forward the letter and copy of my book to him. The publisher assured me that this would actually help my sales. And he was right that sales did improve, but only in the very beginning, and then sales fell sharply and remained so ever since. (I have to add that I am not very good at marketing, to boot!)

Also, at the same time my book which always carried a five-star Amazon rating since 2008, immediately went down to a 4 ½ star average due to two sudden 1-star reviews placed right around when Dyer's book was coming out—it was very odd. And for years my book always came up first when one would do a title search, and was eventually forced way down in the list (although it varies). Furthermore, for two years people would write me that they left a great review, but Amazon would not accept it, the reviews got flagged somehow even though it was fully within guidelines and they were verified purchases. So my book also missed out on several reviews that people took the time to write, and that I knew of. It was all so odd.

To be clear, book titles can't be copyrighted, but the known author etiquette is that if the books are on the same subject matter, you just don't replicate the title. Here was this world renowned author with the same title. While I am not a big name, my books have changed many lives for the better. People often write me that they see life so differently because of them.

Why do I bring all this up? Because the other reason I requested from Dyer that his title be reconsidered, was, as I told him, it was my dream for years to make *I Can See Clearly Now* into a movie. This dream has been simmering within me for many years. but it wasn't time then, but now... now it appears that I need to start thinking more seriously about this. I also share this to describe the deeper reason for that yellow balloon synchronicity at The Manago, as described in Chapter Six, when I symbolically took my book out of the "shadows of stagnation." This sign helped to breathe new life into my movie dream. I still don't fully know the purpose of the synchronicity of our same book title—sometimes it takes years for the understanding to fully unveil. I truly didn't plan on bringing this subject up, but my gut tells me to.

A few weeks into these reawakened feelings of wanting to break into movie creation, as well as entertaining these recollections, I came across a prophetic video by Penny Kelly talking about the coming changes in our world, and in literally 30 seconds had some wonderful synchronistic validation that I am on the right track!

In her video on YouTube: "Penny Kelly Patreon: Current Events – 14 April 2020," Penny states: "Independent film makers are going through what the book publishing business went through twenty-five years ago with the advent of print-on-demand publishing. With the right technology, anyone can make their own movies, and this expands exponentially with a lot of feel good movies being put out as a backlash to the Hollywood programming of a nefarious kind."

Goodness! This is *exactly* how I feel and have felt for a long time. So it was nice to hear it recognized and corroborated by another. Movies are still a great vehicle to reach people. This is not going to go away, in my opinion, but we need *a whole new paradigm in movie making.* The violence and brutal subject matter simply needs to cease as our planet is upgrading and people will no longer be in that 3D space of aggression and hatred. We are moving fully into the Age of Love, as noted earlier.

What's so much worse is when you go down the rabbit hole of children's movies—even in the classics and seemingly innocent stories—is the subliminal sexual programming and symbolism. This is just one of the many ways children have been targeted to be groomed for pedophilia. This will not exist on our New Earth! But we have to face this reality as responsible parents and citizens. In all these cases, it is very hard to process that this has been going on under our noses for decades.

So perhaps this is one reason I am here, *to be inspired* to help shift, even in a small way, the visual arts from darkness into Light—whether I remain in this area or not. New Mexico inspires me, plain and simple. And many artists of all kinds have gravitated toward this enchanting mecca to live and create.

Recently, I had a dream that I was painting a tree and it wasn't very good, so I painted it again and again over the same canvas to improve my interpretation. I do have artistic abilities, and felt I wasn't tapping into them. It felt as if my soul was telling me, through this dream, that I need to delve into a different level of creativity. To pitch this canvas, and create a new vehicle in line with my talents. And so I feel I'm in the right place for that, for now. And movies will eventually be the new vehicle.

[*I must interject here.* A few months after writing this, I had a skype meeting with my friend from another country. We were talking about world events and I brought up how Hollywood is coming down as the dark truths continue to get revealed. I felt to mention that part of the reason I feel I'm in New Mexico is because there are several studios anchored here in recent years, and I want to make spiritual, uplifting movies. A psychic recently told me that I absolutely will do this. She even phrased it just as I do, "in my new life within this life." It feels so overwhelming to me as I do not know the first thing about making movies, and yet I told my friend that I always, in particular, wanted to make *I Can See Clearly Now* into a movie somehow.

The very next morning after this conversation, I woke to an email sent the night before. Subject line: "A Movie Trailer for your book, 'I Can See Clearly Now!'" WHAT?! I get all kinds of marketing emails from businesses wanting to help me sell my books over the last dozen years, but never anything like this. The company creates video trailers for books. So even though it of course wasn't about a motion picture trailer, what are the chances this email with a most synchronistic subject line was sent just hours after proclaiming my long-time desire to turn my debut book into a movie?! I'll take that as a most sublime sign.]

Two months after arriving in New Mexico, I led a Zoom event called "Magical Hawaii… and its Royal Call!" I wanted to introduce this royalty message to anyone already feeling drawn to it. This was much more than just a travelogue of my seven-month journey on the Big Island. It was my first public gathering to sound the call of our royal soul heritage, and participants responded very well to it.

On the day before the event, I felt to run an errand in town, even though I was busy getting ready for my event. I clearly heard that "Leave now!" from Michael, and I anticipated the magic ahead. On the way back home, I was blown away to see this crown-shaped cloud. It was complete with many beings and with their outstretched arms. They are often seen in this way, as I described in *Look Up!* It felt like an amazing wink of support from the Heavens.

Justina was among the royalty in attendance. We've been friends via social media for almost a decade, but it wasn't until the virus and lockdown that we began communicating on a regular basis. I was delighted that Justina would be joining in, and she ended up creating a whole lot of magic on this day of May 23, 2020.

I share the following exchange especially as a grand validation of the royal message. But also as an example of how a stunning, constant thread of synchronicities can occur within a very short period of time. And it's often when two or more are gathered, and in synch. I will always treasure these synchronicities between us as extraordinary magic!

Very soon after the event, which spilled into an over three-hour-long gathering, Justina messaged me at 2:12 p.m. my time. (I remind you, or in case you skipped around the book, that I consider 12:12, 2:12, 12:02 all potential winks from Archangel Michael.) When I was speaking during the lecture part of the event, I caught

12:12 on the clock, and giggled with delight letting everyone know. At that very moment, I was just starting to tell the "Chihuahua" story, as seen in *I Can See Clearly Now*, and *heard* to look at the clock! Here is the first of Justina's messages following the event, beginning with this photo and these words.

BALLARD STREET JERRY VAN AMERONGE

Once home, Gwen can't wait to slip into something more empowering.

Justina: Mary, I wanted to share some things with you. Right at the beginning (I'm in Central Time), you were talking about synchronicity and my good friend texted me at 12:12. And then you caught it on the clock... an hour later. Also, I have another girlfriend I hadn't connected with in about six weeks... I sent her a quick message yesterday and she texted back during our Zoom meeting... she has a granddaughter named Lily! That could be the only Lily I know. A few times, whether it was from you or someone else, and in many other places, a message that keeps coming up (for me) is Balance. This is especially relevant with prosperity. Bartering will be used more, once again.

During the gazing, I didn't quite "see" but I was aware that Mother Mary and Mary Magdalene were present… at least I was thinking of them, and then I thought you could be called "Mama Mary." I also emailed a photo to you. I was quite entertained by realizing it was right in front of me (on a bulletin board above my computer), and has been for years! [Cartoon is seen on prior page.]

Mary: Unbelievable, Justina! I just love how we are connecting lately. Amazing about the 12:12 and Lily! Michael and our friends above have to be laughing so hard at times.

Ohhh yes, balance is so important, and I'm not good at it (but learning)! I could also cry, because I just referred to someone as "mama" in my comments on Facebook just a bit ago, when I normally write it as "momma." I asked myself why I did that. Then I come here and you say "Mama Mary."

It brought up emotion because my beloved grandma, whom I speak of in my first book, we called "Mary Mama." I was named after her, so I felt as if you gave me a wink. Thank you so much for your insights.

Justina: Oh my… and I never really use the term "mama." So yes, it was for you. I guess I only use it when it's in reference to a creature in nature like a mama bear.

3:23 p.m.

Mary: Oh my God, I'm just having a very late lunch while watching *The Mary Tyler Moore Show* on Hulu! (Rhoda is seen in a crown and robe, holding a staff!)

Moore Show

IT'S YOUR CLASS
WITH A CAPITAL "K."

4:43 p.m.

Justina: A Chihuahua just walked by my house.

4:44 p.m.

Mary: Oh my God, and it's 4:44 here! Ask its name! Hurry, run out hahaha (joking)

4:49 p.m.

Justina: (Justina provided a link to an article: "The pandemic is changing how human beings think about status" discussing the very things I was referring to during my talk! Specifically, on FastCompany.com dated 5/15/20, it delved into the status change we are going through right now. "Just a few months ago, people might have awarded the highest status to those people with the most money, or to those who wear the biggest diamonds or drive the most expensive luxury cars. Celebrities and athletes have held high status in society due to their wealth, fitness, beauty, and performances.")

(What I said on this same day during my event was that "There's extreme darkness in the British royalty. There is extreme darkness in the celebrity royalty, that's known as Hollywood. People are going to freak out when they know who their beloved stars really are. I hate to say it. Not all, not all! But there's a lot of darkness. And it's all about the fake royalty stepping down, and all of us elevating ourselves. That's what this whole message is about. Freeing ourselves. The tables are going to turn.")

4:56 p.m.

Mary: Sheeeeesh! You are MAGICAL, Missy! My God.

8:22 p.m.

Justina: OK Mary, I have one more update for today! I just finished another webinar (with a psychic) that I've been familiar with for many years. He mentioned "crown" and they even showed an image of a crown. He mentioned the sword and raising it to clear. And he said the words "mama bear"! During the webinar, I grabbed a deck of my cards. I don't use this one very often, it is the Angel Tarot Cards. I think you'll enjoy what cards came out. [There were three cards "The Wheel: Archangel Michael" "Queen of Air" and "Queen of Fire."]

10:28 p.m.

Mary: Mind Blown!

7:36 a.m. Next Day

Mary: I'm rereading this. Justina, I cannot get over all of this. You will be in my book! Thank you, thank you, thank you for making yesterday extra extraordinary. Here we've been friends all these years and suddenly find we are incredibly in synch. Smiling ear to ear...

We are mysteriously linked to the perfection of Divine, universal timing. Just like when you buy a book, but it sits on your shelf for months, or even years, until it is the absolute perfect time to read it. I'm finding this kind of perfection with friends—old friends suddenly reconnecting, as well as new, like-minded friends magically appearing, to help each of us move through these times. We are helping each other piece together the clues, connect the dots, all while supporting each other as we all navigate through these unprecedented experiences. Similarly, many Divinely orchestrated connections brought us together to name, develop, and grow this royal message for this very book. It is utterly fascinating to witness and experience.

The lovely Magenta Pixie's YouTube video created on July 8, 2020 speaks of things right in line with my royalty messages in this book. The group she channels—"The Nine"—came through to her to say:

"In the new earth reality, there is no hierarchical structure where you have a royal family and you have subjects. That's not how the organic reality works. That's not New Earth, and that's not the 5th dimension. The royal individuals are those who hold the royal code which is an indigo code. It has other colors to it. But it is a warrior spirit. It is a psychic code. It is a code that gives you the ability to radiate your DNA frequency for others to catch. So it's an activation code and it's a code of service. As a royal, you are in service to the whole. You put the whole not above you but as you, as equal to you."

And then came my favorite part that gave me validating goosebumps. "In the fifth dimension, that is the code that everyone holds. It's a unity structure. So, everyone is royal in the new earth. We are all princes, princesses, queens, kings, whatever. You choose your royal form."

This mirrors what I have experienced, felt, lived, and received from the Heavens and synchronistic messages, since this new mission began. Interesting that, before viewing this, I had read and learned about the possible new King of England (who may or may not be the real deal), and I thought to myself—this kind of leadership and decorum will no longer be needed!

We are all royal. No one is better or more important than another. And we will all shine. Just like the angels all shine, and are never in competition with each other. Remember Archangel Michael's words as shared in Chapter Four, about the *pedestals for you all to stand taller, raise higher, connect with us and with each other from a higher standpoint!*

Chapter Ten

We "Crazies" Are the Most Sane

These times are particularly hard on those fighting for truth. Truth that is ignored while incessant lies flood hypnotic mainstream media and their believers. The following quote was seen on Facebook posted by Jeff Brown. I believe that this will highly resonate with many truthers, whistleblowers, Lightworkers, Lightwarriors—all of us working so hard to get the truths out into the world.

"It has been my experience that the one that families call the 'crazy one' is often the sane one. This is particularly true in very dysfunctional families where ideas of healthy functioning are turned upside down. In these families, members often repress their authentic feelings and turn against anyone who reminds them of their unresolved issues and patterns. As a result, the truth-speakers, the ones who refuse to contain their feelings, those who challenge and humanize the toxic status quo, are often scapegoated and vilified, made to feel crazy by those who lack the courage and insight to see beyond the family's madness. If you have been labeled the 'crazy one,' take heart. You are truly not alone. Most great creators and paradigm shifters were met with fiery resistance by those afraid to grow. Whatever you do, do not allow your voice to fade away in the face of their messaging. Your voice, your vision, your ways of being, live at the heart of your unique soul's journey and are the key to collective transformation. No one has the right to bury them under a bushel of shame. No one! And remember, what is crazy to an unconscious person is often brilliantly sane to one who is awakening. Without you, we are lost. Blessed be the 'crazy' ones!"

This is where we are at right now in the big picture. The world family is filled with such massive divide, between the "crazies" and those fast asleep. The easiest way to explain the division? In my opinion, it firmly lies between people who seek and trust mainstream news sources—the true virus of these times—and those who seek truth outside of the mainstream narrative.

So, we find ourselves in a most unprecedented divide, certainly over this virus, ranging from how it started, whether it was planned or naturally occurring, rejecting the tyranny to falling in line with it, etc. And many of us seem to be considered the black sheep in our one big human family. That is, until big truths come out soon and in a big way—because they absolutely will. They already have, to those who seek it. The truth always surfaces, eventually, and the masses need to hear it.

It has been the story of my life that my strong intuition combined with the courage to understand the raw truths in the microcosm and macrocosm of life would lead me to then speak out—and my naming the vital truths would often bring great turmoil. I have always been one to passionately sound the alarm and give a heads-up, even when people around me often weren't ready for it, or perhaps would never be ready to hear. Even when trying to prevent people from, say, getting a flu shot or using toothpaste containing flouride.

The result of spreading hard truths has caused deep suffering in my personal life. But that never stopped me and especially won't stop me now, during the greatest collective crisis of our time. I *know* that many of you relate very well to this! Everything is quickly coming to a head now, in our ever toxic status quo. Truth is king, and it simply must be spread to those willing to hear. My training as Archangel Michael's warrior and leader of a spiritual army has prepared me for just this. We raise his sword of truth while in a state of Love. And I know I am joined by millions around the world in this massive mission for truth, which probably includes you.

It became very apparent to me that, basically, those who watch and believe mainstream news are steeped in fear, grief, and despair; and those who do not, and rather independently seek truths, are not. Why? Because the latter group have divorced themselves from the programming. We desired to step outside of the matrix, as best as we possibly can. So we have this dichotomy and divide, and it severely hampers our collective momentum toward revelation, revolution, and evolution. People are losing friendships, and even family connections, right and left over this divisiveness, and unity is sadly going out the window in many ways.

This is exactly what the dark wants, and has most purposefully designed. Conquer and divide is an ancient technique, and we are falling for it, again and again. It's also "bread and circuses," from the Roman times, where we are paralyzed with complacency and by distraction. We must do our best to awaken as many as we can and to unite as much as possible under a common thread, to quell the dark's continuous attempts to control us.

Now, I do not at all believe that it will get to a point where we won't ascend into our New Earth, yet this is conceptually possible. We must fight for truth. We must fight, especially, for our freedom and sovereignty now. We must dispel many of those concepts fed to us via the dark side of the New Age doctrine, especially those that promote complacency. Just sitting in a lotus position, alone, isn't going to change our world into its promised destiny. The many positive changes happening are *because* truths are being revealed and people are taking action.

Instead of looking outside of ourselves for leadership, and people to look up to and do everything for us, we need to elevate our own selves and start seeing ourselves as fully capable of venturing forth and making change happen. We can do this without constantly seeking approval, leadership, and heavy-handed government. *It is time we finally learn to follow our own drummer, which will be our natural way of being in the Golden Age.* That being said, during these chaotic times and until we get to that solemn place no longer run by psychopathic globalists, Trump is absolutely needed to bring down the deep state. He is needed to reverse the many dark ways that caused mayhem for us all—and he is accomplishing this quietly! We can assist in this process by joining Team Light.

The way we have lived has not worked as power, corruption, and dark forces have caused great devastation of life on earth. Once the swamp (the darkness) is drained—thanks to the strong maverick leadership that is absolutely necessary now, that we ever most gratefully have—we need to grow new possibilities of living, much more community oriented, with equal say and equal rights for all. I immediately think of empowering visionaries like Michael Tellinger. As you may know, he is the founder of the Ubuntu Liberation Movement of Unity & Higher Consciousness that promotes new ways of living in true community.

Chaos around the world now is showing us that the old ways not only did not work, but these ways will become obsolete. Everything needs to come down and be rebuilt in a new way where we work with the earth, and nurture the earth, each other, and all of life. The dark control will be over. We become creators, not destroyers. We create a symbiotic relationship with all that is, as we finally grow our spiritual connection beyond what most humans have ever experienced before.

In order to get there, we need to recognize and break away from the conditioning and indoctrination of the past. We can start doing this, knowing that these dark days will indeed be over. In order to step into our sovereignty, we need to relinquish the covert effect of the dark's behavior over centuries, not just in this unprecedented lifetime. So where to begin? Well, it's no wonder that so many of us have been consciously and unconsciously clearing the ancestral pasts in our individual lives. But once we clear the past and make way for the new, will history become obsolete?

This question makes me recall Indira Gandhi's words, as seen in *The New Sun.*

This channel is surprised that I am coming through, for she doesn't really know anything about me as a former leader in India, and she at first thought I was Mahatma Gandhi. But it is me, Indira Gandhi, former prime minster of India, and I have an important message. Forgive your leaders, your past political leaders, all those who have had tremendous responsibilities and power and in many ways led this world further from love, rather than toward it. As you read these words, specific names will come to mind, perhaps mine among them. It may even bring up anger and your body may tense, and that is not my intention, although it may be a necessary step in the process of letting go of the past, in this way, as well. Forgive our mistakes, often horrific mistakes. Forgive our straying from God's will and rather enforcing our own will, or the will of those with lower vibrations that have wreaked havoc on countless lives as well as the earth herself. Both individual and collective energies created karma that plague not only people, but regions, countries, and all that is. As you move toward peace on this planet, this karma will be released. You can help this process through your forgiveness and higher understanding. One day, these will be distant memories and a very old and obsolete history, because you will be in a very new existence. So let go and let God. Be well and free.

Connect with your beautiful heart and consider how these words feel to you: "One day, these will be distant memories and a very old and obsolete history, because you will be in a very new existence."

I believe this to be absolutely true. Just as we are ridding all the parts of ourselves that will no longer resonate with the New Earth, as the lower, old parts of us are dying away to incorporate higher ways of being, the same will be for history that will no longer be relevant. We are living the caterpillar to butterfly metamorphosis. It will be like moving onto another planet with new lives within our lives, and the old isn't necessary anymore. We need to consciously let it all go.

We also need to release competition. Clearly, competition has run our world in the collective, as well as in our personal lives. We will find that competition will be out the window—no one will be better than the other. After all, we are *all* royalty. There will no longer be anything to prove. As Archangel Michael said in *Michael's Clarion Call*:

When one is in competition, one is out to prove something. When you are aligned with your souls, there is nothing to prove to yourself or to anyone. You are this Divine spark of God, and there is nothing more you need to do other than just be who you are. Can you accept that finally you will all know you are good enough?

Competition is not desired when living in a higher vibration. There is no point to it. When you live in the third dimension, you may be unaware of the greatness that lies within you. Competition can bring that understanding forth, but it can also hinder it depending on your judgment regarding how well you perform. Once you see who you really are, there will be no desire to compete, nor feel envious or jealous of another. You will feel complete just as you are.

Part of stepping into our royalty is learning to fully trust ourselves. I cannot stress this strongly enough. Because, countering that is the rampant gaslighting that presently occurs in our culture, a sneaky manifestation from dark forces that makes us constantly question. Mass media are experts at gaslighting, and we all have been subject to it, at least to some degree. We simply must understand what gaslighting is, and how we've been victim to this practice from the distant past until now.

We continue to be gaslighted as a society, actually now much more than ever as the dark grows ever desperate! The dark has created so many situations that make us question our own sanity—and our thoughts and belief systems. Life is increasingly complex, most especially in this year of 2020, and some people can easily deem the truthers as paranoid and out of touch. The genuine, responsible truther is always open to refining and revisiting belief systems as they research and uncover the hard truths. But truthers, too, can be vulnerable victims of gaslighting. So we need to be ever cognizant of this tactic.

We can also be deceptively gaslighted as individuals, in the microcosm. When I met Monique, the equine horse therapist from Holland (as seen in Chapter Seven), she shared a story I was meant to hear in that orchestrated meeting. This woman had just summoned the courage to leave her boyfriend who turned out to be a narcissist, to cut him 100% out of her life, and then soon after flew here to Hawaii for a visit.

She immediately meets, on this very beach we met, someone very special, a certain deep soul connection. They had just nine days together, and it quickly developed into a significant relationship! I expressed great joy for her, fully amazed how things shifted so quickly for her once she bravely faced her challenging situation. Even though this new man ended up not being "the one," they are still very much connected, and she recently found someone who is right for her.

This is something I have studied over the years, the classic, very commonly occurring situation where a gaslighting narcissist targets the empath, as the empath is the only type of personality that can stand to be with them. Learning that Monique broke away from the toxic relationship and immediately found love, albeit briefly, still gives me goosebumps. In my own life, I've witnessed people devastated by toxic narcissists, as well as psychopaths and/or sociopaths, and so this is a tender subject for me. I was meant to hear Monique's story and I appreciated her following the nudges to share with me. It gave me faith for those caught in the spell. There is always a way out. And you can make new dreams come true, even this quickly!

Five years ago, an acquaintance of mine was dealing with her narcissist brother who was causing absolute hell for her whole family. She wrote me often and I supported her, but it got to the point where she was inundating me with countless articles about narcissism and telling me that it is something that cannot be cured. I was a bit frustrated by the constant influx of information she sent, but I eventually realized that I needed to understand this for my work and life—it was actually a heads-up, and thus a gift.

When I had a booth at a metaphysical exposition a couple of years ago, an older woman said that my Archangel Michael books and sword display drew her right to me. She immediately began sharing that her life was taken over by her narcissistic, psychopathic husband. It was hard for her to see that she was losing herself by being with him, and for so many years. She asked me for help because she felt that even though she left him, the effects of his damaging personality were still creating havoc and upset in her life.

The woman was also aware of the entities and attachments that resided within him and eventually around them both, and they were still affecting her. I helped her to the best of my ability. And I am still saddened to this day by the fact that this woman, who is probably in her late 70s and should be enjoying her golden years in peace, is desperately trying to find herself again. But at least she had the strength and courage to free herself. And those entities and attachments can indeed be cleared from her. I feel confident she got the help she needed.

As I write this and feel led to share it, I feel it is also because we ultimately need to 100% cut off all attachment, trust, and engagement with those toxic in the macro who are gaslighting us. Whether they are mainstream media (journalists and celebrities) or those running (or previously ran) governments from local to national political posts, etc. Just as we must say "no more" to relationships not serving us, we need to say "no more" to the matrix puppets! We need to put a halt to being controlled by the gaslighting dictators, and then we will find a freedom we have never known before. We may think we have been free, but it is a colossal illusion.

It is no coincidence that while I was working on this part of the chapter, I received a call from my friend, who is a psychotherapist. Without my bringing the subject up, she reminded me of a situation when she was in practice with a group of therapists, managed by a total narcissist. The boss was clearly gaslighting all of them and they all ended up quitting their jobs over a short period of time. It was a miserable experience for my wise and sensitive-souled friend. But the bottom line is that they all left—they put a stop to the toxicity!

[Note: Through excellent teachers like Dr. Judith Orloff and Dr. Christiane Northrup, I learned years ago that empaths are always targeted, often finding themselves in very unhealthy relationships with narcissists, psychopaths, and/or sociopaths. I made a mental note to myself to name these two wonderful women, top in their field in a holistic way, in this very chapter, and yet forgot. When two friends sent me a link to the same interview with Dr. Northrup, by Joanne Griffiths, on October 6, 2020 via Facebook, I knew I had to listen, and mention them here.

Dr. Northrup nets it out on this very subject. "I realized that about one in five people has a personality disorder. And right now, the globalists that are running the planet are all sociopaths. And once I understood how they work and the fact that people like me, empaths, were their target... Every empath I know has been in a relationship with a narcissist or with a sociopath. Every one of them, and I've had my share. Because we just can't believe people are as bad as they are. We have blinders on. We can't believe that a doctor would say this or a government official would say this. So I've had to learn that, indeed, there is evil on planet earth and right now it's all coming up." How validating is this?

Literally after praying for the right words used in this book, to help so many empaths who are either caught in the spell by the mentally ill, or to prevent them from being so—because this is a worldwide, rampant issue—I then received more and more validation that this simply must be discussed in this book. I was led to words and messages, effortlessly. The overall goal is that we get past these karmic and ancestral cycles in order to birth our New Earth. One of the validations that happened nearly immediately following my prayer was seeing this woman's post of a picture of a spaceship with the following commentary. "How about we take all the conscious women and men for a ride until all the narcissists and psychopaths get over their childhood wounding? They have not learned how to relate nor share nor live without thinking the whole freaking world revolves around them. We evolve or repeat the madness."]

Wow. This mirrored the significance of spreading this important message; it is time for us to evolve from this pattern. This is a cycle being repeated and many are suffering. Empaths, simply be aware and perhaps educate yourselves on this pattern, if this is new to you. I know of several women and even men who have suffered deeply, being empaths, and thus attracting this into their lives. They eventually figured it out, and left the relationships in almost every case.

I was forced into a personal acquaintance situation with a narcissistic psychopath. And he, even knowing of my work as a channel of Archangel Michael, tried to convince me of the benefits of satanism, yes... me. That was the first huge clue among many. He later turned a picture frame of me face down, symbolizing his intentions. This is what those aligned with the darkness do, both in the macro and micro, they broadcast their intentions in some way. And they sneak their way into lives, creating hardship for others.

This guy proceeded to try and take me down in the absolute worst possible way. So this is happening on individual and global levels. The darkness works through the mentally ill and, obviously, through truly dark people. But it's so important to realize they can even work through susceptible and totally innocent people, as well, which can aid in bringing down another's Light.

This... *this*... is the reason we absolutely must not let anyone steal our joy. I do not care what it occurring, do not let them win. This was my lesson, to not let the dark win. Do not let anyone break you... ever. To the best of your ability, don't give them the negative emotions they will then feed on. The more Light you possess and the greater your mission in this world, you need to be especially cognizant of any potential attacks. Just keep your shields up, your vibrations high, and own your immense power. Of course, always know that you can call on Archangel Michael for his protection.

One of the biggest challenges Lightworkers and Lightwarriors have is to stay in balance. We simply must be aware of the truths in our world—the numerous crimes against humanity. But as Archangel Michael tells his warriors, know enough but not so much that you bring down your vibration. So, especially for those working for the Light and fighting for truth, a delicate balance is necessary as we go down the rabbit holes of truly evil things going on in this world that most people don't know about, and don't want to know about.

If you are being severely messed with by the dark, you must be of great value to this planet, especially during these shifting times. The sooner we realize that the dark is trying to bring down those carrying great Light and heart, the sooner we can offset their attempts. I lived this, partly, so I can share and help others.

This bears repeating because it is that important: if you are having thoughts that do not feel like your own, it is probably because they are not your thoughts. And just as an angel can whisper a thought that is beneficial to the receiver, a dark entity can whisper a thought that can lead to negative feelings, choices, behavior, and challenges in your life. They can even mess with a pendulum (just call for the Light of God, Jesus, Michael, a high being, each time). Stay above their attempts, keep your vibration so high that they cannot mess with you in any way. *The excellent news is that it's getting harder and harder for them to do so, because we are raising our frequencies!*

When I was being consistently messed with in my sleep, Archangel Michael guided me to create a protocol that keeps these influences out of one's auric field. It is all about surrounding oneself in the Merkaba—the star tetrahedron. It consists of two triangular pyramids, male pointing up and female pointing down spinning in opposite directions. Activate it by spinning them in your imagination, seeing what is really there in the unseen, enveloping you. I can raise Michael's sword while awake and deal with any interruptions in my life, but while sleeping we can potentially be vulnerable. What I shared has helped many, including myself.

Another way that non-serving entities and attachments can disturb our peace, as mentioned, is through other people, knowingly and unknowingly. Anyone in the helping professions, need to be particularly aware of this. A psychotherapist or psychic reader, especially if young or inexperienced, can have most honorable intentions, but they can be influenced via thoughts "fed" to them. And if they aren't aware and advise wrongly, they can unwittingly cause chaos in people's lives.

Now I may lose you here, but please bear with me. The dark is always looking for a crack in your auric field. Once this happens, they can enter and cause mayhem. I had a literal crack in my field when I had the first concussion in my life, four years ago. Many things in my life went quickly awry, soon after. I was clearly under attack. I briefly discussed what led to my understanding the need to carry Michael's sword in my last book, but I neglected to share about my concussion until I had greater understanding that convinced me of my theory.

In October 2016, I experienced this concussion by severely banging my head on something while I was in Europe. Especially after my return home, negative occurrences were suddenly happening even though I was on a high from my travels. Dark people in disguise as being of the Light suddenly sought me out, deceiving me. I was clearly under dark attack. When I wrote a friend about my mishap, she responded that it was crazy the number of Lightworkers who were suddenly getting concussions. Hmmm. While traveling, I was out of touch with what was going on, and those words stuck with me.

Over time, I personally learned of others whose lives were deeply affected immediately following concussions, even repetitively so. Did that crack in their auric field create ensuing havoc? The dark targets the Light, and when we are aware of this, we can take measures to protect our field and make sure that any holes in our auric field are dealt with. They also know our weaknesses and can target them ruthlessly. When we are aware of this, we have the upper hand and see what is being played out.

When I shared my theory with a friend, who is a gifted psychic, about concussions and the dark getting in, I prefaced it with "I know this sounds crazy, but when people get concussions…" And she responded that it is not crazy at all. In fact, she experienced a car accident, suffered a traumatic brain injury, and she had horrific dark thoughts that were not hers and yet trying to control her. But then Archangel Michael swooped in and brought her to the Light, truly saving her! While I felt so very sad to learn of her experience, I greatly appreciated this validation. On the bright side of this, it was the accident that resulted in an influx of her psychic gifts!

Now, here is the saving grace… No matter what is thrown at you, remain in a true state of Love. Be immersed in Light. And, again, find any way you can to be in your joy, even if it is just staring at a flower or appreciating a beautiful, sunny day. Seek joy deeply, like you never have before. *I feel dramatically less affected by dark influences these days by really getting this!*—just by maintaining awareness, seeking joy, and keeping my vibration high. And forgive those who have hurt you. Often it is not even them, but rather confusing negative interference behind the words or behaviors, messing with people's true thoughts and beliefs, due to gaslighting. I cannot stress this strongly enough!

You see, the dark does not have the greatest power in the world that we are privy to. They do not have souls like ours, *nor do they know what love is*—or compassion and empathy either, for that matter. So, this is our response... Love. I tell you this from the most painful, unimaginable experience that I have been enduring. I was definitely planning on writing about this, but when I came across the following words on 1.20.20, it was a great segue and inspiration to begin sharing:

"Find a place inside where there's joy, and the joy will burn out the pain." ~ Joseph Campbell

We are all unique and we have our individual ways of seeking and being in our joy. Connecting to nature is a top choice for many of us. For me, in the last quarter of a century since I woke up, it's especially while seeking, experiencing, and celebrating magical synchronicity (which, as we know, often occurs in nature).

And of course, connecting to our angels and unseen friends is a sacred gift that keeps giving. There are no words good enough to describe this blissful, ethereal connection that we are all invited to engage in. Our angels and guides exponentially expand our awareness on so many things for our joy, *but also for our needed understanding and growing wisdom.* I've shared many joyful signs in this book, but here's an example of how angels can give us a heads-up.

In *Michael's Sword & You*, a key point that Archangel Michael led me to share, via a profound thread of powerful synchronicities which I then decoded, was to describe to readers how sacred symbolism has been hijacked by the dark. And this is a key issue that we have raised Michael's sword on. One of the sacred symbols that has been greatly taken over is the all-seeing eye. This symbol has been hijacked by the dark, as you probably know, and as you can see right on the back of every American dollar bill (which will apparently be changing!).

The synchronicities mirroring this need to reverse the hijacking and treasure the sacred, included finding a rock that looked just like the Hamsa symbol, a hand with an eye in the center which I shared in the book, and will share again here. Hamsa is a protective symbol commonly seen in the Middle East, known to ward off the evil eye. Interestingly, the jpg number randomly assigned to this photo is: IMG_ 5222. 5 stands for change and 2 (in triple digits) for duality, such as Light and dark. And here I was literally guided to this rock, seemingly placed by Michael with his "Leave now" that led to it. But it had a dual meaning—I found it during the time that troublemaker was sneakily trying to take me down, while causing harm to my close friend I've known since my younger years. My warnings to her fell on deaf ears. So Michael gave me this very rock as a reminder of protection and faith.

Extraordinary synchronicities repeatedly showed me in very clear ways that I was most accurate in my reading and intuition—although the constant signs that I couldn't do much about deeply burdened me. Such as, the song by Nina Simone, "I Put a Spell on You," repeatedly went to the beginning of the same song, on my car's radio at a most synchronous time. It's a great song, but the sign sadly verified my very thoughts about this person.

One night, when very close to where this guy lived, I told my friend who was driving that he lived right off of the expressway exit just ahead. Suddenly, a car with his plate cuts in front of us and exits. A few seconds later, a second car, all black with blackened windows had the license plate CINOMED (I spell it backwards, here, so you won't be as jarred as we were) abruptly cuts in front of us and exited there, as well! This synchronicity really shocked us, to say the least. Never before or since had I seen any plate so dark in my life. And I have sought license plate synchronicities on a daily basis, for 25 years.

Some people are under severe dark influence. It won't be this way in our New Earth just ahead! But this is an example of how intensely synchronicity can mirror the state of things, and just one example among so many in this particular case. I could not deny what this guy who was extremely sneaky, and yet a coward in person, was up to—heartlessly causing mayhem in happy people's lives because he was so unhappy in his own life. The intensity of dark attachments and entities within him were hidden to many, but not me. Just as Dr. Northrup stated, this is a very real concern and targeted empaths simply must be aware. Remember how that one narcissist owner took over a whole practice of empathic psychotherapists.

On September 3, 2018, I met with a healer and intuitive to discuss this person's antics, and to together send him healing on his childhood wounding so he would stop causing such immense harm to others. We, of course, especially sent healing to my beautiful hearted friend who was unknowingly caught in his spell. Afterwards, I stopped to get coffee at a place I hadn't been to in about four years. I was surprised that it was open on Labor Day in America, but I felt so guided there and for good reason, due to what was there.

Walking out with my coffee, I see this wonderfully wild looking chair—in the shape of Hamsa in 3D! The timing, yet again! I felt I was being assured that my dear friend I tried to warn, as well as myself, were ultimately being protected. With all of these signs, the odds of these occurrences were way too astronomical to happen without Divine meaning and intervention.

I consider synchronicity to be an exact science of the Universe, but how we decipher it is largely subjective. This is where our intuition reigns supreme. For when we tap into our gut feelings mixed with Divine influence, we arrive at understandings we may never have considered before. And that is the point where awe-inspiring magic can occur. What a gift for each of us to behold, whether it is a wonderfully positive and happy sign, or a sign of necessary understanding or warning.

Out of experiencing and transcending deep pain and suffering comes great opportunities that beg to enlighten others, such as I was guided to do here. Certainly, you can relate in your life when getting to the other side of rough challenges and experiences, that make you want to help and support others in their lives. We are all waking each other up, and we all have pieces of the puzzle that will help us do that. I worked with well over a dozen intuitives and psychics that each gave me validating pieces of the puzzle in this situation, for which I'm grateful.

On August 30, 2015, AA Michael said:

Do you see the Light at the end of the tunnel? Do you see what will come out of all the chaos and huge, seemingly insurmountable challenges before you? These challenges are driving the change. When you shake your head at the reality of a given situation, re-frame it in your mind that this is helping people to wake up and that is helping people to wake up. Because people are waking up. As a collective you are waking up to your reality and you are each deciding how to be in that broadened space of understanding. When you make sound choices based on your new understandings, you are putting energy on a more enlightened choice. And that is a contagious energy. As you make more enlightened choices, you are growing your Light, and that is helping the collective. When you do not acknowledge the reality of what is before you, your Light is remarkably lessened. There are many ways to increase your Light; this is one of them. Stay in your heart and know that the wisdom you need is within. Trust yourself and if you feel swayed from that food or that location or that person, honor the feelings. Your feelings do not lie. Honoring your feelings also grows your Light! These times are of great challenge to all, but you have the power within to endure, transmute, and transcend these challenges.

Clearly, we are in spiritual battle, in the microcosm and macrocosm. The following is yet one more example of how the micro and macro mirror each other. For twenty-five plus years, I've been battling the whole Roundup pesticide product in the micro. Just before leaving Colorado for the Big Island, I sold my first ever trailer home which provided cheap and easy living for a year and a half.

I closed on the home with much success, even amidst outside forces fighting it so hard right up until the sale. After closing, my realtor, her assistant, and I were all happy, having a good and celebratory time. We were standing in front of the beautiful tree on the lot because the realtor wanted a picture of the two of us, holding a "Sold" sign. The moment was nearly ruined when a neighbor, and of all times, starts coming toward us spraying Roundup for the trailer community.

When I asked him to please not do this now, or at least start in the other direction because I could smell it, he proceeded to walk with it right toward me saying he will walk past me, demonstrating his dominance. Sorry to say, but it felt like I was watching a dog marking territory on my lot. In the past, I've seen him spray, wait a day, then spray again on everyone's properties a ridiculous amount and never putting up those pesticide warning flags—which frustrated me, especially with kids in the area. He knows very well how much I am against this product, to please keep it off of my lot, and that I use only vinegar on the xeriscaping for weeds.

The crazy thing is that on this day he is wearing a military hat and fatigues. In the year that I've known him, I never once saw him in these. So, this is a symbolic example of literally being in battle in the micro—for here he is in army fatigues with his weapon of known absolute poison completing the battle picture. I truly didn't feel well after that and I wonder if while we were inside the home closing, he was outside spraying on my property, because I could taste it in my mouth for the rest of that day. We always got along fine until I was firm on the pesticide not on my lot, and he simply did not like that.

I immediately asked the angels to protect us from consequences. After he rejected my request, and right when walking by us, the realtor's assistant said really loud "It is poison!" And I responded, "Yes, it is!" So he looked really silly. I contemplate this in the macrocosm which this mirrors. Does it not mirror how ridiculous it is that this product continues to sell and be used in countless public and private places, despite scores of lawsuits and already significant wins against the manufacturers Monsanto/now Bayer? Well, needless to say, I couldn't get out of there fast enough. I pray this transmuted some energy for the collective, as well as on a personal level. Because of course, that is what we are doing now in every situation that calls for it—transmuting the dark into Light.

A few days later, a friend of mine told me that I have to check out this popular restaurant here before I leave for Hawaii, because they took this casual burger place and changed the name to make it look more upscale (but with the same food, apparently), and he found this funny. Well it wasn't too high on my list of priorities to see this as I prepare to leave Colorado, but when he mentioned it a second time when we were driving together, I felt that there was something to it.

Upon arrival, I peeked through the window and was floored. When I immediately saw the large mural, I had to go in and take a picture of it! Basically, this symbolically mirrors the cover of *Michael's Sword & You*! With a Big Eye and triangle! Plus, if you notice on the ceiling near it, is a surveillance camera (or big eye)! Just wild. Was it a reminder that my warrior mission will continue as I leave for Hawaii, and it's time to scale up?

I was preparing to leave for Hawaii that following day, but found time for a walk that was actually guided. As I began walking, I was thinking how every step toward this new journey was challenged, and yet magical. Things always worked out so well in the end, no matter how complicated! I sold my home even though forces were fighting it, and I did extremely well. Everything came together in the nick of time. It was a great reminder to hold the faith no matter what countering influences may appear.

Just then I come across words written out of chalk on the sidewalk: "One step at a time," with a heart shape drawn below the words. About twenty feet ahead, I see this twig that holds the shape a human taking a step! It was so random, but I cannot help but make connections within the absolute humdrum of life that is actually never really humdrum. This is an example of following the wind of your soul as the Universe's messages light the way.

Note: It's 9.20.20, and I just edited this very part of the book. My Facebook friend Steffanie posted a meme of twelve different twig representations, similar to mine above, found in different "poses." The funny thing is that I never saw a post like this nor witnessed anyone share this particular type of random sighting, and here I see this at the perfect time to validate my own inclusion in this book.

I used to wonder how people judge me for how I see into *everything*—even a random twig at the perfect time. But it never stops me and I won't stifle the way I see. I talked about synchronicities with license plates and numbers when no one else was, so many years ago when people probably really thought I was crazy, until they too started noticing the magic. So, it's more than okay to look into the randomness. In fact, I happen to believe that it's encouraged by the angels. Anyways, this synchronicity was a beautiful and unexpected wink!

Everything is speaking to us. Our trials, challenges, successes, and choices speak to us. And the Universe speaks so magically to us, through synchronicity. As you may gather from my island experiences, sometimes the message was immediately clear, other times I'd piece things together as I went along, and yet on more rare occasions there were profound occurrences that could only be fully appreciated by focused reflection over time—such as how we were clearing the rich/poor man divide, with the prolific money and coin signs.

One thing is for sure. No matter where you are on the planet, synchronicity is heightened now—it truly is and has been on the rise. And our gratitude for signs, just like for anything, brings an abundance of them into your life. Yes, you can actually attract more synchronicity by appreciating it. I still get excited like a kid when signs occur. And I truly believe that being in this excited state is why they are a constant in my life—as well as having acute awareness, while always seeking them.

Feeling gratitude, no matter what is going on in your life and the world around you, is absolutely key. One of my many favorite messages from Archangel Michael is seen in *Michael's Clarion Call*. Michael says:

God wants you to have what you desire. Your gratitude for every desire that manifests itself is actually felt by God. God connects with you through the heart. The heart connection allows God to maintain a direct relationship with you that is always present, but something that is your responsibility to nurture. It's like a plug in a socket that allows the energy to continuously flow, but if you don't turn on the lamp, it just sits there and there is no Light. So turn on the connection through feelings of gratitude. And when you feel grateful for the synchronistic gifts in your life, you will turn on the magic as you bring God closer to you.

Have you ever won a big lottery jackpot? I mean, at least a million dollars? What? No? Not even one of you?! (Wink.) The fact is that you are winning the lottery of life every single day through magical synchronicity, blessing you constantly. I venture to guess that the astronomical odds in so many given signs often beat those odds of winning a big lotto jackpot. So, in this way, we are all lucky winners, every day!

I am in utter love with synchronicity and I hope you all feel and appreciate the richness of it, too. I created the "Wink" chapters in this book to communicate and highlight how glorious, connected, and stunning signs are. I truly did not plan for these two chapters, they just happened. And then I got really excited about it as I laid them all out in chronological order. Synchronicity is a great friend to have when going with the wind of your soul—seeking and gleaning from them can make your endeavors pretty effortless, not to mention utterly miraculous.

In *The New Sun*, this is what Archangel Michael has to say about this state of being:

You will 'go with the wind' of your soul. Your soul will lead you to your actions, your passions, your meetings with others. Your soul will direct you toward achieving your goals and manifesting your desires. Never again will you have that 'I should have' feeling because you simply will be so aligned, there will be no reason to regret anything anymore.

I love that, have lived it, learned a lot from it, and still continue to learn. Part of this process of going forward in these times is not caring about what people think. Going with the wind of your soul is just that... *your* soul. You may be deemed irresponsible, foolish, a total nut case, or the like. But it comes back to the point this chapter began with. The "crazies" may just be the most sane.

The "crazies" will bravely go out on a limb again and again, and help make change happen in their personal lives, and thus within the collective. Personally speaking, I will never stop going out on a limb because I care more about all of life than I do my reputation or what people think of me. All of us "crazies" are needed, now more than ever, to change the ever toxic status quo. I love and deeply appreciate my "crazy," but actually most sane, friends and acquaintances; I truly treasure all of them in my heart.

Chapter Eleven

The New Mexico Winks

Of course, universal and angel winks continued their magical dance, never disappointing, once I returned to the high desert. The following is a sampling of my sharings with the Michael & Mary Group, after leaving the Big Island for my new beginning in New Mexico.

March 14, 2020. *A royalty wink.*
With such concerning and unprecedented things taking place suddenly, I was wondering if I should perhaps reconsider my moving plans and stay closer to my family—although it is crazy expensive here in Colorado and I simply feel that I must be in New Mexico for the second part of my book. I went to Craigslist and saw a

halfway decent and yet pricey place. Something told me to look at the map to see exactly where it was; probably because the address on Sir Galahad Drive was intriguing. It intersects with Merlin and Excalibur streets, and near King Court! Just wow.

I heard that only about 10% of the food is left in the grocery store by us here. Amazing. Have you all stocked up? The funny thing is that I have been over prepared for my family, for many, many years, always "just in case." Of all times in my lifetime, the one time I am not, I am not settled at all, don't have most of my things, have no home or car to my name yet, is when I really needed to. I have to laugh!

How are you all doing with such wild things going on in the world? I'm just blown away as I witness such changes, restaurants starting to close, events cancelled, and on and on. I feel so very optimistic that good things will come out of this amidst the challenges, a true worldwide reset.

March 23. *A Big Island wink.*
I just got my Internet installed this morning... PHEW! I was going to have to wait at least 20 days with most everyone working from home now—of all times for a warrior and truther to be without Internet. I asked if there was anything I could do to get an earlier date because I need to be online for my work. The only way I could get an appointment set in a few days was if I bought a $200 package, so I agreed to it, even though I only need internet service. Then someone cancelled and I got it even a day earlier. Thank you, Michael! (You bet I was praying for help. I can go to a cheaper package later, but I'm willing to do this for now.)

All the beaches and bays are closed on the Big Island, including all commercial boat trips, right now. It's interesting that people are being social distanced even from the social spinner dolphins and precious beings in the sea. I've been so busy that I haven't had the time to miss Hawaii. I know it sounds weird, but after that incredible last dolphin encounter, it's as if they are helping me to "handle it," even though I felt like I just up and left my many dolphin friends so prematurely.

However, I have many things here that make me feel like I am still on the Big Island, now on the Big Desert. Dogs roam free, in many rural parts of the island. Here I have two resident dogs who come visit me here, often sitting outside my front door.

In Hawaii, two of the most memorable sounds are tons of roosters "cockle doodle doo-ing" constantly, as wild chickens and roosters rule the island; and the other is the coqui frogs who are very loud at night. While I got used to these frogs not native to the island, they can be crazy loud especially when there are many in a loud chorus. I'm sensitive to sounds when sleeping and don't miss the frog sounds at all, to be honest. Anyways, as it turns out, my landlords have a tiny barn across from me with a bunch of roosters and chickens running around. Yesterday, the chickens came into my courtyard (the landlord said he never saw them there before) and put on quite the show.

Much more to come about these times. I have tons of catch up to do on my work and the book, now that I'm just getting settled. The guy who delivered the mattress, and who has connections, says that they are indeed preparing for lock down. I was wrong about this weekend and probably could have gotten my things in storage in Colorado, but I'm very tired and my body just wants to rest, so I forgive myself for being "off" on this. I won't stop focusing on and sharing the magic of the Universe with you. It's more important than ever to notice it, and to keep our spirits high through these times.

March 19. *Another P.O. Box wink.*

When I get a P.O. Box from a small-town post office, I can sometimes pick the box number from what's available. But with bigger cities, not usually. When I went to the Santa Fe post office yesterday to rent a box, I asked if I could choose from a bank of available numbers. Once again, I explained that numbers are very important to me, they carry energy, and that I love numbers in double or triplicate. She said that the computer would generate one for me. The numbers that came up were in ascending order, but nothing that got my adrenaline going. Well she left for a long time to get the keys (like 15 to 20 minutes! and her associate went to check on her because it was so long), and it turned out that she found a different box for me. P.O. Box 22333!

My new phone number ends in 333 too, ironically. She said she never does this, but since she wasn't very busy she sought a good number for me... and I was so grateful! It was very sweet of her. And, of course, I had to share with you. I was going to miss 1234, but now I'm excited about 22333! Never say never... never.

March 28. *A Eureka wink.*

My friends, so much is happening behind the scenes. Things are not what they seem at all. I've been following all of this for a long time while trying to make sense of so much: Who is President Trump, Q, the Alliance, especially; The Democratic Party not being the one we grew up with; The Massive Crimes of Mainstream Media; the Vatican, Hollywood and many of its stars, are not what and whom we think; the Federal Reserve being dissolved into the Treasury as our money becomes gold backed, and on and on. I've kept quiet and just slowly shared here and there little glimpses via YouTube videos especially. Well the cat is out of the bag, it is time to talk about this. I know I will lose some of you on this, and let me tell you I didn't always feel this way. But as I sat and observed for a very long time, it is ever clear as a bell what is going on. Humanity is being FREED, and not by who or in the way we would probably ever imagine. Truth is Boss now in these times.

This virus crime is being used as an opportunity to reset this world and ourselves, mass arrests of the bad guys are happening, and we must continue to pray and raise Michael's sword through these times. We simply must be willing to reconsider our beliefs and take a new look at what is really going on in our world. The deception stops here. The only way to free ourselves is through truth, and the truths are coming out now at full speed. It is so exciting! We are here for exactly this.

It is time for the dark to lose their crowns as we each crown ourselves. This is no coincidence that I was led to write this book about stepping into our royalty. As you know, this all came into being so magically, and guided by Archangel Michael. This was all most unexpected. I will start to share a little more now, starting with this from Grace Solaris on Facebook, March 26:

"Was with none else than Donald Trump in dreamtime last night... I knew from the start of his inauguration that he is not who he appeared to be and displayed as. I knew he was cherry picked by the star alliances to do the job, that no one other than a true master can do. To voluntarily walk into a 'devil's nest' to assist in freeing humanity from thousands of years of unimaginable atrocities can only be done with the highest forces of light behind you and within you. So many will be surprised and shocked to the core when all comes into

the light. My heart rejoices and screams with joy as the fragrance of liberation spreads across the planet... more and more are beginning to feel it, though the majority are still hostage in the mind control fear poverty hologram, an awakening wave is sweeping across the planet with unprecedented momentum... time to face the facts and wake up to the true story not the fake news fear propaganda. We are going to witness sooooo many falling from grace as their masks are pulled away in front of our eyes. However, there is a higher plan that is playing out now in the midst of the global lockdown and it serves every one better to stay away from the streets and be indoors, so that the network of deception can be dismantled and those behind it can be arrested and made accountable for their crimes. No one is going to escape this no matter how much money or status they have... the "crowns" are going to fall. No reason to panic. Stay calm, do things that makes you joyful, share kindness with others... be the eye of the storm and hold a space of peace for all those that are challenged right now. Sending love and healing to all. Let's calm the waters and be grateful that humanity is coming together as One and that when we are thru this, we can truly start creating the heaven on earth of peace and equality and unity and abundance, that we came to build. All is in the hands of love.
- Grace Solaris

March 31. *A Michael wink.*

For Everyone... from Archangel Michael today.

Do not think for a moment that the Heavens are abandoning you. So many doubt, but we are in fact with you more than ever. Life on earth is changing fast now. I have asked you many times to get in the habit of embracing change, and now all of humanity is forced to change like never before, as a collective.

For those of you working with the changes, you are most

excited. You know in the depths of your being that this is what you have waited for. This is what you have worked towards. And now much of what you thought and ever imagined could happen is playing out, as the Light confronts the dark like never before. It may feel very scary for others. So, I ask you to know what faith really is. It is your trust in God. God is not abandoning you and neither is this Archangel. Oh, on the contrary.

Ask me to help quell your deepest fears, and I will. Ask me to hold you in my arms, and I will. Ask me to take you to the top of the mountain to show you what is really going on, and I will. Go into your heart and imagination and feel me right now. You are not alone. You are not without support. You are not without Divine life force. I tell you, you will be amazed at what humanity as a whole will do next as they delve deeper into Love. That is the key, to keep being Love to yourself, to others, to the world. Please put being Love as your highest priority, as that is the antidote to any virus of darkness. You'll see.

~ *Archangel Michael*

March 31. *A double check wink.*

People are overwhelmed and making more mistakes, so it's a good idea to double check everything. For instance, a $500+ return on an appliance that malfunctioned never made it to my credit card balance. It was so good that I checked. No apology, just okay it's done now. Reminds me of when I went to the bank to deposit the check for selling my used car earlier this month. A $4400 deposit is what it should have been. I check the receipt, and it's for $44! I noted the error and got no apology, no words at all. This was before things got crazy and people in the service industry became overwhelmed. It is always so important to check. I had a father who instilled that into me, for which I'm grateful. Although I wouldn't be surprised if I got an angel nudge, perhaps without realizing it. I truly feel for all those out there in service jobs dealing with the public. I always go out of my way to ask how they're doing and to thank them for their service, especially during these rough times. Frankly, I'm impressed by a lot of the wonderful, positive attitudes out there.

April 3. *An alert wink.*

There was huge news we are starting to hear about in NYC a couple of days ago, and here is more. Thousands of kids are being rescued from underground tunnels under Central Park! It's so incredibly horrific and the world must now face the rampant pedophilia, sex trafficking forced onto so many children for too long, and around the world.

No wonder Michael gave us signs about the "White Hats." The ones on the front lines are saving our kids in many places around the world, as well as working to free Humanity, and especially all of the children! This is all so surreal. The swamp, as they say, is truly being drained before our very eyes.

Massive things are happening. The truths are coming forth rapidly now, to free us. Prayers.

April 6. *A reminder wink.*

I just wrote the following for Facebook friends, as I see so much growing fear.

"We have to laugh no matter what, we have to continue to seek our joy. Fear is the dark's game and they are playing this card so hard right now, and too many are falling into the trap. It's a very scary world, no question! But we are here for this, to transmute such evil darkness into Light. To turn this very apparent manmade virus on its ear. It takes each of us spreading LOVE. None of us have all the answers, and it may be hard to not feel vulnerable at times, but I do believe with my whole being that we will persevere and win this spiritual battle. The positive effect of the global meditation felt by so many on

April 4th was a big clue of not only the immense power that we are individually and collectively emitting, but the absolute legions of the unseen that are helping us through. Let's try to focus on that and not give energy to the fear via dangerous MSM spreading their lies. Please seek truths outside of the mainstream news until that is turned on its ear too."

March 6. *A presidential wink.*

Regardless of what anyone thinks of the U.S. President, I found it extraordinary that this tweet I found on Facebook was written at 5:55 a.m. with the words "LIGHT AT THE END OF THE TUNNEL!" Although he/they are always writing in code and with attention to numbers!

April 7. *A heart reminder wink.*

I thought things were confusing before, in so many aspects of society and day-to-day living. Just take the subject of food and nutrition. Can any experts agree on anything? It seems that too many nutritional experts have their own unique answer to right nutrition, and often a marketing plug to go with it that they make money off of, which is especially difficult for those desperate to lose weight. And we are led all over the place to all kinds of extremes regarding what are the right answers for our individual bodies.

Now we are in these wild times with all kinds of information coming at us from every angle, especially regarding this virus and what is really going on behind the scenes. It is indeed overwhelming and complex. But it is also as overwhelming as we allow it to be. What has worked for me and calmed me down a whole lot is the "maybe yes, maybe no" way. That it is *okay* to not know exactly but simply observe and feel your way to truth. Ultimately, and what really gets me excited about these times more than anything, we are being forced to navigate from our hearts. Whenever I think about this, I imagine this huge smile on Archangel Michael's face, because this has been one of his biggest messages for years. We are learning more and more about our heart's wisdom. This crisis is evolving us; no question about it.

April 8. *A Corona beer wink.*

Signs aren't seen as often when holed up at home, but they are still there! Taking a walk to pick up trash along the road revealed some gems today—a smashed up Corona beer bottle, perhaps symbolizing the virus biting the dust? Do you hear a car's honking horn at the same moment you are about to do something, and it alerts you to something positive and supportive, or perhaps the opposite and it's a warning? This happens to me all the time, it's crazy how accurate. Or here where I am, just when is that rooster "cockle doodle doo-ing."

What bird is flying close to your window at the same moment you had a significant thought? At the moment that I was telling my friend Anne via a phone call that I'm feeling that New Mexico is where I need to be to write the second part of my book, a falcon flew right by her window. When she took a picture of it for me, it looked surreal and had an etheric quality. As we know, we are messengers for each other, too, with signs. May we listen closely to it all. Recognizing the magic is ever more valuable now. Validations, blessings, and Divine guidance is abounding. "Signs often carry specific personal meanings to individuals... Our angels know exactly what our favorite signs are." ~ *I Can See Clearly Now*

April 9. *The most bittersweet wink.*

My beautiful mom joined my beautiful dad in Heaven today. Right on the 5th Anniversary of my dad's passing. And they were both 88. What happened yesterday clued me in as I felt this overwhelming urge to watch *Father's Little Dividend*, that old movie with Spencer Tracy and Katherine Hepburn. I used to watch old movies with my parents all the time, and haven't in years because it would make me sad not watching with them. And yet, I know it was my dad whispering to watch it. So I watched with him (truly, in spirit) and laughed at all the parts I knew he'd be laughing at. Not even an hour later, I found out that my mom was in the hospital. I just *knew* she would transition today. Extraordinary! For it is a great testament to their immense love for each other. I know they are having one beautiful reunion right now. I am so deeply sad and yet so extremely happy for them!

"My parents have one of those marriages that last forever. Observing them as a married couple over the years has been like watching two people dance a beautiful waltz—flowing with sure step, independent as two separate beings, and yet in sync, one complementing the other, classy, engaging, an effortless meld."

~ With joy and honor, from *I Can See Clearly Now*

April 11. *A wink from my parents.*

Yesterday, on Good Friday, I was driving home after visiting a place where I could relive happy memories of my parents when visiting us—near our former home in Placitas—when both of my parents suddenly came into my awareness. I could feel them, knew it was them no question, and which made me cry with joy. I *heard* to look at the clock and it was exactly 12:00 p.m. on Good Friday! This gave me the most incredible feeling of peace. I can feel how happy my mom is being back with my dad. And just as all who transition into the loving, grand Light.

April 15. *A hummingbird wink.*

We often seek the signs after a loved one's transition. And while I'm not sure yet how my mom will choose to signal a message to me, whether by a type of bird, a flower, or what, the following felt auspicious. My mom was buried on Monday in Michigan, not open to the public because of the virus, and, of course, I was unable to attend. I've had my few hummingbird feeders out for at least ten days, yes, a bit ambitious this early, perhaps. But finding those feeders was a priority when I got some things from storage. And here, after beautiful, sunny weather we suddenly had a gorgeous snow on Monday, and that is when the hummingbirds appeared!

[Rereading this, before going to print, I recall what happened when I was 17 years old, shocked over the passing of my beloved grandmother Mary. We were in the car as part of the long funeral procession and I recall looking up at the telephone line for miles never seeing so many birds (sparrows) lined up on the lines, an extraordinary number, as if to pay respect to my grandmother.]

April 19. *A wink from my mother.*

I moved one of the hummingbird feeders closer to the window, where I write. And boy, are they being the messengers for me. They haven't been hanging around the feeders for very long for the last week, just seconds before they are chased off by another.

Last night, I wrote a tribute for my mom. As soon as I finished, I looked at the clock and it was 7:33:49. My mom was born on 3.3 and passed on 4.9. *Just then*, a hummingbird comes to the feeder now near me and sips for a full six minutes! I then especially wondered if my mom will indeed use the hummingbirds as a sign that she is around.

April 19. *A Michael wink.*

In a personal channel to me today, Archangel Michael said: *The world is changing so fast now. Even the Heavenly realms are having difficulty catching up with all the shifts. Would you believe that? But this is how profoundly positive change is happening on your planet, and I can tell you that it is exceeding our expectations! I know that this news is filling your heart. And please do share this knowledge with anyone you wish.*

I can *feel* this, can't you? Exceeding Heavens' expectations is *very* encouraging! No matter what is going on that we do see and experience, as we awaken, we learn that so much is going on unseen and 'behind the scenes' beyond that which we know. This is where our relentless faith steps in. We are each so very powerful and I believe that many of us are really "getting this" now.

April 21. *An air pressure wink.*
With all the banks closed except for drive-through, it took me about four hours yesterday to be able to find a bank that allowed shared branch banking so that I could deposit a check. I haven't yet been able to open up an account here yet, and I couldn't wait on the check, so I was on a mission to get it done. Well that time being out in my car ended up unveiling a super amazing synch that would not have happened under other circumstances.

The tires' air pressure light for my new used car went on suddenly. I didn't take it too seriously because my Subaru often did the same thing and when the pressure was actually fine. I parked the car and when I got out, an odd alarm sounded? I'm still getting to know this unique car. Well, maybe I should have this checked, and I happened to note that oil change places are open and busy, during lockdown.

As I thought these things, I looked up and laughed! Right in front of me was a Firestone business with a huge banner sign promoting "FREE AIR PRESSURE CHECK!" Crazy! The guy kindly and immediately checked my tires and the psi was 43-45, when they are supposed to be set at 35. I don't know why the alarm didn't go off in the month I've had this car, but I'm glad it did now. And I was grateful for the supreme ease of checking it out! The timing and perfection was simply... 5D ease.

April 27. *A ladybug wink.*

I took a walk along the shoulder of the dirt road near me this morning and stopped to watch a ladybug hanging around on a weed. I then knelt down to put it on my hand and connect to it. A man in a pick-up truck and with a look of concern on his face, asked if I was okay. I said "Hi" and "Oh yes." He asked if I was sure. I said I just stopped to see this ladybug. I guess that sounds really weird. I guess I always look weird. The older I get, the younger I get. The older I get, the more unconventional I get, too. hahaha But it was sweet that he showed concern.

April 29. *A little bird wink.*

Earlier this morning, Lillian was guiding me to take an action in my personal life. She has actually been doing so for some time. And just at the crux of it all, just when I was literally about to do something that I feel in my heart will be good for me, I hear something lightly hit the window. It is a little bird. And it sat on the narrow ledge (between the two vertically placed windows) looking into my place, back and forth, for least five minutes and chirping. It was very unusual behavior.

Oh how I wanted to get a picture, but I didn't want to chance it flying away if I got up to get my phone. Just before it flew away, it pooped, and on the screen were two lines that made a perfect 11 (and 11, as you know, stands for illumination). And, by the way, the deposit is now almost completely gone? This sweet little bird appearing had to be an auspicious sign, certainly Lillian coming through that bird!

But how about the bird leaving a deposit? I was exhausted as I haven't slept well for two nights for some reason. So, I took a needed nap. I had this dream where I was lying in bed and someone from above was telling me that something great was going to happen. The roof collapsed and nothing hurt me at all but a bunch of bird poop mixed with snow from on top of the roof fell onto my legs! I just had this clear awareness it was bird poop.

I thought this is either a ghastly sign or an amazing one—even though I was told just that something great would happen. Ever since seeing the movie *Under the Tuscan Sun*, I leaned toward the positive view of this type of occurrence. In that auspicious scene, a bird left a deposit on the main character's head, which was immediately deemed a great sign to sell the house to her, by the old Italian woman proclaiming "Segno, segno." As soon as I woke, I looked up the sign and it was as I thought, a sign of good luck.

One description read "The main omen associated with a bird pooping on you is that it is a *sign of luck*. Luck, prosperity and good fortune are all yours to come with this symbolic experience." I like this one too: "Some people assume it is bad luck and therefore a bad omen to have a bird poop on you. Yet this is the precise type of thinking which can prevent one from experiencing the luck and abundance to come."

So, I'm going to ride on the positive because this has been a difficult situation that I feel is now raining with Light. And it's not just Lillian, but Michael and the Heavens have been supporting me on this, too. The timing of the bird was such that it would be huge odds for it to land on my tiny window ledge at the perfect time, and stay there looking in for over five minutes. Oh... synchronicity.

May 1. *A wise warrior wink.*

I believe that all of you are Warriors of Michael, part of our mission. So yesterday, in the sword raising announcement, you saw that I led it with this:

A fellow warrior in our mission, Jackolyn, wrote me and I greatly loved and appreciated her process: "I raise the sword as well as multiply myself and the group 100 billion times." Now that is stepping into your power! Let's do this!

Not only did I love receiving this from a fellow warrior, but I used it during the raising, playing with it, and will continue to not just in future raisings, but, well, the applications of this are endless in our ability to create! I find it to be fun, *empowering*, and exciting territory to say the least. I'm so grateful to this fine healer for sharing her process with me. Imagination is everything. As we know Michael wants us to work with our imaginations when we raise.

We are being called to step it up, play it big, as we are awakening to the true power that each of us are, while the forces tried to hide, snuff out, and condition us away from our power. Those days are over.

May 1. *A Michael wink.*

Michael just came through with this message, and my patrons see it first!

I stand here with the highest of the high taking a bird's eye view of all of humanity, and do you know what we see? So much courage. And so much strength. So many of you have 'naturally' stepped into new roles. How? What? Why? Your souls are guiding you. You have been in dress rehearsal for these very times. You have been preparing to be the way showers for eons of time!... by now voicing truths, awarenesses, and cosmic understandings. That sounds very grandiose, doesn't it? But you truly have. Everything that you have experienced in your lifetimes on this planet has prepared you for

Now, dear humans fighting so hard with all your hearts. NOW. This is no time to play it small. Like I have repeatedly taught you: connect to your soul, all of us, and your greatest wisdom through that beautiful heart of yours. Oh, yes, you will still encounter many walls, scared people taking all their frustrations out on you, anger, upset, fear, so many emotions primarily. BUT, those very walls are coming down. SEE THEM coming down. As this is the time to bring down the divide and bring up the UNITY! Stay true to who you are. And that includes not being perfect all the time. We see you, we see your hearts, and we tell you to keep on keeping on. You are making such grand headway now, and as I eluded to before. Be strong, be joyful, no matter what is going on outside of you. Seek peace in every opportunity you can, and anchor that within. Love shall win. But it takes everyone committed to living and being this most powerful force.

~ Archangel Michael

May 2. *A crown wink.*

Our Joy wrote me yesterday about my upcoming event, stating that many synchs with crowns and royalty, among other things, validated how I was truly guided to be in Hawaii. I was eating lunch while watching a little bit of a movie (I have a habit of watching mostly funny, old television shows while eating), and felt to read her email right away. Just then, I see these crowned people acting as queen and king in the movie. Later in the afternoon, I get a Happy May Day message. "Every girl is a queen. Each boy is a king." Relates to the movie scene too! The Crown signs continue!

[Joy emailed me quite often, supporting the winks shared in this book. Her loving support of my work has been a constant, and so deeply appreciated!]

May 3. *A Lily and Marie wink.*

Okay, two days ago on May 1st, I was on the phone with Natalia, who I met in Hawaii. You may recall that she channeled my guide Lillian, who then left a penny on her seat after we got up from the table at a restaurant, and proceeded to leave us both money for days after that.

I told Natalia that I want to eventually adopt a Chihuahua and name her Lily, after my guide and adopted aunt. She said to ask Lillian to help me find the right Chi. After I hung up, Lillian whispered, "Consider it done." I kind of already felt this, but the validation was so sweet. About 15 minutes later, I thought what the heck, I'm not ready to get a dog yet but let me just see what dogs are up for adoption at the Santa Fe Animal Shelter. My jaw dropped. There were 2 Chi's. And of them, not only was one named Lily, but the other, Marie. Marie is the name of Lillian's mother-in-law, my friend's Grandma who I have also connected with in spirit! To me it was just another wink and a crazy sign, given the timing!

May 12. *A thunder and lightning wink.*

Yesterday, I was feeling out of it from the moment I woke. I wondered if I was unknowingly taking on others' "stuff." As soon as I asked Michael to help me, I realized the answer. Someone sent me energetic cords. He said to cut them, and of course he would help me.

The second, and I mean the second we cut them, I heard an extremely loud thunder strike so close to my home. Validation... wow! It was so powerful. And yesterday was the first time I heard thunder since returning to New Mexico. I could see the lightening, so close to my home. So that made an imprint on me to always check for cords, because it sure took a toll on me yesterday. I felt immediately free, by the way, once the cords were cut. So, I share this as a reminder.

May 12. *A Michael wink.*

I love this memory from four years ago. I believe that we can change the world from this place.

On May 12, 2016: Archangel Michael was whispering to me in my sleep last night, and he would like this to be shared, as it is for all who wish to hear. He basically said (from memory, I wasn't fully conscious) "What if there were this magical place, this one very spot where, when you stand in it, you can ask for anything... a certain feeling, something you desire, a dream come true... and it would come forth. Would you seek this place?" (Yes.) "Well it is within you."

The way we create is changing. So is the ease that comes with creating. It is up to us pioneers to move into full conscious creation. We can learn together.

May 15. *A Lily and an 11 wink.*

Goodness, my friends! Yesterday morning, I was on my way to downtown Santa Fe, and a car's plate with key letters and numbers in front of me clued me in to a *positive* sign. It was related to what Lily was talking about, in late April. Remember, that bird landed on my ledge for five plus minutes the second Lillian was encouraging me to take action on something? So, I was excited at first when I saw the license plate, but then my wandering mind started to doubt. And just when I doubted, a rock hits my windshield strongly, and yet didn't do damage. New Mexico is the king of rock damaged windshields by the way, and yet the timing was spot on. I follow this car off the exit and into Santa Fe, and suddenly a car darts in between us. The personalized license plate it sported? ELEVEN! I was blown away!

But it wasn't until I reflected on the email I wrote you, back on 4.29, that I realized the additional message: "Just before it flew away, it pooped, and on the screen were two lines that made a perfect 11 (and 11, as you know, stands for illumination)." I totally forgot that part, and now make the connection!

May 21. *A Lily and prosperity wink.*

I took a spontaneous trip to Colorado for a belated Mother's Day celebration this weekend, which filled my soul. As soon as I got onto the highway to return back to NM yesterday, I see a Chi cloud in the sky! Look at the perfect placement of that eye, and raised ears. This has happened again and again where there simply is no coincidence or question in what the sighting is about, especially when you see the perfect placement of the eye(s). I will never cease to be amazed. Anyways, I thought of all of you right away, and had to share.

[For readers to understand the significance of what happened on this drive back to New Mexico, first I must share this related memory.]

May 20, 2018: The spirit of Lillian continues to connect with me and prove she's around me since she first "came through" when I was in Canada last Fall. But today… today was over the top. Yesterday, I led my workshop in Albuquerque with a beautiful group of new Warriors of Light! This morning, I was on my way to Santa Fe to visit with friends, and I heard a whisper "from above" to "Look for the 'Lily' truck today." This trucking company name has served as a symbolic sign of her.

Sometime later, I headed for home. When I was on that hypnotic drive through the desert between Las Vegas and Raton, New Mexico, I see none other than the Lily truck right in front of me! What are the chances that I'd encounter this truck which is few and far between here? And I'm following it! When I went to pass the truck, I crossed the Canadian River (Canada is where she was from)! Then I see mile marker 444!

Once I got to the Colorado border, I realized I should get something to eat. Yet, it took a couple of hours due to a couple of phone calls. But as synchronicity goes, the timing was divine. I called ahead to pick up a sandwich at the perfect place, because the young woman answered, "This is Lily, may I help you?!" Wow! Our passed loved ones are helping us through! Even ones who adopt us as family, from the Heavens!

[Now, fast forward two years later, on the way back to New Mexico from Colorado.]

I was nearing that memorable place in New Mexico where I saw a Lily truck, that striking place where a big hill was cut through to make way for the expressway. While recalling this memory as I drove by, and in the same place that the Lily truck was in this photo, a different truck appeared and to my shock. It had the word FORTUNE in big letters with a pot of gold and a rainbow! Are you kidding me? Remember how Lillian left a penny under my friend's seat when we were having dinner and she *heard* from Lillian, because she is psychic? And she kept leaving us money signs after that? And we did deep healing work for the collective for the rich/poor divide? Well how could I not tie this synchronicity with all of that prosperity meaning? Then, three days after seeing this FORTUNE truck, I *heard* to go to my memories on Facebook, only to see this original memory posted on May 20, 2018. This same day, two years prior!

May 22. *Queen and 11 winks.*

Carol wrote me yesterday blown away by the latest Lillian wink. And she had lots to share in response! As you know, Carol and I have had a lot of synchs in tandem, most notably when the Queen messages began appearing.

Here is just one of Carol's synchronous recollections: "On May 2, I saw a young woman wearing a T-shirt with QUEEN on it. Later, I was in a parking lot and thought I'd better send myself an email to remind myself to add it to my 'signs list.' Almost *immediately* after I typed the message and pulled back onto the street, I was behind a van or SUV with this license plate: ELEVN11."

Just Amazing, Carol... all of it! Thank you for letting me share your continual magic with our group!

May 26. *A reminder wink.*

People are rethinking how they spend their day, what their choices are, and what resonates and no longer resonates with them; a constant reassessment that ultimately leads to a change in their actions and behaviors. The reason that it is easier is because as they are already releasing much of their past, those habits which are connected to their old beliefs and actions, just dissolve naturally right along with them.

~ Archangel Michael, from *Michael's Clarion Call*

These words from Michael have never been so true as they are now. We are being called to grow closer to our souls, and thus our choices and habits that don't resonate will fall away. We are moving into who we really are, and away from societal conditioning. It is very exciting. In many ways, don't you agree it is happening quite naturally now, where we are kind of just done with a lot of the 3D aspects of life? It's great to take notice and just let go of what no longer serves—with ease.

May 31. *An old royalty wink.*

Two days ago, I went to Albuquerque to run a couple of errands. As soon as my thoughts went to my book, I see this "ROYAL" truck in front of me. I laughed out loud. I haven't seen the word *Royal* on a truck since Hawaii.

Then yesterday, I inserted into my new book what I shared days ago at my royalty event: "And it's all about the fake royalty stepping down, and all of us elevating ourselves..." etc.

After that, I learn on this very same day rumors that the queen of England abdicated the throne on May 10th? And there's a possible new king claiming heir to the throne? Still looking into this, but how's that for synchronicity?

All the world is a stage right now, more than ever. And this is making us trust our hearts, our intuition, more than ever, too.

June 3. *A seed wink.*

Start seeing yourself as a seed. For you are each preparing for new growth, unprecedented growth for humans, due to your rising vibrations. Get ready to shed what you think you know about life and even yourself, as you grow your understanding of truths. This takes tremendous courage, and so summon this courage. For you will be rewarded in many ways; it's endless, really. For every shift will spawn new possibilities simply because you had the courage to grow. Trust yourself and give yourself the freedom to expand. What you do for you, you do for the greater good… always.

~ Archangel Michael, on June 3, 2017

June 6. *A Lily and Mary wink.*

Remember the Chihuahuas listed for adoption at the shelter near me, one right next to the other of Lily and Marie? They were the only Chi's available. And then I just posted the Lily and Mary signs with the lilies by the 55 post, a couple of days ago?

Well, Carol sends me this yesterday! "OMG, Mary. I'm looking at cats on petfinder.com, and I just came across two kittens, their pictures/descriptions SIDE-BY-SIDE, and their names are, respectively… LILY and MARY! And they are at a rescue RIGHT BY ME!"

"I am looking at them on my phone, otherwise I would have taken a picture! Another WOW — or, more appropriately, a MEOWOW (sorry… haha)!"

So, I went online myself to see them, and my search came up with 34 pages of cat listings in Carol's area, and 40 on each page. That's a lot of cats. *Now what are the chances* that these two cats Lily and Mary would be side by side and on the top of the very first page? They even look like they are from the same litter. It was a MEOWOW moment, for sure. I have no question that Lily is connecting with Carol now, and maybe you too!

Lily	**Mary**
Kitter • Domestic Short Hair	Kitten • Domestic Short Hair
1 mile away	1 mile away

June 15. *A breath wink.*

Good morning, everyone! Right now, in this moment, check in with your breath. Is it shallow, or are you taking breaths that are deep? We know how important it is to have conscious breath that supports deeper breathing. I discuss this in my new class that I created in Sedona. When in Hawaii, I became more conscious of my breathing. And I would do little checks, only to find out how shallow it was. Snorkeling is what woke me up like never before to the benefits of deeper breathing. I found myself naturally breathing so deeply when breathing through that snorkel, as I needed that extra oxygen to swim. You can really hear and feel your breath more, through that tube. And it felt great! More about this in the class... but just a thought if you don't do this, to simply check in, and then, perhaps, breathe deeper.

June 16. *A wink in my sleep.*

Many of us are working hard in sleep time, on unconscious levels, and probably even working together. This mask spell is serious and doing too much harm on so many levels, and we need to be aware of what this is really about.

I woke out of some kind of work regarding this in the wee hours. I have no idea where my spirit goes, but I suddenly become half-awake with some kind of understanding. And today it was all about the masks specifically, raising awareness in some way, and doing energetic work. Next, in my mind's eye was the widest rainbow descending over land. It was so extraordinary that I wanted to capture it with a camera, and then realized that I wasn't seeing it in waking life. And to me, this was a sign of the mask mandates ending. Or, at least growing awareness of the truths behind it. Archangel Michael and other beings can actually put visions in our third eye, as wild as that seems. I've experienced this so many times. For me, it is often extraordinary cloud scenes. But I felt this rainbow was put there to symbolize success and to keep the faith. And so I share with you.

June 19. *Nature winks.*

Nature is sitting *still* around me at times, lately. Are you noticing an increasing presence, as if the birds, animals, trees are speaking to you louder than ever?

Remember I told you about that lizard I saw in Sedona, where it stood still when I was standing right next to it? Therefore, I knew it had a message for me since lizards normally scurry if you get anywhere close to them. And sure enough as I stood there talking to it, asking what its message was, it went from dark (standing in a shadow) into the Light (moving into the sunlight). I have the scene on videotape.

I also filmed a dragonfly who let me get very close (again, not normal). This happened when creating my new class, while in front of Cathedral Rock. I put my finger right next to the dragonfly standing on a rock, and it didn't budge. It wasn't as dramatic as that one that stayed on me for over ten minutes, years ago in Colorado, but still. And it happened soon after I said to the class to let's go and find some magic.

Two days ago, I went right up to my little frog pond and was just looking into the water, and was shocked to see a sweet, little sparrow sitting on a rock when I was right next to it, and it did not fly away! Normally, as soon as I open the front door, all the birds flee. But this one just sat there for a long time and I was talking to it, asking if it was okay. It looked at me several times. It then flew off, flying just fine. That's three meaningful, well-timed signs from nature right there. I'm listening. There's something to this, because it seems that nature is speaking to us louder than ever.

June 24. *A Mother Mary wink.*
Yesterday, while deep in meditation, two memorable things happened one right after another, almost as an 'as above so below' feel to it. And it felt like it was for the masses, not personal.

Mother Mary appeared and had a message. I'm sorry, I don't recall it except the feeling of joy that she appeared and because of what she said that I lost recall of. Right after that, below her were all these baby chicks hatching to overflowing. It felt very positive, whatever it meant. My eyes were so heavy that it took a really long time to open them. When I did, I looked at the clock and it was 1:11 p.m.!

One of the first things I did was to look up the spiritual symbolism of chicks hatching. The first thing that came up in an internet search was: "Coming out of the shell means giving yourself to a new world, new experiences, and new sensations." With the subject of our new Heaven on Earth continually coming up, that surely resonated.

After some very difficult days lately, I woke yesterday morning feeling oddly excited, like some big, positive things are happening for our world that we don't see yet. The meditation sure validated these feelings.

June 25. *A Mother Mary wink.*

When I was in Sedona, I bought a Mother Mary statue, about a foot and a half tall. I've been wanting one, as well as an Archangel Michael statue. I've been looking for years and can never find the right portrayal of him, namely one that doesn't have a devil beneath him. But when I saw this Guadalupe version of Mary, I felt I was meant to have it as a reminder to maintain more connection with her, as well as to have a symbolic representation of her.

Mother Mary is on my angel team but I've been getting the message from many places, to *consciously* connect, even more so. People I have gazed at have seen me morph into her on so many occasions, or just see her around me, including at my recent zoom events—thus, more reminders.

So, I literally told Mother Mary that I want to grow my connection with her, and then she came into my meditation! I'm sharing this as a reminder and, surely, she is actually nudging me to do so if you too are feeling the same—or perhaps you already are in touch very often!

June 28. *A Michael wink.*

The following words from our Michael are especially telling now, with the very times we are in. Those who rely on the mainstream narrative are particularly fearful, and those seeking truth outside of the conventional narrative are not, for the most part.

Many of you are so relieved that you are finally seeing things happen, things that you have been waiting for: the dismantling of all that does not serve your world. For those of you, well, you are in your glory now. However, for those of you who do not understand, panic and shock are in your midst. It behooves you more than ever to remove the blinders for good now, and see the changing world exactly as it is.

~ Archangel Michael, from *The New Sun*

July 2. *Eye winks.*

A couple of days ago, our Joy gave me feedback on my class "Navigating Between 3D and 5D Energies" that I filmed in Sedona. She wrote:

"The meditation was very peaceful—-the scene of the water was like a Monet painting! And finally, when you did the gazing, your eyes went from brown, to green, to blue, and back to brown again! Has this happened to others that gazed into your eyes?"

So, I wrote Joy that while recipients often comment that I morph into others, I don't recall hearing, specifically, that my eye color changed... interesting!

How ironic (but, not really!) is it that the next day I see a post from a Facebook friend who stated that her eye color is changing? She wrote: "Strangest thing, my eyes are changing color. They used to be really dark brown, and now I have lots of golden color in them."

Is this coming up for anyone else? Please let me know if so, and I will share with the group. Fascinating!

July 3. *Eye winks.*

I heard from our Jane yesterday morning regarding eye color change, after asking if anyone else in our group has experienced this.

Jane wrote, "Yes! My eye color has been changing since the end of last year. I have hazel colored eyes and they're getting lighter from the outside in and in a circular shape. I had just seen my eye doctor before it happened, or before I noticed it, so I don't feel like it's a physical issue. I had heard that physical detox can lighten your eyes. But I do wonder about it all the time so I'm loving this email!"

So I responded, "Jane, that's amazing! I've heard that about detox too, but I do believe in my heart it has to do with our evolution!"

Jane wrote back, "I have read that the whole eye color changes at once. [Jane is referring to effects from detoxing.] Not like how mine is changing—only the outside circular rim is lighter. I, too, came to the conclusion it has to do with ascension."

How exciting is this? Thank you so much, Jane, for letting me know this exciting information and giving permission to share with the group! And thank you, Joy, from my heart for noticing this, as it created a segue to discuss these kinds of amazing changes! Bring it on.

July 7. *An arrow wink.*

Back when I created the class on demand in Sedona, I shared the arrow metaphor. As the words just came out of my mouth, they felt profound and guided, saying that humanity is like the arrow in the bow, being pulled backwards which we definitely are, but only to be thrust further forward than ever before.

Last night, I was listening to Magenta Pixie on her YouTube channel, and she used the same arrow metaphor! This is happening so often where I feel we are all getting the same downloads. And we all deliver in our unique and individual ways to people we are meant to share with, and who are drawn to our particular style and messages—such as the queen/king/royalty/sovereignty messages. It all came out of nowhere to become the focus of my new book, and these messages are now everywhere... Everywhere. Are you noticing this, too? We are mirrors for each other! And it's exciting because we know these messages are being Divinely sent, to guide us to unique and necessary understandings.

When we go through these unsure and unsteady times, it's things like this that give us such comfort that we are on the right track.

July 16. *An energy shifting wink.*
In my class I created in Sedona, I discussed shifting the energy of the mandates (such as mask wearing). I do my best to shift everything surrounding this. "I can breathe!" And one of my many frustrations is the "X"s placed that arbitrary 6 feet from each other, inside and outside of many stores. Yes, they want us 6 feet from him, 6 feet from her, 6, 6, 6... yep. It's intended for us to succumb like sheep to social distancing, which in my firm view is all about control and something nefarious, not for the sake of our health. Just like being forced to wear masks, a mandate that is also about control and not about our health. The masks actually make us sicker according to scores of doctors pleading with us to understand. We can agree to disagree, and I sure do with love. But I purposefully don't stand on the X's because no one controls me, and I will stand to the side of it somewhere (maybe 7 feet away haha).

When I went to Trader Joe's this morning and walked over to stand in the outside line to get in, I was thrilled to see for only the second time no line at all. And then I saw something that made me so happy. Someone created adorable chalk art out of the X's, which made the X's dissolve! They shifted the energy from those cold X's!

July 22. *A purple and gold robe wink.*

Yesterday, I connected with a reader, who remote views, for a 30-minute appointment to get another opinion, helping with the mold exposure symptoms. When it was completed, she asked if I had any other questions, that she could give me another five or ten minutes, which was really nice. So, I asked her if AA Michael had anything to say to me that I'm not hearing.

The reader responded, "Yes, I do keep seeing them put this purple and gold robe on you."

"That's the queen theme," I replied. (I already mentioned my new book to her).

She went on, "I think it's absolutely beautiful. And they keep putting this piece of jewelry on you. It's a symbol, but I don't know what the symbol is. She described this image a couple of times accentuating the purple and gold robe saying "It's just brilliantly beautiful."

Funny, because I'm such a casual gal, yet I appreciated being adorned in this way as we all are, without our knowing! I recall that time after sitting in the Seat of Isis, the ancient stone seat, located in a magical forest above Rennes les Bains, in the South of France. I was hiking back down the hill and I heard church bells ringing in the town, and just then, Michael said they were crowning me. Interesting, because it was right after connecting with the Goddess Isis energy. I cannot remember if he used the word "Queen," but he was making me feel this was about assuming my royalty.

I also remember him placing a seal of some kind of significance on my forehead... my third eye. Perhaps it was the same symbol seen in the piece of jewelry that the reader noted. This all felt so grandiose that I never told anyone this before. Of course, I did not know about the royalty message—they were planting seeds, yet again.

July 24. *A new beginning wink.*

The following is a great reminder to stay full of faith no matter how we may be feeling in the moment. These last two years have been the hardest on my heart, bar none. And even so, Michael has taught me to stay in my joy no matter what, and the dolphins sure taught me that. Last night, Metatron came through with a very positive message. This message has come through in many ways, that all will be well and a new beginning is right before me. Then, I dreamt very vividly last night that I had a baby. A baby represents new beginnings!

This morning, as I was leaving the house, I had this premonition that a gray pickup truck was going to come barreling around the corner, cut into my lane, and nearly plow into me. I saw it, felt it, knew it. Not even a minute later, I get into the car and a gray truck comes barreling around the corner and nearly plowed into me. Crazy! There was barely a foot clearance before his sudden stop. Because I had the premonition which then made me cautious, I knew I'd be okay. It felt like a metaphor, affirming that even though these have been scary times, all will be well!

When on my way into town, I see the "Lucky Truck" (that truck with shamrocks I've told you about) in front of me, then when I later had Lily-related thoughts, the Lily truck was in front of me. Then I see the Lucky Truck, again. So even though things haven't changed or manifested yet, this all replenished my already strong faith big time, beginning with Metatron's message. Faith is everything. We may not know exactly how or when things will work out, but we just know that they will.

July 29. *A Queen's throne wink.*

Oh goodness, I couldn't wait to share this with you. I was working on my book last night, while recalling some

Queen synchs. My landlords called and had something for me, so I drove to their house. They are such warm and good people. When I got there, they were seated in front of their house waiting for me. As I walked up to them, the wife points to the large, unique chair next to her and says, "We have this throne for you." Seriously? They know I'm an author but I then had to tell them what my book is about! And not only that, but the husband said that the woman who gave them the chair lived in Hawaii.

July 31. *A leap of faith wink.*

I was working on my computer when I see a grasshopper hanging upside down from the bottom of the ledge of my window. That's about five feet up! They represent good luck, taking a leap of faith... many things. It then walked right into a spider web! What was this telling me? I was having a challenging day helping myself and some personal friends through deep frustration over what is going on in the world. Did I fall into a web, was I too vocal on social media trying to wake people up, or did I help clean up the web of lies out there? Because suddenly, as I'm taking pictures of the grasshopper, it and the web fall and there's not a remnant of the web left on the window! I'm still not sure and will keep feeling into the meaning. I always want the truth. But I feel like I am taking a leap of faith taking down the web of lies—that's for sure.

August 5. *JFK winks.*

Yesterday, I saw a picture of Trump's desk in the Oval Office. It made me think of the picture of "John John" peeking out from under JFK's Resolute desk—that iconic photo from almost 60 years ago. *The very next day,* I see Trump in a video on social media holding a photo album in his hand, standing by his desk, and showing that very photograph! He was describing the photo, saying that it was "John John," and specifically uttered the words "who *is* a friend of mine." Not *was* a friend of mine, but in the present.

Many of you may be aware of the theory that JFK, Jr. is still alive. That his death was staged. It sounds crazy but there is a lot of evidence and connecting of dots that many are piecing together, including myself. Was this indeed staged and Trump was leaving us a clue letting us know that this is indeed true? What are the chances I see a picture of Trump's desk, which made me think of little John John, and then Trump shares that very picture and refers to it in a most unexpected way, only the next day?! Trump speaks in code, clues, and symbolism to communicate to the truthers.

Also, on this same day was the horrible bombing in Beirut, Lebanon. When researching it, I happened to find out that just two days later was the 75th anniversary of the Hiroshima and Nagasaki bombings! I got really weirded out when watching video accounts of this present day attack. Because just prior to hearing about it on this very day, I was rereading and editing in the book the very part about the Pearl Harbor bombing. And how Lightworkers have been drawn to New Mexico to balance out the karma, being that the atomic bomb was created here! What are the chances? I hadn't read the part about Pearl Harbor in many months.

August 8. *A spider web wink.*
I get a lot of flies in the house. They usually just zoom past me and all around the place. But yesterday, this one kept landing on me relentlessly for a long time while I was on the computer. I said to myself, "That's it, I'm not going to sit back down until I catch it." So, I got out my butterfly net, and yet couldn't catch it. I then watched it fly right into a small spider web, this time the same

window ledge as the grasshopper under the outside ledge the other day. What are the chances of all of this? There's a definite message there!

August 10. *Film making winks.*

This is a great example of what can happen when you call out what you desire, both in 3D and otherwise, and messengers and synchronicity magically appear.

I shared with you a few days ago that I changed my company name from Twelve Twelve Publishing, LLC to Twelve Twelve Productions, LLC in order to create the space for my movie dream. In response, our Saramae [in the M&M Group] wrote me about someone she met who is a film maker, and was so kind to give me this person's phone number. What is utterly striking is that they met at a hotel in Las Cruces, New Mexico last year, and neither of them lived in New Mexico! Things often happen for many reasons, as we know. So, were seeds being planted here, through others?

Saramae wrote, "I had a conversation at breakfast in the Drury Hotel with a woman who is a film maker. Our conversation reached a spiritual level and I mentioned you and your work." I was quite floored and very grateful for this unique meeting that would turn extra synchronistic a year later, and Saramae thinking to share with me! Because here I am literally in New Mexico now, and taking a first step toward my movie dream.

Then yesterday, I went back to Abiquiu to enjoy some scenery. I stopped at Bode's, a country store. Outside of incredible natural beauty, there isn't much to see and do in Abiquiu, but I like this store that has a little of everything. I walked by the cashier and heard a customer talk to him about movie making. The cashier asked what studio he worked for. This was way too coincidental to ignore.

After they were done talking, I told the customer I happened to overhear their conversation, and boldly asked what he did. It turns out he works for a union in the movie business. He gave me the website and I wrote it down at the store but can't find it. Sometimes synchs like these are just winks and nothing more.

I truly have no idea how I will pull all of this off. I'm a very determined, independent person, but this feels utterly overwhelming. And yet, I feel this drive. What is it that you are dreaming of? Do you feel ready to start a new life within this life? What does it look like? Common sense is not as key as intuition these days, in my opinion. More about that in the new book. Sometimes I like to keep things private... until the right time. But sharing with you sure did something! Anyways, I felt to share this experience with you, for whatever its worth. Following the wind of the soul is exciting, even during such crazy times in this world.

August 11. *Bird winks.*

This continues to happen... where I recall some kind of event or synchronicity, and it happens to be on the exact day (or within a day) of something years ago. I bet you are noticing similar things!

Yesterday, I was just marveling at the number of birds who visit my pond for a drink. I think I told you, I placed a clay pot bottom filled with water, so that the birds aren't all fighting to get to my little frog pond in dry New Mexico. And even with this little mock bird bath, I have to fill it at least twice a day because there can be as many as ten or more at a time.

My hummingbird feeders are now further from the house because it is ant city with the sugar water, but the hummingbirds will still come up to my window where I work a few feet from, and look at me. And yesterday, two appeared together, which is rare! When things like that happen, I immediately consider what my thoughts were in that very moment. So anyways, it all made me think of the following quote, and Michael said it almost five years ago in a personal channel, but it came up in Facebook Memories today!

"On another note, you are about to hear a new calling. A call from the animal kingdom… the birds! They will be showing you some amazing synchronicities and they need to be promoted. The birds are an important part of your transformation on earth. Why do you think you are suddenly surrounded by so many birds?!"
~ Archangel Michael, August 16, 2015

(AA Michael was referring to my sudden desire to place several bird feeders around the home, when we moved to Sedona.)

August 17. *A Chihuahua and Queen wink.*
Soon after I got onto a beautiful trail in the Jemez mountains yesterday, I set up to create a new video. It will be controversial, no doubt, but I was called to do this.

While setting my camera onto the tripod, I was gathering my thoughts, deciding that I would start with the royalty message. I was just about to begin when a young couple walk by and the woman yells "Queen!" WHAT?! I was situated close to the trail and decided to just stop the video whenever I heard hikers walking by. I spoke to the woman and verified, "Did you just say 'Queen'?" "Yes," she said. I basically told them that I was just about to speak about royalty, so thank you for creating this synchronicity. They got a kick out it, and were so lovely to talk to. I then just began to introduce the video, but stopped it again, only to see a couple walking *three Chihuahuas.* I also saw a Chihuahua later in the video, and yet another when putting my tripod away.

September 6. *Number and dolphin winks.* This is just too good that I must share with you. It's a long one.

This morning, I went back to the wetlands. Check out this amazing light show. [In the picture on the prior page, the colors in this unique ray of light spanned from red at bottom moving through all colors of the rainbow, with violet on top.]

When I parked my car returning home, my trip odometer read 888.7 at 10:44, it was 78 degrees out and the odometer read 57878! I knew something was up, especially with the 144 reference. But what was with that 1/10th of a mile less than perfect number on the trip odometer? (wink)

Then after working on the book, later in the day I recalled that I wanted to quote from a book that my dolphin sister Hydee gave me, *Change We Must*, by Nana

Veary. I randomly opened to a page and it mentioned the 144,000 in the bible. For some reason, my thoughts went immediately to the dolphins and about how I would love to go back and learn so much more about them. I then imagined writing a whole book about the crystal beings. My heart wanted to have a deeper understanding of why I was so irresistibly drawn to the spinners, why I had to swim with them as much as possible, and more about what role they are playing in these times. I heard Michael say: "Look up 'Lemuria and dolphins.'" Right then I look at the clock and it was 4:44!

When looking at the internet search results, I intuited which one to open and saw this post at www.elementalbeings.co.uk/lemuria/.

"Lemuria was an ancient civilisation predating Atlantis. The souls incarnate at this time were very spiritual, vibrating at the 8th and 10th vibrational levels. They created reality by dreaming it into existence and during this time co-existed with Elementals, Angels and worked in harmony with the Dolphin race."

"Dolphins are 12th dimensional beings who hold the grid of light Earth Matrix in their brain structure. The dolphins communicated with humans during Lemurian times in holographic form patterns, sending transmissions from their brains to assist Humans in holding Gaia's light grid matrix."

"The Dolphins hold within their brains the holographic structures and symbols which allow more light to enter the Earth's domain at this time. As part of Gaia's evolution she requires Ancient Lemurians to reconnect to their sacred Dolphin knowledge and re-establish connection with them to assist in the next evolutionary stage of the Earth's progression."

"Ancient Lemurian Dolphin Temples existed where

Humans and Dolphins would exchange healing codes of love which the Dolphins 'sang' and tuned into Humans central core matrix. Many of us remember these communications and you can experience once again Dolphin/human symbiosis allowing your heart to sing with joy."

"The Dolphin temples are connected to energy vortexes of Gaia which Dolphins work within to charge up the ley line energy deep within the sea. By reconnecting to the Lemurian Dolphin temples we can assist Gaia in visualising to bring into being in the physical realm symbols and patterns required in humans to allow more light to descend as part of the new dawn after the 21.12.12 shift. In Lemuria twelve Dolphin temples were created, these temples still exist ethereally and are in the areas of Hawaii, Bali, Fraser Island, Florida Keys, Yucatan Mexico and Samoa."

This resonated ever so strongly, in so many ways. Thank you, Michael, for the nudge! Next, I went to www.gailthackray.com and read Gail's wonderful and revealing article, "The Healing Power of Dolphins."

"Have you ever heard of Lemuria or the lost continent of Mu? Many spiritual messages have been channeled about this ancient time. Some believe it was one of the first civilizations on this planet even before Atlantean times. That was a time that people understood energy healing. Illness was known as an energy in-balance and was easily 'healed' by the adjustment of one's energy using colored lights. Some believe Dolphins came to Earth to help the Lemurian people. That Dolphins and Whales came from Sirius B, a constellation in another dimension. Sirius B being a water planet was inhabited with Mer people; half human, half dolphin. The Dolphins came to planet Earth to teach love and they have continued through the generations to support us and teach us to love one another."

"Whether you believe in this or not, I am sure you will agree Dolphins are very special, beautiful creatures that bring a sense of peace and love. They are known to be highly intellectual beings able to communicate with each other telepathically and talk to other dolphins several miles away."

"Swimming with the dolphins helps to open one's heart chakra so one can receive love and feel more connected to Divine. Perhaps in ancient times they taught the Lemurian people to open their hearts and were an intricate part of the teachings of Lemuria and Atlantis. Those who had past lives in these ancient times have a particular affiliation with Dolphins and Whales. If you love these creatures, love the ocean and the color turquoise you probably have once lived in these times. Meditating with pictures of Dolphins can then open your heart and help you to receive a stronger connection to Divine."

"When I first swam with the Dolphins I was amazed at how they swam together in synchronicity. It wasn't as if one was a leader and the others followed. Rather, they moved as one. Swimming down then making a 90 degree turn, perfectly timed and in synch. As one turned, they all turned together. It was obvious they were connected telepathically, perhaps subconsciously, perhaps as one consciousness. Their minds almost seem to work as one. Yet once in a while, one would break out and play with you. Swim towards you, roll under you on their belly, and then swim off as if to say 'catch me if you can.' They'd join the others and continue in formation. I was especially touched by the mom who brought her baby right underneath me to show her off. Perhaps she knew I was a mom."

"I found you could hold a thought in your mind, perhaps a problem. It was as if a wave of knowing, a wave of love would come over you and you'd feel a sort of release. A feeling that as you swam with the group of these beautiful beings, you were receiving waves of love and a sense of peace was being instilled."

"I found mostly I couldn't connect one on one, rather my plight was taken by all of them together. Are these beautiful beings able to open your heart somehow? Are they able to heal?"

"There are certain places in the world where your vibration is higher, where you seem to be more able to connect with the Divine. For me, the Dolphins place you in sort of a high energy love bubble that opens up your heart and allows you to connect with the Divine. If you can't be there with these beautiful creatures, meditate on their presence. Surround yourself with photos and paintings of these creatures and ask for them to open your heart."

Another superb article! It touches on so many things I've felt deep inside. It's so true that they appear to be of one mind, intricately connected. When one would come to you—to connect, to heal, to telepath, to play—it wasn't only that one. They appeared to work together, in unity. They are supporting the actual connection with the human, I could feel it so deeply and I believe that you will sense it from the few YouTube videos I share. It's unlike anything I've ever experienced. This dolphin and Lemurian connection is so key to our further understanding and appreciation of these beings' role in the ascension of our earth.

~~~~~

While this chapter needs to cease, the winks for us all continue to bless us daily.

It will be impossible to not notice the magic of the Universe. There will be a profound intensity of miraculous occurrences experienced by each of you, such that the way in which you each see the world, the Universe, will intensely change in a multitude of ways. It will be glorious.

~Archangel Michael, from *Michael's Clarion Call*

Chapter Twelve

The Arrow Metaphor

On September 21, 2019, I sent a message to my warrior group. Things are getting increasingly obvious. It's all in our faces. Truth is everything, and true knowledge sure is power.

"If we're watching mainstream news, we are simply being had, manipulated, and conditioned. As warriors, we are fighting for the truths, and one of the big truths is to see the Climate Change hoax for what it is. When the well-organized climate change marches occurred around the US yesterday, and suddenly a young girl is thrust extra heavy into the spotlight to lead the youth, the people to protest, we have to wonder just how does that happen? How did she get there? Because the deep state is actually behind it? And she is being used *as a pawn*? The weather has been manipulated for too many years—*that is the main climate crisis!* Why don't politicians ever talk about this? Why aren't they talking about climate engineering (chemtrails) above their own heads, HAARP, and all weather manipulation? I've talked about this before. There's tons of proof and it starts by simply looking up and seeing the unnatural lines in the sky. Cognitive dissonance is a real thing, and very much alive and well right now. We are being led to believe the crisis is all our fault. And 'they' are leading us on a path that will require us to make most concerning changes using fear and manipulation to save a planet *that more than anything needs the dark to stop messing with it*. Yes, of course, all of humanity has definitely created many issues, and was covertly led to create many issues too—as this was by dark design in the making for a long time. My feelings about this aren't popular, but everything inside me was screaming yesterday as I witness where this is going. And I know that I am not alone in this reaction. We simply have to question everything right now. We are being hit by the weather manipulation, 5G, vaccines, the poisons in the foods, on and on—they are all intricately connected to bring us down. Truth and awareness are the first steps to fighting this. And we will win in the end. Keep Michael close by… with his sword."

"Again, when it's big and sudden, all endorsed by big media, famous people, politicians, etc.—these are the red flags. Swords Up, my friends!"

This was written well before the "plannedemic" hoax and the inciting of violence, destruction, and racial tensions all by sick design. We've all been played and had, again and again. History keeps repeating itself until we collectively wake up.

The fact is… just like with an arrow in the bow, we are being pulled backwards. But in that being pulled back, *we are only to be thrust forward, further than ever, into new and wonderfully uncharted territory.* I shared this very metaphor that seemed dropped right into my heart from Michael as I was filming my class in Sedona, in June 2020. Or, perhaps he gave me the visual, too. Whatever it was, the metaphor was so immediately clear to me.

We are all arrows being pulled back, way back. And in that pulling back, we are awakening to our personal truths, flaws, and shadows, in the microcosm. As we are simultaneously awakening to the truths of extreme evil in this world run amok that most of humanity has been unaware of, in the macrocosm. Then and only then, when we finally face our true reality in this 3D world, can we release it fully and propel into our 5D and beyond New Earth existence. We can let go of the aspects of ourselves and this world that are not aligned with our royal future!

Regarding those aspects of us that are engrossed in the synthetic way of life, certainly materialism—everything that has taken us too far from nature and God is shifting right now, as we speak. When in lockdown, we could no longer shop for frivolous things, only what we needed for survival, primarily. In an odd way, it made us face our true needs and desires. It certainly made us more appreciative of everything that we have. It also made us aware of what we no longer want. I was watching, in shock, a video of Manhattan after all the rioting with store after store boarded up; all those businesses suffering. And yet consumerism appears to be falling.

A lot of things are falling now, things that won't be aligned with our bright future. When Archangel Michael said that competition will not be a part of our New Earth, in *Michael's Clarion Call*, I responded:

"I imagine this will make a lot of sports fans upset."

AA Michael: *That is because they will be viewing this from a third dimensional mindset. Just as we spoke earlier that the need many have for coffee, alcohol, or other drugs will vanish, this is also hard to imagine from your present mindset. See from a higher perspective what it will be like. That you will feel such joy, peace, and bliss that your present needs will simply vanish.*

While I don't watch sports at all, knowing there are so many huge sports fans out there, this was hard for me to conceive of. But look at what is happening to sports right now. Many professional sports organizations are falling! Everything Archangel Michael shared in *Michael's Clarion Call* and *The New Sun* about our approaching New Earth is coming true! And in very unexpected ways, in my view. I published these books well ahead of their time to help prepare us for what is happening now and directly ahead.

To get there, we need to face the reality of that which needs to go in our present world. Mainstream news is the biggest virus in the world, in my firm opinion. Conventional news sources are clearly the vehicle for the dark to control, manipulate, indoctrinate, propagandize, and create fear and divide among all. I haven't owned a television set in years and I'm so grateful I made this decision to rid of it. And, by the way, it's all media—mass media—not just the news. But nothing has the massive hypnotizing effect that the news provides these days. It seems to have put too many of us in a literal spell.

When something is repeated often enough, it goes right into our subconscious minds and runs us like a computer. This is especially true for children who haven't yet developed their "critical factor," but it's also true for adults. This is what the mainstream news does. They repeat and repeat to no end untruths—often blatant untruths—which then runs our thoughts, beliefs, and subsequent actions. And this is why so many of us truthers, Lightwarriors, and Lightworkers are repeating the truths as often as we can, to counter this war on our minds and souls. This is a natural inclination that so many of us seem to be adhering to.

Whether you like President Trump or not, they most unfairly slander this man throughout every day. No matter what he does, which is often greatness and like nothing we've ever seen because he is not part of the establishment, they spin, lie, falsify, and skewer everything to the point that people are massively programmed to hate him. Those who do not watch the news, and rather watch his actions, see Trump completely differently.

This whole virus-created chaos sure appears to many as one big psyop, from the mask ritual to social distancing to certain states setting up contact tracing where we snitch on each other? Instead of snitching on each other reporting those not wearing masks, perhaps we do more real and beneficial reporting of the real culprits. Yes, perhaps we should:

- Photograph every person behind child sex crimes, and send to the state or country
- Photograph every chemtrail we see, and send to the state or country
- Photograph every food that contains allowed gmos, pesticides, and other dangerous chemicals, and send to the state or country
- Photograph every Roundup application on school, local, and state owned property, and send to the state or country

- Photograph before and after pictures of every vaccine damaged child, and send to the state or country
- Photograph every cell phone tower on school property, and send to the state or country
- Photograph every pharmaceutical that is damaging our bodies, and send to the state or country
- Photograph every crime against humanity, and send to the state or country

Okay, I think you get my sarcastic, but necessary point. The created virus is real but the "pandemic" is clearly a scam seen by so many who research all levels of it. And these mandates and practices forced on us are dangerous in so many ways.

Experts are coming out of the woodwork telling us so many things contrary to the politicians causing mayhem. Thousands of medical experts are speaking out that mask wearing not only doesn't prevent a virus, but is actually making us sick. The wildly inaccurate and unsafe testing is being used to further their scheme by making decisions and mandates based off of them, and is not to be trusted. And even the taking of temperate at the third eye is not good for our pineal glands.

All three of these things I knew from the get go and spread the word to beware, and yet was attacked and ridiculed by several. Yet, listen to the doctors, especially virologists who would know better than anyone. A top virologist in their field would certainly know better than top leaders, governors, and mayors—all politicians! We each have a right to wear a mask and socially distance, but the masks should not be mandated.

The ramifications of this created, fake pandemic (fake as in the pandemic, not the virus) is most concerning for our youth. Children wearing masks and being forced to social distance is, for me, the hardest to witness. They are generally not affected by the virus and, rather, these mandates are potentially causing great harm physically, mentally, socially, emotionally, and spiritually.

Personally speaking, it is the hardest on the heart to watch these kids being forced to do things that are completely against their free nature. And I know that many of you feel the very same about this. When we are kids, everything we experience goes right to our subconscious minds without a buffer, and then runs us. So this all needs to be stopped and reversed so that kids can breathe vital oxygen freely, hug, play, see everyone else's faces and smiles, and simply be kids again.

When I was in 5th grade, I wore a body brace from chin to pelvis, for three years because of a spine curvature. That alone changed me for life. To this day, I still have to wear loose-fitting tops, not to ever again feel uncomfortably bound up. I despised for my body to be so confined like that, and it was painful. Not to mention that I felt I was sticking out in a social way; perhaps why the orange car triggered me.

I recall this as I ponder the effects of what this insanity is doing to children because it acts on the same principle. This affects the subconscious which can then run the person like a computer through their adult lives, unless they consciously address it. May this all stop immediately and children be healed from this insane nonsense forced on them.

How nice that the states in the U.S. are suddenly "caring" about our health so much (more sarcasm). But where have they been? We must cease being so fooled. This is all about control, not our health. We are smarter than this to blindly succumb to these mandates, snitch on each other, create more conquer and divide, all while the real culprits continue to tyrannize us.

We get so emotionally triggered and go nuts as a country from what appears to be a fully created situation designed to incite racism, violence, and the tearing down of our cities, especially in the U.S. Too many fell for it. And it was all guided and promoted so well by the deep state, mainstream news, and many Hollywood celebrities. And yet this and so many more millions of crimes against children are happening while the media and those same celebrities are completely silent about them!

There lies the worst evil. The most heinous and horrific of all crimes—child sex trafficking, pedophilia, satanic ritual abuse, adrenochrome creation and usage, etc.—go without any, or barely any, attention from MSM? May we turn off the tube, if we haven't yet, for all our sakes, but especially for the kids.

Like him or not, President Trump and the white hats are fighting and bringing down pedophilia, child sex trafficking (as well as human trafficking), ritual abuse, all of it. Again, you won't hear it on the mainstream news, but millions of children have been saved, and tens of thousands of arrests have been made with many more in the process. It's all documented and, tragically, you have to do research to find this information because the news won't cover it, for the most part.

No other president has tackled the most horrific of crimes on this planet, and here, the man who is most bravely leading this, endures being blasted day in and day out. He's vilified not just from the media reports. But their damaging programming then seeps into the public, purposefully creating immense hatred of the man who is doing so many great things for our world. Great hearted people are pulling for the dark side, without realizing it—

they are being fully played. The horrible lies and corruption of the man running against Trump are coming forth as I prepare this book that goes into production a week prior to the U.S. election. The MSM watchers don't seem to know about it because, again, it's hidden and censored, whereas the truthers and a small number of brave media outlets are on it. You don't have to agree, just please bear with me and hear me out.

While I am not obligated to share with anyone my personal political views, I am willing to because I feel it's important that we all get very honest now. This isn't about U.S. politics, republican or democrat—this is about LIFE. And politics has been ruling our lives especially in this year of 2020. But I digress… In 2016, I went from being a life-long democrat (while never liking politics) to removing myself from it all, never again to support any party. Once the election was stolen from Bernie, there was no way in the world I would vote for the truly dangerous woman running against Trump. The democratic party is not the one we grew up with, not that it was ever great either, but things were getting outrageously out of hand. And that goes for both sides of the aisle, for that matter. But the radical left is unrecognizable now.

Yet I will support a president who is saving the children! And who is stopping all wars and bringing peace to the world! And who is working to put a stop to our being financially cheated and enslaved! And who is bringing down pharmaceutical crimes. And who defunded a most non-benevolent organization that is supposed to safeguard our health but has done the opposite. And who appears to be uncovering hidden, magnificent healing technologies to us. And who is treating us all as equals. The list goes on and on. Too many people don't know this because they are being constantly thrown lies, absolute lies, on the news.

I also honestly say that I didn't care for his "tweeting" at first, *until* I realized that this is the way for him to have a voice for what he is doing! He has to self-promote and get truths out there. Because you will hardly hear any real truth from conventional news sources.

Thank goodness for Twitter, in this way, for Trump has created his own news channel! And he then has truthers around the world acting as digital soldiers fighting to get the truths out. Over much time, I researched his true actions, and soon realized that MSM was manipulating our minds to hate this guy when he was accomplishing things that no president ever has. So, I joined in the digital soldier movement, as well as leading our spiritual army with Archangel Michael.

We've been manipulated day in and day out. And this needs to stop. And I believe it will stop because it will get to the point where the truth can no longer be hidden. Rather, it will be in plain sight. MSM will have to change. Until then, we have to dig and dive and traverse through a heavily, ridiculously censored internet to gain an understanding of what is really going on. *And we have to have the courage to accept that we've all been played*—it's okay. This was an awful, cruel setup and we all pretty much fell for it at some point!

I get into this more in *Michael's Sword & You*, but we also have to be especially cognizant of those falsely appearing to be on Team Light, but, in reality, are not. They hook you in to their narrative with some absolute truths to gain your trust, and then feed their suddenly large followings with all-out lies and propaganda for an agenda not so full of Light. We can get so tired of not knowing who to trust which is another reason why connecting to our intuition is so very key! The massive attempts to coerce and confuse won't remain.

You who are on earth are presently being bombarded with dishonesty and untruths coming from so many directions that you often do not know what to believe about earthly things, let alone spiritual ones…this will change.

~ Archangel Michael, from *Michael's Clarion Call*

Politics is literally taking over our lives right now. And, thus, politics must be talked about, even in a spiritual book. Especially so. The depths of darkness are being revealed on this beautiful planet. We must see this big picture in order to project our arrows into a much better place.

Again, it is vital to understand that part of being a Lightworker on this evolving planet *is* facing the existence of extreme dark—evil people and evil non-humans—and their evil actions. And this battle is not being fought just on land. It is being fought in other dimensions! I never wanted to see this, and rather only focus on Light. And we needed to focus on the Light to raise the frequency of our planet, as well as all of us on it. We accomplished that, and now we are in conscious spiritual battle as everything comes to a head.

Look at our beloved Archangel battling evil for us, an aspect of him I avoided. It took me a long time to really get this and accept the existence of evil, and then Michael gave me his sword mission, and that's when everything became especially clear. Humanity has to play the hand it is being dealt, we have no choice. Complacency and avoidance of truth are out the window.

We must look at where all the allowed and encouraged rioting is occurring in states and cities across the U.S. They are democratic-led states and cities. This is hard for many to see, but there is a dark satanic stronghold in this party that wants to bring down this country, get into office, and create a most ominous future. (They tried in 2016 with their candidate and failed, thank God.) I do not at all see this happening, or I would not have written this book! God wins.

The extreme darkness must be seen and dealt with so that we can build on a new and clean foundation for our New Earth. It's an absolute necessity. I broke through the conditioning myself to see what Trump is actually doing. Trust me, I do not agree with all of his policies, but... and it's a big *But*... He is fighting and defeating the dark cabal, a seemingly impossible task that he is somehow actually accomplishing. JFK was assassinated for trying to bring down the deep corruption.

Again, the satanic cabal must be defeated and he is the only man who has had the audacious courage, desire, and capability to lead this mission. Call him crass, an egomaniac, whatever you want, but what if it takes a person with his type of personality to accomplish the near impossible. So we need to get past media's horrifically erroneous claims and deceptions constantly forced on us about him, and support him in my firm view! Funny how the past leaders with smooth, likeable personalities have behind the scenes caused immense harm to the U.S. and world. It is all coming out.

I am publishing this book just prior the U.S. presidential election, and many question if there will even be one. What a crazy time to publish a book, and yet it seems to be the perfect time. The truths about Trump's opponent (who is not whom many think he is) and much more will shock the world. The push to make the U.S. a communist country is being stopped by Trump. We need to pray hard and support (not bash) this president working tirelessly for not just the U.S., but the world.

No one has to like Trump but I hope everyone loves that he is saving our children! And he is bringing peace to our world. I have to stress again, this is not a fight between left and right, this is a fight for life. A fight so that our enslavement ends, dear readers. The successes accomplished thus far are stunning and massive. This anti-establishment leader absolutely must and will win the presidency again. I know in my heart that Trump will TRiUMPh. *President Trump is leading the way to our New Earth*, like him or not.

What just happened after writing the above passage is pretty mind blowing. Today is August 20, 2020. On my desk is the book *The Complete Reader*[10], by Neville Goddard—a compilation of several of his books which are all completely new to me. It has sat here for about two months because I just haven't made time to read more than a few pages. Archangel Michael just told me to open the book and that I will want to put what I see on that page into the book! What? So, I closed my eyes and opened the book. It happened to be right where Chapter Seven begins, titled "The Greatest Prayer," on page 199. The subtitle reads: "Imagination is the beginning of creation." I was utterly astonished by what I read next.

"You imagine what you desire, and then you believe it to be true. Every dream could be realized by those self-disciplined enough to believe it. People are what you choose to make them; a man is according to the manner in which you look at him. You must look at him with different eyes before he will objectively change."

---

[10] Goddard, Neville. *The Complete Reader*. Audio Enlightenment Press, 2013.

This is exactly what I did regarding Trump! I looked at him with different eyes and saw a man polar opposite from what media wants us to see. It took time and lots of research, but I see him so differently. And I know of many who went through this same process. I am gobsmacked by this synchronicity… Michael!

The second paragraph from that is a royalty reference! "'The king that sitteth on the throne scattereth the evil with his eye.' Sympathy for living things—agreement with human limitations—is not in the consciousness of the king because he has learned to separate their false concepts from their true being. To him poverty is but the sleep of wealth. He does not see caterpillars, but painted butterflies to be; not winter, but summer sleeping; not man in want, but Jesus sleeping. Jesus of Nazareth, who scattered the evil with his eye, is asleep in the imagination of every man, and out of his own imagination must man awaken him by subjectively affirming 'I AM Jesus.' Then and only then will he see Jesus, for man can only see what is awake in himself. The holy womb is man's imagination." This is so very beautiful, powerful, and aligned with what Archangel Michael has taught us about imagination and creation.

Clearly, the way to our royal new lives and our New Earth is enhanced and co-created through the imagination. Every sword raising that Michael's Warriors of Light raise with Michael to, ends with the following: "Raise the sword for our New Earth. Visualizing, Intending, and Proclaiming the Coming Forth of Our New Earth Full of Love, Light, Peace, Freedom, Joy, Great Health, Abundance for All, etc."

Regarding just health alone, our health has been compromised by all the toxins forced on us, including this created virus. But things will change! President Trump is

318

quoted as saying: "In one year, every treatment that we are now using in the hospitals will be obsolete." What does he know that we do not? Trump is already changing the medical status quo that has been responsible for immense suffering and loss of life. We know that all kinds of cures to disease have been held back because medicine is such big money, and the powers that "be" (to be "were") do not want us healthy. Medical doctors have barely been trained in nutrition when food is thy medicine, as Hippocrates taught us in B.C.! Everything has become switched, so backwards—which is exactly the dark's way.

Even hydroxychloroquine, deemed by scores of doctors as a safe and most effective treatment for the virus (as it has been for malaria and many other afflictions, for decades) was actually being banned from even being prescribed, at least in the U.S., according to many reports. Rather, the software developer's dangerous vaccine was being pushed with the protocol to just wear your masks, socially distance, destroy all small businesses, etc., until it's ready?

Have you heard of Med Beds? Med Beds are advanced Artificial Intelligence technologies that will reportedly scan the body and then regenerate it. They have the capacity to remove disease, and will even anti-age—and in just minutes. These are technologies created by off-planet ETs, so far advanced from anything we know.

There is both the Light and dark side of AI. This obviously represents the Light side. Is this what we have to look forward to? Is this what Trump was referring to when he reportedly stated "In one year, every treatment that we are now using in the hospitals will be obsolete"? I think of and imagine these Med Beds every day. We have much to look forward to while enduring these unprecedented, challenging times. Just imagine what this will be like! And imagine what we will be like once we ascend into our New Earth and we harness the growing Light—the Liquid Light which will eventually, over time, fully sustain us as foretold by Archangel Michael nearly a decade ago.

AA Michael says in *Michael's Clarion Call*: *"In the Golden Age, your health issues will wane, as your bodies are able to allow more light within. Light will heal, as it has healed many of you, but your physical bodies must be able to hold this Light. This is why I say there will be a shift in health as you raise your vibration.*

As far as abundance goes, we are heading into abundance for all. No wonder the angels and Universe kept symbolically sending me prosperity signs. Our money will literally be changing. We will one day not have to work too many jobs or unhappy jobs, just to survive. We will spend more of our time in joyful and creative pursuits, instead of working jobs that do not fulfill us.

Debt will no longer be enslaving us. Eventually, after we experience abundance as a collective, we will one day, on our New Earth, no longer need money. But until then, if you haven't heard of GESARA and NESARA that we are on the precipice of gleaning from, you will very soon.

We are in the process of seeing much change in these areas regarding finances. Many people are already reporting their mortgages being mysteriously wiped clean, their college school loans with a zero balance, and their credit card debt vanishing. This is a slow and quiet process right now. There we go with the arrow again, having been pulled back including when it comes to money, but only to experience a level of abundance so breathtaking and new.

First, we simply must see and acknowledge the truths of our enslavement within the matrix. As awareness of the evils of this 3D world reach the tipping point, the extreme dark loses its stronghold (it's happening now!) and we prepare to shift our world forevermore. May we harness our imaginations at every opportunity and see our new royal lives with our beautiful hearts in action.

This leads me to recall a message I received from the sleeping prophet Edgar Cayce a couple of years ago! I've been drawn to him ever since my spiritual awakening in 1994. I was up in the wee hours thinking about Edgar one night. So, I posted on social media one of my favorite quotes from him that next morning.

"Forces of light on earth shall overcome the force of darkness. Complete spiritual enlightenment on earth will occur." ~ Edgar Cayce

I also recently shared his prophecy about Larimar, the healing stone, which I've been most drawn to for years. He simply kept coming up in my mind. I had this feeling he was wanting to provide a message through me when I had just sat down to listen to a videotaped meeting. One of the speakers synchronistically mentioned him, and so I immediately paused the meeting, knowing and feeling without a doubt he definitely had a message for us!

"My name keeps coming up to you, dear soul. And part of the reason is that I have a message to impart through you. Many people are growing so weary, especially those well aware of the dark forces wreaking havoc on the planet, and are losing faith in their future. This is exactly why you were led to your sharing of my words today, as an important reminder of what lies ahead, what you are all working towards, individually and collectively. So I ask you, those reading these words now, to claim the magnificence that you are. Do not put me up on a pedestal, nor any other. Put yourself up there and strive to reach higher with powers within just waiting to be tapped. When you really get in touch with your Light, there are no limitations. The limitations the world of lower vibrations placed on you imprisoned your Light, but it is your responsibility to free yourself. Claim your power now! Feel and act on the drive to shift and change your world for you are all needed. These are not just fluffy words I impart, for you were here lifetimes to prepare for this lifetime! These are most difficult and yet also magnificent times because the human being is evolving! This is a most complex and miraculous shift you are working towards. For every heartache you experience in this beautiful world, there will be the miraculous successes that will keep you aligned to persevere through the challenges. Do not sway from your faith now. I among many prepared you for these times, so draw on our wisdom and move forward without fear. If fears seep in, face them, do not run from them, for then you will understand the true power of your Light. Simply reside in the Light that is you."

~ Edgar Cayce through Mary Soliel, September 2, 2018

Over a decade ago, I had an extraordinary string of synchronicities regarding the Titanic, as shared in the "What's with Molly and the Rose?" chapter in *I Can See Clearly Now*. "I now see that we, the billions of us on the planet, have metaphorically been passengers on the Titanic. We have indeed been sinking; but we will be saved. We must surrender to a Higher Power. We must trust that we will indeed have peace on earth as well as a healed earth. We must believe that this will occur no matter *what* is going on, *even if things keep getting worse before they change.*"

It is written in sacred prophecy that our destiny is set, and nothing will stop our promised shift into a New Earth. What is up to us is the timing. The more of us that awaken to the difficult truths, take action, and while working to co-create our new Light-filled reality, then the sooner our miraculous New Earth will appear. It is time to assert our sovereignty now and direct our arrows toward magnificence.

May I leave this with you, dear reader. Please place your hand over your heart as Archangel Michael has taught us and encouraged us to connect to, again and again. Now ask the wisest part of you, "What is this earth's destiny?" Tune in to find the answer which should be immediate, truly instantaneous; whether via words, feelings, images in your third eye, etc. Then ask your beautiful heart, "What is my royal destiny?"

Lightwarriors and Lightworkers are playing many roles at once. We are anchoring in the Light, transmuting darkness, being truthers by researching and spreading awareness, taking action, meditating, and imagining and dreaming in the New Earth, to name a few. We are in the midst of juggling many tasks until one day, more ease will come. The freedom will arrive. The abundance will overflow. And a level of peace and joy we never knew will fill our hearts. Seek that bliss. Everything we are enduring will all be worth it, and the Universe is counting on us all.

I honor each and every one of you, queens and kings, and your royal families. See you on the other side… on our New Earth.

ABOUT THE AUTHOR

Mary Soliel is an author, visionary, spiritual teacher, and self-described "synchronist." Her three-time award-winning book, *I Can See Clearly Now: How Synchronicity Illuminates Our Lives,* is a groundbreaking exploration of the phenomenon of synchronicity.

As a channel of Archangel Michael, the publishing of *Michael's Clarion Call: Messages from the Archangel for Creating Heaven on Earth,* and *The New Sun,* highlights Mary's mission as a teacher and messenger to globally raise awareness of the Golden Age before us.

Her fourth book *Look Up! See Heaven in the Clouds* demonstrates her pioneering exploration and visual proof of this movement toward a new and Heavenly earth.

Mary was clearly led to Canada in late 2016 to spread a powerful message for humanity. *Michael's Sword & You* is a guided manual to help Lightbearers take action with Archangel Michael to transcend the chaos in our world and co-create our Heavenly New Earth. All five of Mary's books are award-winning, and this book won the 2018 Body Mind Spirit Book Award.

The birthing of *You Are Royalty* came as a surprise after Mary felt the call to the Big Island of Hawaii. There, she gained a whole new level of understanding of the immense power of the Light to transcend the darkness, as humanity finally learns to free itself from the grips of enslavement, and gain their destined sovereignty and royal heritage. Her sixth book details in a most magical way how she was synchronistically led to this new mission and resulting awarenesses, during her unique, seven-month long journey living on the island, and then culminating in enchanting New Mexico.

Mary is available for U.S. and international speaking engagements and workshops, and radio/print/television interviews.

Please visit Mary at **www.marysoliel.com**. Contact her at **alighthouse@mac.com**.

Made in the USA
Columbia, SC
06 January 2023

75570205R00189